# Head over Heels

**other memoirs by Hugh Lunn:**

Vietnam: A Reporter's War
Over the Top with Jim

# Head over Heels

## Hugh Lunn's

HIGH-OCTANE, GIRL-CHASING
SCOOP OF A '60s SEQUEL TO

*Over the top with Jim*

*best wishes,*
*Hughie Lunn*

University of Queensland Press

First published 1992 by University of Queensland Press
Box 42, St Lucia, Queensland 4067 Australia

Typeset by University of Queensland Press
Printed in Australia by The Book Printer, Victoria

Distributed in the USA and Canada by
International Specialized Book Services, Inc.,
5602 N.E. Hassalo Street, Portland, Oregon 97213-3640

This work was assisted by a writer's fellowship from the Australia
Council, the Federal Government's arts funding and advisory body

**Cataloguing in Publication Data**
*National Library of Australia*

Lunn, Hugh, 1941-
  Head over heels.

  1. Lunn, Hugh, 1941-   . 2. Journalists — Queensland — Biography,
  3. Queensland — Social life and customs — 1945-1965. I. Title.

994.305092

ISBN 0 7022 2418 9

# Contents

# 1
# *The green vegetable reporter*

Four years after I left school at the end of 1959 I had become a pretty rare commodity — in fact, so rare that nobody was unkind enough to mention it. I had become a Fourth-Year cadet reporter: the only Fourth-Year cub reporter anyone on Brisbane's *Courier-Mail* could remember .... although a friendly old sub-editor told me he was sure he had met one "down south" 30 years before, in 1933.

The reason my position was so unusual was that — although reporters were supposed to do a four-year cadetship — apparently it didn't take most people that long to learn the secret of how to write stories.

So cadets were always made into reporters within three years.

For example Jack, my older brother, was very proud of the fact that he had been graded after two years, seven months, and five days. And Bob Macklin, even though he had started his cadetship six months after me, had already been made a D Grade reporter by the Editor. Which, no doubt, everyone on the paper had duly noted, seeing as so much time was spent discussing cadetships and gradings. All reporters on the *Courier-Mail*, even the really old ones, could rattle off exactly, to the hour even, the tiny amount of time it had taken them to get graded — and then how quickly they had moved from D grade to B grade, or even that loftiest of positions: the A grade.

"I was once the youngest B grade reporter in Queensland," was a phrase that could be heard nearly every day in the Reporters' Room, in tones that squeezed through beneath the constant high-pitched staccato clicks of dozens of old typewriters.

So what was I going to tell people for the rest of my life?

By the end of 1963 I had already been a Fourth-Year cadet reporter for nearly six months, so I was getting pretty worried. The only thing I was totally sure about in journalism was that there were no Fifth-Year cadet reporters. You either got graded or, it was rumoured, the Editor called you in and told you to try something else.

The problem was I couldn't think of anything that would suit me, even if journalism didn't.

Not that I told my parents, Fred and Olive, of my fears.

I was 22 and, as they worked away in their cake and pie shop, both Fred and Olive thought that their number two son — as I was often called since starting work at the same place as Jack — was doing better than anyone ever dared hope. "Writing articles for Brisbane's biggest newspaper," was how Olive so grandiosely put it to the relatives, who thus kept suggesting exclusives I should dash off on my trusty typewriter.

They had no idea that I had spent most of the four years of my cadetship typing out horse-racing fields and lawn bowls results. I couldn't write a feature for all the rice in China.

At least Fred wasn't impressed by my job.

Fred claimed that, although he was only a pastrycook, he knew all about newspapers.

"They write 'em up; and then they write 'em down," he would say as he made his pies. "They've been doing it since the year dot." I wasn't sure what this meant, but I couldn't ask Fred, in case he realised just how little I knew about my job.

What worried me whenever Olive started boasting about her two sons, was that she didn't seem to realise that there was a good chance, a very good chance, that I would go down the gurgler and again let her down. Just as I had done when I failed Junior, and when I failed Senior the first time round, and when I failed both University subjects in my first year out of school.

So I ached inside every time I watched Olive's face light up like a feast day altar as she told customers — who had merely stepped in for a pie-and-peas — how both her sons were reporters on Brisbane's largest metropolitan newspaper: fighting for truth, liberty, justice, and the Australian way.

Hell.

Poor Olive had no idea that I was a deadbeat who was only just surviving at the *Courier-Mail*. Or that my time to be graded as a reporter was rapidly running out.

Part of the reason for my survival was that I had spent most of my cadetship performing repetitive mechanical tasks. Things like collating the overseas cables off the telex machines for the Foreign editor; working out the dividend yield for shares for the Finance editor; checking the arrival times of ships and mail for a section called the Diary; finding out the moon and tide times or sunrise and sunset times; or typing out the Weather Bureau's report in *Courier-Mail* style, which they called "House" style.

All of these tasks were much easier than trying to write a story, because you did the same thing over and over again every day.

The tough part about writing stories was that every story was different.

Most of the time it was hard to work out exactly what the story was.

It was shortly after my arrival at the *Courier-Mail* in August, 1960 — eight months after passing Senior at my second attempt — that I found that writing stories was the hardest part of being a cub reporter.

The first job the paper gave me when I arrived, aged 19, on the third floor — called the Literary Department — was the one Jack did when he started there nearly three years earlier: "Markets Reporter".

It was a tough job.

The Markets Reporter was invariably a male First-Year

3

cadet — female First-Year cadets were assigned to a large room full of women reporters with "SOCIAL" on a sign above the entrance: the only room on the floor I never went in.

Almost everyone on the paper started at 2.30 in the afternoon, or six at night, to ensure the morning paper had the latest news. But the Markets Reporter, unfortunately for me, had to be at work by 10 a.m.

I had two main tasks. One was to type out the radio programs for every station for the next day — even though I couldn't type — with a story on one of the programs kicking them off.

This was more difficult than it appeared because, while every station sent in stories on their programs hoping to get some publicity, there was a standing instruction that most of these stories had to be about the *Courier-Mail*'s own radio station, 4BK. So you couldn't just write the best story from the seven stations.

Mostly the stories were about the plays that were on the wireless each night, like "Forbidden Planet" or "Lost Without Trace". There were also "Radio Novels" and popular record shows like "Platter Chatter with Bill Gates" on 4BH. Bill was very popular in Brisbane because he drove a white sports car and made public appearances at the O'Connor Boathouse, a dance-hall surrounded by wide verandahs which was built out over the Brisbane river on the riverbank at North Quay.

One of my first stories was about a competition to win a new-fangled five-valve radiogram by coming closest to guessing the National Top 40 on 4BK in correct order.

After doing the radio programs, the Markets Reporter then had to walk up to the city's fruit and vegetable Markets at Roma Street to find out what had been going on that day. The Markets were in a couple of huge sheds on a small rise between the front of the City Hall and the Roma Street railway station. There the reporter collected a copy of all the fruit and vegetable prices for the day. These then had to be typed out in House style for a special page produced just for the first edition of the *Courier-Mail*, which only went to people in the country because they were interested in these prices.

That was how I found out that everyone in Queensland didn't get the same morning newspaper, even though they all bought the *Courier-Mail*.

So what you got inside your paper depended on where you lived.

Fred wasn't surprised when I told him about this. He said he would expect the papers to do something like that.

"They only tell you what they want you to know," was one of his favourite sayings, even when he wasn't talking about newspapers.

While at the Markets, the Markets Reporter was supposed to watch out for any stories which might be going on. This meant wandering through the cavernous tin-roofed sheds chatting to the old merchants who sold wooden boxes full of produce from their own wall-less areas, marked out on the concrete floor with their boxes.

I knew Jack had broken lots of stories from here when he was a First-Year cadet reporter under the special by-line "By Our Markets Reporter".

Unfortunately, Jack had used all of these stories up by the time I came along.

Jack had already broken the story of the giant rats which inhabited the Markets. "I counted 22 rats in half-an-hour last night at the Brisbane Markets .... the cats didn't have a chance," Jack wrote — and received a two guinea bonus from the Editor. He even found a story next door as he was leaving: "I could have stolen 20 railway trucks with their keys left in their ignitions at Roma Street."

No wonder Jack had already been graded as a journalist by the time I joined the paper.

But, even if Jack had left some of these stories over for me, I wouldn't have had time to write them anyway. By the time I typed all the radio programs and the fruit and vegetable prices out with two fingers on an ancient typewriter it was always after 9 o'clock at night. I had to get everything

5

done by then because the markets report and the radio programs were in the first pages that had to be ready to go and get printed each night: to be "put to bed" as everyone on the newspaper said.

Jack explained that there weren't enough people to put all the pages together at once. So, if the paper was to be printed on time, pages had to be continually "locked up" throughout the night so that page one was the last page to go — in case some big story broke at the last minute.

Despite the long hours, I did like my job.

The Markets Reporter sat near the middle of the General Reporters' Room where there was always a lot happening. I sat opposite the Police Roundsman who talked to the police on the phone, or illegally listened to their radio to find out what the police were up to.

Police Rounds was a job most of the other male cadet reporters aspired to. He got to cover lots of important stories like robberies and murders, and gallivanted around in his own new 1960-model Holden Special with a large black radio-telephone on top of the dashboard for all to see, so that he could talk to the Chief-of-Staff from up to a couple of miles away.

The reporters who did this job were considered hard and tough, and had a lot of pull.

On one of my first days on the paper I heard a Police Roundsman ring up the Police Commissioner and explain that some stupid policeman had been silly enough to book him for going through a stop sign, even though the Police Roundsman had explained who he was.

It was soon fixed up.

One of these Police Roundsmen was a real cool pistol shooting champion who occasionally smoked cigars and continually phoned police up and kept saying "thanks a million, Senior". Another had long black hair oiled down and combed straight back from his brow to over his collar. I used to sit and watch him.

He had long, wide, white fingernails which he kept cleaning at his desk with a pen knife. And every now and then he would reach into his back pocket and whip a palm-sized comb rapidly back through his hair. Just twice. He was as handsome as Clark Gable and, no matter how late at night he arrived at work, he always looked neat. No one ever referred to this Police Roundsman by his name. They just called him "the Count". He worked late at night — long after I had gone home — because part of the Police Rounds job was to take first edition newspapers around to police stations for the police to read to help keep them awake after midnight: and so they would tell the *Courier-Mail* when a story happened.

While being the Markets Reporter lacked the panache of Police Roundsman, at least I got to go for a walk through the centre of Brisbane every day whenever I liked from our four-storey skyscraper which was directly opposite the GPO in Queen Street. As I left the building, I couldn't help but look up each time at the inscription etched in gold on marble in the foyer: "Our liberty depends on the freedom of the Press and that cannot be limited without being lost — Jefferson".

Unlike the terrible first job I tried for eight months after leaving school, here no one minded what you did all day — so long as the work was done in time.

Jack only occasionally showed his nose in the office because he was always out looking for stories. But when he did he came over to my desk. For some reason he started calling me Brother, instead of what he had called me since I was born, Hughie.

One day, about three months after I started work as the Markets Reporter, Jack came over to my desk in his immaculate tight blue suit which featured four buttons on the jacket, his black hair combed back in a cow's lick away from his slightly freckled face, his black shoes polished. "How goes it Brother? Listen I hear there is a story at the Markets."

He handed me a folded piece of paper, and left.

"See my old contact Ted Tipper. He has a story", the piece of paper said.

7

Jack was always very secretive about stories. Even with me. He said you never talked about your stories to anyone, "anyone at all", until the story had appeared in the paper. Otherwise someone else would scoop you with your own story. What could be worse than that?

"Scoop" was one of Jack's favourite words. I wasn't sure what it was, though I knew it was a good story: and I was still looking for my first good story.

Mr Tipper was easy to find.

He was a fruit and vegetable dealer at the markets with a large sign above his stall, although I hadn't noticed it on my daily trips before.

Mr Tipper was next to the men who concentrated on vegetables like pumpkins and turnips, the type of dealer known at the markets as a "heavy vegetable man". Jack had warned me not to use that phrase in any story. He said another cadet, Bill Richards, had been hauled into the Sub-editors' Room where there was much mirth as the sub-editor read out selected parts of Bill's story, and invented others: "The number of *heavy vegetable men* at Brisbane Markets is increasing. *Heavy vegetable men* can be seen gathering in groups to discuss their problems .... Brisbane is under threat from *Heavy Vegetable Men*, according to ace reporter Bill Richards."

I liked Mr Tipper immediately because, like Fred in his cakeshop, he wore an apron: a device Fred called his "badge of servitude".

Like Fred, Mr Tipper didn't bung anything on, and he liked me because I was Jack's brother.

After a few minutes, the aptly-named Mr Tipper pulled me aside into the shadows of a tall pile of boxes next to some dusty chaff bags full of green pumpkins, shoved a watermelon under my arm, for-nothing, and slit open a bag of potatoes from Esk. He cut open a rotten potato with his pen knife and stuck the contents too close to my eyes.

The price of potatoes, he said with a long wink, was about to soar.

I couldn't believe my luck.

Here was a rip-snorter of a story.

As I hurried back through the city to write my scoop I did wish I didn't have the watermelon. It was slowing me down.

Back at the paper I put the watermelon on the water cooler, grabbed a typewriter, and started my story.

I had to remember lots of things all at once.

Not only did the "intro" have to be typed separately, but each of the first three sentences had to be typed on a different sheet of paper. This was in case the page layout required each sentence to be set in a different typeface, since different typefaces were set at different linotype machines down on the Composing Room floor below: or so Jack said.

Also, everything had to be done in triplicate.

The original of the story was for the Chief Sub-editor, who decided if and where he would use the story in the paper. One of the carbon copies (called "blacks") went to the paper's Queensland Radio News Service — which supplied several radio stations in Brisbane, including our own 4BK, with news. The third copy went into a special basket so it could be sent to our other papers in Queensland or, if it was a big enough story, down south to Sydney and Melbourne.

Even as I typed I could hear the radio announcer in my head — since I really wanted to be a radio announcer — saying, as he had done all my life: "Here is the news from the worldwide sources of the *Courier-Mail* and the *Telegraph*; these are the main headlines .... the price of potatoes in Brisbane is about to soar, sources at the Brisbane Markets have told our on-the-spot Markets Reporter."

It was very exciting.

However, every time I typed the first paragraph of my story (the newspaper called a sentence a paragraph), I found nothing was coming through on to the second and third pages of my copypaper.

Even stranger, the first page had something typed on the back as well as the front. Yet there was clearly nothing on either side each time I started.

Luckily, Jack had popped into the office for a visit. He

explained that the carbon paper came up the opposite way around after it was wound through the typewriter roll. It was because the carbon paper was in my typewriter back-the-front that I was getting a mirror image copy of my first paragraph on the back of the first sheet of paper. This was also preventing any blacks being made.

At night several pensioner "copy boys", some of them retired policemen who had been good contacts in their time, were employed to pin these sheets of paper together for the reporters. During the day this job was done by the pretty young copy girls in their tiny mini-skirts. Copypaper consisted of three sheets of poor quality white-brown paper with two sheets of much-used carbon paper in between: all held together by a silver pin in one corner. Reporters went through hundreds and hundreds of these as they made mistakes, or tried to improve their stories.

There were lots of rules about how a story was to be presented.

You had to put your name in the top left corner of the first page so they knew who was responsible if anything was wrong.

In the top right-hand corner you typed a catchline, or "slug" as some called it, to ensure each page of the story could be identified once it went down into the chaos of the Composing Room on the floor below to be set into various typefaces.

The first page was always numbered 2, which seemed stupid to me. But Jack explained that this was done so that when the sub-editor wrote the headline, and pinned it to the front of the story, the headline would become page one.

Thus I began my story:

---

H. Lunn                                    potato 2

Watch out Brisbane! You don't know it yet, but the price of potatoes is about to soar.

more

---

I was surrounded by a thick pile of used copy and carbon paper by the time I got that much done, yet even then I had forgotten to do it double-space, and had to start all over again.

But at least I had made the opening paragraph less than twenty words.

Jack had warned me that it was said that if your intro was longer than twenty words "your copy will beat you back out the door".

Apparently an over-long first paragraph was so obvious, once you entered the Sub-Editors' Room, that by the time you had dropped your story into the basket in the middle of their table, and opened the door again to leave, it would have been picked up and tossed out the door ahead of you.

Then you would have to do it again.

So it was with some trepidation that I took the original of the potato story around to the Subs Room, after remembering to put a "gate" (-/-/-) after the last "para" to show the story had ended.

Sixteen to twenty ageing men sat smoking around a big oval table, silently thumbing through thick piles of typed, pinned copypaper and making marks with blue pencils or, for the younger ones, with biros.

This was the room said to be best avoided by cadet reporters.

I could see the room had been deliberately designed so that there was no way of putting your story in the basket without actually entering the room far enough for the door to close behind you. When you did, every head would look up with an involuntary frown. There was never a hint of recognition. Then with unseeing eyes, these old men would scan the walls of the room over and over again as their minds searched for unseen words to fit the headline spaces allocated by the Chief Sub.

It was said these sub-editors all hated reporters. Reporters got to go places and meet people and were plied with free drinks, while the subs sat all night in this room struggling to put the newspaper together: to get it out on the streets just for the benefit of the reporters who could then skite about the story some sub had re-written for them.

All of these strange elderly men looked the same to me, perhaps because they all wore plain shirts and ties and each had an overflowing bottle of sticky, thick, foul-smelling grey paste in front of them: plus a small paint brush and a double-edged blue razor blade.

The blade was so they could chop your story up.

The paste was to stick it all together again the way they wanted it.

One of these old subs was a real misery-guts. He was famous for bawling out cadets for mistakes in their stories. He wore a white-and-green tennis eye-shade on his forehead and elastic metal shirt rings around his sleeves to keep them up away from the glue, the razor blades, the carbon paper, and leaking biro ends.

He used to say he was angry because he was dying of cancer.

Every few minutes one of these sub-editors would — without saying anything — hold up a finished story and an ever-alert even-older copy boy would scoot around the table and fetch it. The sub would then reach into the common basket for another story to sub according to the Chief Sub-editor's instructions, which were written on the front.

The Chief Sub sat at the inside bend of the big kidney-shaped desk which kept him close to all the sub-editors around him. He continually thumbed through the small plans he had drawn of each of the next day's news pages — called "layouts". I was surprised to find out that the advertisements were drawn in first, then the picture, then the page lead across the top, and then all the other lesser stories .... right down to tiny ones called "fillers". The subs used to send lots of these fillers downstairs in various sizes so they always had something to fill exactly any holes that were left in the pages.

It seemed a shame to me that all the fillers that didn't fit were simply chucked away in metal and never seen by the public.

12

After being handed a completed story the copy boy would roll it up, put it into a steel cannister, and lift the lid on one of the many steel pipes on the wall, creating the sound of rushing air. He would drop the cannister into this pipe and the story, and the cannister, would be sucked away at great speed to the Composing Room on the floor below. This hissing and sucking of air continued constantly as stories went off to be set in type, or as other steel tubes arrived every couple of minutes from the GPO across the road with news telegrams from around the world.

This gave the Subs Room an eerie atmosphere in which the noises were so loud that the soft whispers of the subs could barely be heard below them.

It was as if a team of accountants were working away blissfully unaware that they were sitting among the machinery at a large factory.

After leaving this heart of the newspaper I took the blacks of "potato" to the two baskets on a shelf which was half in the General Reporters' Room and half in the Chief-of-Staff's office. Every half an hour these baskets were checked by reporters from radio news, interstate service, and country press.

And, occasionally, by the Chief-of-Staff himself.

Mr Kevin O'Donohue, the paper's ace reporter, was Acting Chief-of-Staff and he called me into the glass-fronted office which looked out over the grubby green General Reporters' Room.

From this office you could see the reporters sitting at more than a dozen timber desks with drawers which overflowed with piles of paper from stories done decades before. The edges of these tarnished, varnished wood desks were all burnt black from cigarettes left too long on the edge. The reporters sat behind typewriters tipped over and balanced precariously on their backs as if they no longer worked. But reporters did this with typewriters to make room on the desk for the three copies of their stories when they had finished typing.

K. O'D, as everyone called Mr O'Donohue, was holding

a black of my story in his hand, no doubt about to praise me up.

His large frame filled the door completely and he twiddled his glasses in one hand. With his glasses off you could see his large, smiling blue eyes standing out against his ruddy, soft face below a thick shock of wavy silver hair. Unlike other chiefs-of-staff he never wore his jacket while in the office.

"Hugh," he said, motioning me over, "why is the price of potatoes about to soar?"

Because, I replied, as it says in my story they are in very short supply.

"But you don't say why are they in short supply?"

I had to admit I didn't really know.

"Back up to the markets, Laddie, and find out," K. O'D said.

When I got back after running all the way to Roma Street I breathlessly explained.

"It's because of all the wet weather."

"Good," he said. "But why does rain send up the price of potatoes?"

Back at the Markets, I was glad Ted Tipper was still around.

The rain, he explained, had turned all the potato fields into seas of mud as far as the eye could see. It was a disaster for the farmer and for the consumer.

"And when will things improve?" I asked Mr Tipper, trying to anticipate Mr O'D.

"When it stops raining," Mr Tipper said.

So that was it! The wet weather had turned the potato fields to mud. This made the story even better. Everyone was interested in the weather. Every day the *Courier-Mail* carried a story on the weather, and it was always written by one of their best general reporters.

"Why do muddy potatoes cost more than non-muddy potatoes?" Mr O'Donohue asked nonchalantly as he leaned back in his head-high chair and flicked through my waning scoop.

14

"Spuds might weigh heavier because of the mud?"

K. O'D looked over his glasses unimpressed.

"The cost of washing the mud off the potatoes could be high?" I suggested.

But K. O'D just pointed.

At first I thought he was pointing at my watermelon on the water cooler, but then I realised that beyond the water cooler, the window, and a dozen buildings, was the Markets.

Ted Tipper this time drew on a box of oranges.

He drew a potato field, and little men. He showed how muddy fields would make it much harder to find and pick potatoes.

That was why the pickers had to wait for fine weather. And it was why a lot of the potatoes rotted in the ground in the meantime.

K. O'D smiled.

"Hughie, now you have your story," he said.

But my potato story didn't make the paper.

Jack consoled me by saying my story missed out because we had something called "a big news day". He pointed out that at the same time as I was writing my potato story the Americans were sending a chimpanzee called Sam into space.

Apparently this story was a pearler.

I heard them talking in the Sub-editors' Room and they reckoned that this was the biggest story that had happened in their lifetime — which was a long time for all of them.

When I asked them why it was such a big story, they said if the Americans could send a monkey into space then, clearly, they could send a man.

I didn't think it was very good news since it kept my potato story out of the paper, but everyone else was happy to see that the United States had at last got ahead of the Communists in the space race .... since losing out when the Russians surprised and frightened everyone, except Fred, by sending the first satellite into orbit around earth a few years earlier.

15

Unfortunately, just two months after my potato story, the Russians again made a monkey of the Americans by sending the first man into space: beating the first U.S. spaceman by a whole month: which I knew from the *Courier-Mail* cadetship race was a big winning margin.

This space race made it just about impossible to get any markets stories into the paper, so it was fortuitous that at this time I got off the markets, though I would have preferred a more dignified exit.

I bought a new grey suit with a thin grey-and-red striped tie on time payment, plus a new pair of grey suede shoes to replace my old school ones. Someone had told me that a journalist was a reporter with two suits, so I thought I had better at least get one.

After walking up to the Markets for what turned out to be the last time, I did my rounds, and was walking out of the barn-like building into bright sunshine on the side of the hill facing the City Hall when I rolled. Over-and-over I went, rapidly down the hill and into a small mobile newstand perched on the corner.

I had gone over on my left ankle and couldn't walk.

The woman paper-seller helped me up, and I found my first use for the city's new-fangled parking meters as I hopped from one to the other all the way back to the *Courier*.

When I staggered in, my new suit covered in dirt, the Chief-of-Staff rushed out of his office demanding to know what had happened. Our ace Police Roundsman was not impressed on being told to drop everything and drive me to the hospital.

I wasn't much use to the paper on crutches, so each day I had to tear up all the cable stories that came in on two telex machines and put them together for the Foreign Editor, Mr Winders, who sat at his own special desk looking out at the world from a corner of the Subs Room.

The cables were mainly from some organisation called Reuter, which churned out stories about how Russia kept exploding various sized megaton nuclear test bombs; the space race; the Royal family; and airline hijacks.

I was lucky because I was the first person in Brisbane to know about these events as they came straight into the *Courier-Mail*. While I was doing this job the American election was on and I watched the voting figures coming in every few minutes in their millions, with John Kennedy just in front of Richard Nixon.

I wanted Kennedy to win — not just because he was young and handsome — but because he was a Catholic: and the United States had never had a Catholic President before, even though more than one-fifth of Americans were Catholic. It was exciting when the telex machine rang bells and announced that Kennedy was the winner. It seemed the world was now safe from the Russians, and made me feel much more confident about being a Catholic.

I would get mesmerised standing in front of the two telex machines. Watching all these big stories come in from around the world, I kept forgetting to tear them up and put them in order.

One day I was the first person in Brisbane to find out that Gary Cooper — the star of *High Noon* — had died.

That was when I learned about how to sell papers.

Mr Winders told me to watch the poster the next day because it would say "Gary Cooper dead" and so everyone would want to read about it.

"If he wasn't so famous it would say 'Film Star Dead' and people would buy the paper to see if it was somebody famous like Gary Cooper," he said.

When I told Fred this piece of news as he rolled some Lunns buns at our Annerley cake shop he said it didn't mean that Gary Cooper was really dead.

"It means that they want us to *think* he is dead," Fred said.

# 2
# *Kicked out by Uncle Bill*

With other cadets occupying all the bottom positions in various editorial departments, and a new Markets Reporter called David Bentley, I found myself coming back from injury at the end of 1960 rostered on, of all things, General Reporting.

General was the job most of the top reporters had because, Jack said, you had to know something about everything to be a general reporter.

These reporters had no definite beat.

They sat in the big green room on the third floor, six or seven men and one or two women, watched over by one of several possible Chiefs-of-Staff through the glass wall — ready to be sent to cover any story not covered by a regular roundsman: from a car accident to a new road opening.

Because many stories were gathered by phone, a three-woman switchboard was next to the room through another glass wall, so reporters could signal that they were ready to take their trunk calls from around the state.

When not on the phone, these general reporters thumbed through their thick contact books or sat around reading papers and talking until the Chief-of-Staff called them in, one at a time, to allocate the stories he wanted.

These stories could be on anything.

Anything at all.

The *Courier-Mail* usually sent a reporter to meet the Migrant Train when another load of New Australians arrived from Sydney at South Brisbane station. The idea was to write a story about families who had left behind the despair and awful poverty of Britain or Europe to start life anew with great hope in our wonderful state of Queensland. Also, the paper's "Style Book", which every new reporter was given on arrival, said "our newspapers strongly support the immigration policy".

My first assignment in General was to meet one of these trains.

Instead of having to walk or catch a tram, I was given a docket for a taxi and, when it pulled up at the top of the high ramp behind the station, I felt special as I paid for the ride with my signature, adjusted my grey coat and tie, and used my Press Pass for the first time, to get on Queensland's biggest railway platform for nothing.... a pass which was signed by no one less than the Commissioner of Police himself.

The train was late, and when it finally arrived it was much, much longer than I was expecting. It must have had at least a dozen carriages, and hundreds and hundreds of foreigners poured out of every door the moment it stopped.

As I stood near the hissing steam engine I was surprised how badly dressed they all were. How they all seemed loaded down, mentally and physically.

These migrants carried children and parcels and bags and ports of all shapes and sizes.

They seemed to be in a huge hurry to escape wherever they had come from.

Some actually ran along the platform, despite their loads and the heat of the Brisbane summer afternoon, which made me sweat even as I stood in the shade of a train carriage. Others dragged children screaming behind them while yelling in foreign languages as they hurried towards scores of waiting buses, cars, and taxis outside the exits.

There were migrants, and officials, and porters, and children, and drivers, everywhere.

I wasn't sure where, exactly, to start looking for the story.

As I stood on the long concrete platform next to the train I tried to catch the eye of some as they swept past.

But they just wouldn't look.

My mind wandered away, as it so often did, to the outings I'd once enjoyed with my red-haired girlfriend.

This time I remembered our journey together just a year before when we had caught a train of just three carriages from this very station to the Gold Coast. I could see her there on the platform looking beautiful while picking bits of black ash from the cinnamon H-line dress she was wearing and smiling broadly as we headed for her parents' home at the Gold Coast: feeling so grown up on a train by ourselves.

People were still rushing past.

I raised an index finger.

I coughed loudly.

I even gave the car hand-signal Fred used for stop in the Zephyr.

But they all kept rushing past without looking.

I felt sorry for them.

They seemed scared.

I realised that this must have been how my Russian schoolmate Jim (Dima) Egoroff and his family arrived in Brisbane a decade ago when he was nine years old.

It was probably this train that had brought Jim to Brisbane to sit next to me at school for the next nine years. Throughout those years we had cheated from each other, and I thought — as the migrants sped past — how I could have gone on to University to do Law or Medicine myself: if only Jim had applied himself.

I wondered what Jim would have done in my position, looking for a story on this platform.

He would have probably found some Russians and cracked his favourite Australian gag by asking one of them: "Do you want to fight me mate?" .... and then introduce me as his mate. But Jim, I decided, wouldn't have been much use here today.

Only the previous week I had asked him if he knew of any stories I could write and he showed, as I suspected, that he knew nothing about journalism.

Jim was working on an old rust-and-red 1936 International truck he had bought for practically nothing because it was just the engine and chassis. As he did this, he said he knew a good subject for a story.

"Spanners," he said.

Jim reckoned Australia was being flooded with cheap spanners from Japan, and these Jap spanners were no good.

This didn't sound like much of a story to me. I knew that not many people even knew what a spanner was. In fact, if I hadn't known Jim I would never have seen one.

But there was no stopping Jim when he had an idea in his head.

Jim got two large double-ended silver spanners and held them up, saying one was American, and one was Jap.

I should have known Jim well enough, after all those years sitting together at school, not to ask which spanner was which.

But I did.

Jim brought the two spanners together in an instant with the sort of force from such a short distance which only he could muster.

When the impact on the air around us had cleared I opened my eyes.

In Jim's left hand was an unmarked silver spanner, and in his right hand was half a spanner.

He threw the half down into the dirt saying: "That's the Jap spanner."

Well, the one thing I knew about this migrant train was that there would be no Japs on it. Not after what they tried to do to us in the last War. And no other Asians either, because of our White Australia Policy. Boy if there was an Asian family on the train wouldn't that be a scoop?

I decided to watch out for some, but couldn't see any.

Within a few minutes the migrants and their luggage had all disappeared, and I was left standing all alone with no story, next to an elongated steam train, like James Dean on a concrete movie set. It was as if no one else had ever been there at all. My face went very hot as I felt my pink cheeks blush red and I smiled broadly as I always did when I knew

21

I was in trouble. It used to get me into trouble at school because the teachers thought I didn't care.

No one back at the office seemed perturbed when I came back without a story.

But that didn't make me feel any better.

I knew that they knew that I had missed the story.

I knew Jack would know.

And I knew too that it was because I didn't know what needed to be done.

I feared I was like my father Fred, who always said he was a man "who needs to be told". And I found myself getting told a lot of things now that I was on General Reporting.

The Chief Sub, Mr Kev Kavanagh, appeared next to my desk waving my story about a truck accident in which I wrote how the truck driver was killed when he was hit by the prime mover.

He asked if I knew what a prime mover was?

I had to admit that I didn't.

"For your information Mister Lunn," he said quietly and deliberately, "the prime mover is the front part of the semi-trailer. The driver was *inside* the prime mover."

Mr Kavanagh said I should ask questions.

"Don't be afraid that you might sound stupid. We had a hopeless reporter here who was always asking dumb questions — yet he turned into the best reporter ever to work for this paper."

I wanted to ask Mr Kavanagh who the reporter was, and how long he took to complete his cadetship and get graded, but thought better of it.

When a teenage girl was run over and killed by a tram in Adelaide Street I got the job because the Police Roundsman was out. Just like the paper always did for car accident deaths, I wrote two paras.

"Can't you see that getting killed by a tram is a far bigger story than getting killed by a car," I was told after being called into the depths of the Subs Room.

Actually I couldn't, I said.

But I could see that getting killed by Australia's Own Car,

22

a Holden, was a bigger story than getting killed by some other car.

This really upset this sub-editor, who was a bit of a stinker. He said he had been watching me for months and that I had better start taking this job seriously, show some gumption, use my nouse or, or .... but he didn't go on.

No, he said, he didn't want to know why I thought getting killed by a Holden made a bigger story.

"Weren't you the young man who dragged one of our top photographers off a job to photograph a car accident last week where he could hardly find the dint in the car?"

It was true, I said. But the photographer hadn't wasted any film. He just looked at the Zephyr, shook his head, and muttered: "We don't chase ambulances on newspapers son. They only chase ambulances in the pictures," and left.

I told the sub I still thought it had been worth a picture because so many people owned Ford Zephyrs, and would hate to get a dint in their car. I knew a bit about cars, I explained. My father, Fred, had a six-year-old Zephyr Six: and I recalled how devastated we all were when it got its first ding when it was brand new during our heroic drive from Brisbane to Melbourne in 1954.

Luckily he seemed to understand.

"Well for your information the Police Roundsman is having to redo your story because he knows a good story when he sees one," the sub said. "Lots of people get killed by cars. But hardly anyone ever gets killed by a tram. That is why it is a bigger story than getting killed by a Holden. Don't they teach you anything at that University?"

The subs seemed to hate the fact that the cadets went to University at night. But this sub also had a particular set against me. In fact he got me in the poo with the whole subs table one night.

I wrote a story which said police were interested in interviewing "elderly people who lived in the Windsor area 20 years ago". This sub must have lived in Windsor, because he called me in and said the story was ridiculous. "People are not 'elderly' just because they were alive 20 years ago,'' he shouted, and all the subs nodded their heads up and down.

If I didn't know a good story, at least I knew a bad one. So when I was asked by the Chief-of-Staff to cover the *Courier-Mail*'s garden competition, I made sure I didn't over-write.

Jack said over-writing was a major problem with reporters.

Gardens didn't interest anyone in our family.

Owning a cake shop, we never had time to garden. Anyway, Fred disagreed with cutting grass. He said "mowing the lawn" was another way of saying "killing grass". And flowers, to us Lunns, were something you saw on altars in church on Sunday.

I was assigned to interview the winners of the various sections of the gardens competition, and, along with the list of results, I wrote two paras about who won the main prize, where they lived, and why the judges gave them the prize.

I went cold the next morning when I got up and saw the story had made a much bigger splash than I imagined.

It was a page lead — one of the longest stories I had ever seen in the paper. There were more than 40 paragraphs about the various favourite trees of the winners; how they made mulch, propagated plants, and designed garden beds. These people seemed to know dozens of different flowers, whereas at our place we only knew gerberas and gladiolis, both of which grew wild in the back yard. Jack had thought it was such a big story when someone grew a double-double-gerbera that he made it into a scoop.

When I arrived at work that afternoon the Chief-of-Staff called me into his glass office.

"After you went home, Colonel, I had to take another reporter off his round to ring up the winners of our garden competition and interview them all over again. You're proving to be a pain in the neck. You'd better sharpen up,'' he said.

This was very bad.

Jack had told me that the angrier this Chief-of-Staff was,

the higher the military rank he gave you. I had suddenly been elevated from Sergeant to Colonel, and there was only one rank higher to go: General.

My luck seemed to be running out. I could see that in this reporting game we were playing for keeps.

Nothing I had learned at school seemed to be of any use. Not calculus, nor trigonometry, nor chemical equations, nor the laws of physics, nor the vocabulary of Latin. Not even poetry, though I found myself reciting more and more often to myself Arthur Hugh Clough's "Say not the struggle nought availeth, that the labour and the wounds are vain, that the enemy faints not nor faileth, and as things have been, they remain".

For example, when the whole building shook during a shorthand class one lunchtime it didn't occur to me that what was happening was a story until I saw the paper next day: "Earthquake Shakes Brisbane".

And why hadn't they taught us the word "obituary" at school?

When I was told to get the obituary file I went to the paper's library and — trying to repeat what the Chief-of-Staff said as if I knew what I was talking about — asked for the "habituary" file.

Naturally, the Librarian couldn't wait to tell him how dumb a member of his Literary Department was.

What made it even worse was that, when I wrote the obituary, a sub-editor — unfortunately the same sub who got me for writing the weather report as "the whether report" — shouted at me in the Sub-editors' Room:

"Cementary? Cementary? Listen fungus-features, what the hell is a cementary? Are you bunging it on? Have you shot your bolt? Is this a bloody concrete metaphor for death?"

Then, turning to address all his fellow subs, he asked: "What have we got here? Another bloody academic."

I thought I was cactus. But all I got was another lecture from the Chief-of-Staff.

Most of the sub-editors seemed to hate people who went

25

to University because they said they couldn't spell. But I thought they were just angry that the cadets all got to leave work a couple of nights a week for several hours — on full pay and at the paper's busiest time — to attend lectures.

I finally got my big break as a general reporter a few weeks later.

I was sitting typing the radio programs when the Chief-of-Staff for that day came rushing out of his office.

"You with the hair on. A crane has collapsed off the top of a building in Adelaide Street. Bill Tuckey will need help .... you're all we've got," he said.

I grabbed my grey suit coat and ran out of the building and down Isles Lane while putting it on, like a uniform.

He was right.

Just behind the *Courier-Mail* a crane had bent and toppled over from atop a building site into Adelaide Street. The crane was waving around like an elephant's trunk. As I arrived it collapsed further and sliced through some over-head tram wires. The inch-thick wire cable lashed out furiously sending sparks through the air, and whipped into the front of a silver tram. It burnt black holes right through the grey-painted metal above the driver's head next to the glass display for the destination of the tram.

Then another black cable snaked through the air and fell silently and malignantly across the road, and I noted that tram number 510 had stopped in its tracks.

Tuckey's curly black hair and silver suit stood out among police uniforms in the middle of Adelaide Street, as rush hour trams piled up in long queues from both ends.

People anxious to get home were herded back away from the area.

I raced to the centre of the action and Tuckey, one of our ace reporters, said with a note of great urgency and excitement: "Get the number of trams held up, their destinations, and take a note of all damage you see."

This was it.

This was the humdinger Jack always talked about being ready for.

I got my notebook out in one hand and my biro in the other and — standing in the middle of Adelaide Street admired by thousands of onlookers being herded back by police — I started to write down the destinations of the trams hit with the live electric cables and the damage I could see. As I did this, a giant police sergeant strode up, completely blocking out my view of the swaying crane.

He ordered me out of the area behind police barricades.

I pulled out my Press Pass and held it up, but the policeman was my Uncle Bill.

A Press Pass wasn't going to impress Uncle Bill.

Uncle Bill was a huge man who had spent most of his life being the only law in small Queensland country towns. He wasn't used to kowtowing to the Press, or anyone for that matter.

He was used to being obeyed.

Hadn't I been staying with my cousins at the Police Station in Esk the night the whole town closed down while Uncle Bill went down the main street, alone and unassisted, to tell a gang of bikies to get out of town?

When he gave me my driving licence he insisted on describing my hair on the licence as "auburn", despite protestations from Olive and myself. And, even though I didn't want it, he gave me a licence to drive a truck. When I asked if he was going to take me for a test drive, he replied: "Don't be silly son, I wouldn't get into a motor vehicle with you driving."

This time around, just as I was on the brink of a big story, he was even less impressed with my credentials. "I am ordering you out of here," said Uncle Bill.

"But Uncle Bill," I pleaded. "I am a reporter now. I am 19 years old. My boss sent me here. This Press Pass is signed by the Police Commissioner himself."

"Get out of here before I kick you out," he said. "Your mother would never forgive me."

I felt I was letting Bill Tuckey down. In front of thousands I climbed back over the barricades and counted the trams that had banked up. I wrote down their destinations

— displayed in white letters on black — while Bill Tuckey covered the disaster area alone.

Tuckey had everything he needed, but at least he got me to sit next to him while he wrote the front page story in the General Reporters' Room and typed "Tuckey/H.Lunn" on the top of the first page which he slugged "crane".

I was amazed how quickly it all flowed off his typewriter — so quickly that I barely had time to take out the pins to separate the blacks from the original and put the three copies of our story in order. And, while none of the other reporters asked us anything about it — or even looked our way — I could feel they knew we were the most important people in the green General Reporters' Room that night.

The next day the photos and our story took up almost the whole of page one.

Somewhat surprisingly, after such a success, I was taken off General and relegated back to cadet jobs like the weather, the tides, ships due in and ships due out. I did get a day covering the Land Court but there was no story because one of the barristers stood up and addressed the judge saying he understood there were some "very pressing matters that require the attention of the court happening in Brisbane".

The other barrister leapt to his feet and supported his "learned friend", and everyone — including the judge — ran out of the courtroom.

I wandered slowly past Queen's Park and up to Queen Street, which I was surprised to find was practically deserted — except for crowds of people huddled around TV sets in shop windows.

Back at the *Courier-Mail* there was nobody around.

There weren't even any subs in the Subs Room.

Then I found them all.

The entire staff of the newspaper was crammed into the Chief-of-Staff's office — even the girls and women from Social — watching the end of the First Test from the Gabba against the West Indies.

No one could believe it when the Test match ended in a tie

— the first ever in Test history. Except perhaps me. I loved cricket and listened to it whenever I could on the wireless because I knew anything could happen, and often did. I even carried around a new type of small radio — a transistor — to keep up with the Sheffied Shield scores. I had been to that Test on the Saturday and saw Garfield Sobers score a century in which he hit balls so hard they bounced off our fieldsmen and into the white paling fence that surrounded the green ground.

Perhaps because the Editor had heard of my sporting background, early in 1961 I was transferred into Sport. But when I got in there I found it was only to sub the horse racing results. This involved writing on the race details for the compositors (who set the type) the size and typeface the results had to be put in, and the column width in ems or picas. This was, of course, unnecessary because it was the same every week. The comps — who had been setting these horse fields for decades — knew what was required much better than I did. But the system was that the journalist had to write the type and size and column width on each page of copy paper. However, the advantage of this system was that whenever I got something wrong one of the comps would ignore me and set it right.

Perhaps this made me too casual, because even the comps missed my first really big mistake on the paper.

One night I was particularly pleased with myself when I found an error in the typed telex results from a southern race meeting. A horse called Red something-or-other had won at three-to-one. But instead of a semi-colon after the price, two letters had mistakenly slipped in on the telex machine — an ''o'' and an ''n'' — so I obliterated them with my pen.

The next day the *Courier-Mail* got so many phone calls about this that they had to put three people on phones just to explain that it wasn't a scam to rip-off Queensland's SP bookies. Unbeknowns to me, SP bookies throughout Queensland had an agreement with punters to pay out on the Starting Price published in the *Courier-Mail* .... and my error had cost them a pretty penny.

Acting Turf Editor, Fred Pilbrow — a man a funny cadet friend of mine, Cliff Dawson, called Derf Worblip behind his back — stood over me so that his giant frame and belly forced me to look straight up into his unwavering eyes. He was ropeable and asked if I was aware of what the word "on" meant in racing parlance. I explained that, while I had heard that expression, the "o" and the "n" on the stark piece of telex paper had just appeared to me to be one of the many telex machine mistakes.

Derf said I had dudded the bookies who had lost their loot. An SP bookie would pay out 90 pounds in winnings on a 30 pounds bet at three-to-one, but only 10 pounds at three-to-one *on* — nine times as much. My error could have cost SP bookies throughout Queensland thousands of pounds each.

By now my face was bright red.

I said I was really sorry, and added — purely as an after-thought — that, still and all, perhaps it was a good thing to catch these SP men out since what they were doing was illegal.

That was it.

Derf got really angry then.

He accused me of knowing more than I was admitting to. He wanted me to fess up, and seemed to be hoping I would name names and admit to some sort of conspiracy. And, when I didn't, he warned that the Editor would be told of my attitude to what was a vital service to readers throughout the state.

Right then my journalism career seemed over before it had really begun.

My punishment was, he said, that I would no longer be al-lowed to sub the race details.

What a relief.

But I knew it would never happen.

No one wanted to sub the race details. Even when I had to go to University for a three-hour evening lecture none of the graded reporters in sport would touch the race fields, the tipsters' boxes, the jockey names, the weights, and the bar-

30

rier draws while I was gone. These would all be there waiting for me when I got back at 9.30 p.m., if I got a lift. Which made it nearly impossible to get it all done in time for the first edition, which was printed by midnight.

One night I got so far behind after Uni that I could see the race pages would not be done in time.

Worried the pages wouldn't make it, I started tossing pieces of paper up in the air so everyone could see just how much unsubbed material was weighing down my desk.

Throwing the race fields in the air had the desired effect.

Instead of getting angry, as I expected, the Sports Editor, Harry Davis, took me around behind a cupboard and put his left hand on my right shoulder, and told me to cheer up and stop panicking.

He looked me fair in the eyes and said: "Son. Have you ever seen this paper not come out?"

Well .... I had to admit he had me there.

But what about the big hole in my race details page that there would be no time to fill?

What about the tipsters' boxes?

Harry reached into his drawer and pulled out a piece of metal the size of a large book. It had a map of Breakfast Creek racetrack etched into it, and he held it up in front of me: "This'll fill the hole for the first edition," he said, and smiled.

# 3
# *The red-headed stranger*

Even though journalism was such a confusing job, I was glad to be working for a newspaper. Time passed so quickly that there wasn't much opportunity to dwell on the way my life had gone so badly wrong since leaving school.

My first job had been for the Brisbane office of the American oil company, Mobilgas, on the top floor of a three-storey building at the corner of Creek and Adelaide Streets.

After learning things like how to measure the speed of stars in order to qualify for University, I had ended up, aged 18, collecting mail from the GPO, opening it, and delivering the contents to the IN baskets on the desks of various Mobilgas executives.

At the same time, I collected the contents from their OUT baskets, for delivery to other people's IN baskets.

Like school, at Mobilgas you weren't even supposed to talk.

A man everyone called "Creeping Jesus" made silent patrols between the long rows of clerks' desks to make sure everyone was working in silence.

Five cadet clerks, including me, were employed to handle all the mail.

Mail for every Mobilgas station and fuel depot in the state had to be pigeon-holed and posted; thousands of monthly statements were folded and put into envelopes; hundreds of form letters of demand for money had to be sent to slow-paying garage owners ... three possible letters, each more threatening than the one sent the previous week.

Back came the ugly replies.

One was on a piece of brown paper roughly sewn together with black cotton. Inside it said: "This is for you, I have wiped my arse on it."

And he had.

My only break was a weekly trip on the tram to Bulimba carrying a locked port to Gilbarco, the company that made the petrol bowsers, or the occasional message delivery up town. I always took as long as I could, sitting on the grass under a tree in Queen's Park near the statue of Queen Victoria, wondering how to escape my fate. On the way back I would hover on corners watching crippled and lame old men waving Brisbane *Telegraph*s around and yelling out "woop *Tele*, City Final" and ponder how they ended up doing that job. I would read all the strange signs in the street outside shops like: "Casket Closing Now" — meaning all the tickets in another Golden Casket state lottery were almost gone. Casket tickets always reminded me of Fred, because he bought a couple every week and never won anything. The nearer I got back to Mobilgas the more I felt cheated by the Christian Brothers who — having taught me to love Browning and Byron and to write essays on the form and the matter of thought — hadn't warned that work would be so boring.

And hadn't warned that when I left school I would go so quickly from somebody to nobody.

There was no chance of even joining a football team.

I went to work hanging off a bus at seven-thirty in the morning, and came home with the entire Brisbane workforce what seemed like twenty hours later — hanging out of a peak-hour tram at six that night. Two nights a week I didn't get home until after ten, because I caught a bus after work to Queensland University for three-hour lectures in Accountancy I and English I — then a bus back to the city to wait for another bus home to Annerley.

I was supposed to make it to University another two nights a week for one-hour tutorials, but never did.

Why I had done Accountancy, I wasn't sure.

I didn't know the first thing about it. I had even almost

failed Bookkeeping in Junior when I was 15, but that wasn't my fault.

Our teacher — frustrated that our C class couldn't seem to work out which was the debit side and which the credit side of a Balance Sheet — taught us that the debit side was Victoria Street, outside St Joseph's College Gregory Terrace, and the credit side was Princes Street.

The trouble was that, when we walked in for the public examination, the stupid outside supervisors had re-arranged the desks so everyone was separated, turning them all around to face the other way. So, throughout the Bookkeeping exam, I had to continually try to reverse everything as I went along, making profits losses and losses profits. I became totally confused.

It wasn't much better at University.

I didn't understand one sentence the Accountancy lecturer said, and I certainly couldn't do any of the assignments. When I told him I thought accountants had thought up hundreds of incredibly complicated and roundabout ways of working out how much money a business was making, or losing, he didn't seem interested. But when I recounted my experience in the Bookkeeping exam, trying continually to list profits as losses and losses as profits, he seemed impressed.

"That should qualify you for a job with just about every company in Australia," he said.

English, I was surprised to find, wasn't much better.

I had always managed to pass English at school, but when we got our first University assignment in March 1960 — "Write 3,000 words on the Ballad" — I knew I was gone. I was always flat out writing the 40 lines of foolscap needed for essays at school, let alone 3,000 words.

That was definitely beyond me.

Anyway, I wasn't interested. I was the only mail clerk who had done Senior, so none of my younger mail clerk mates — Larry, Jeff, Tony or Scott — had to study at night. I wondered why passing Senior hadn't given me a better

34

start in life because it was such a mighty effort. Something I never really thought I could achieve.

When I said this to our boss he said: "Oh so you're the one who wasted the extra two years doing Senior?" And he told me, proudly, how he had learned "more than enough" by just doing Junior.

I didn't tell him that I had actually wasted *three* years. I didn't want him to know I had repeated Senior.

The main reason I had enrolled at University was because my girlfriend from school days with the ginger-ale coloured hair had enrolled there fulltime in Arts, and I felt I might lose her if I didn't keep up. Also, Jack was going to University at night and Olive expected me to go too.

It was also because of my red-headed girlfriend that I ended up working at Mobilgas.

When I started taking her out at school she told me her mother was petrified I might convert her to Roman Catholicism.

My girlfriend's mother always referred to Catholics as "Roman Catholics" — considered an insult by my religion. By some strange twist of logic, she said Anglicans were the true Catholics, and we were *Roman Catholics* who were run by the Italians. We were part of a rigid structure: whereas the Anglican church was like an abstract painting. Waving her left hand around as if trying to keep her cigarette alight she said we invariably gave ourselves away by saying "haitch" instead of "aitch".

She was unimpressed by the argument I had learned at school that "Catholic" meant universal and therefore to say "Roman Catholic" was like saying "national international". She even took a book down from her bookcase and read bits aloud to me to prove that the miracles at Lourdes — since the apparition of Our Lady there a century before in 1858 — were not really miracles at all.

This was heresy, so I mentioned one day that it was interesting that all of the great religious poets writing in the English language seemed to be Catholics: Chesterton, Thompson, Hopkins.

"Not T.S. Eliot, the greatest of all," said the mother.

After that I went for my first-ever visit to the State Library to see if this was true, and was surprised to find all the poets we studied at school had written hundreds and hundreds of poems: not just one or two each — the ones in our school books.

I was even more surprised to find she was right about T.S. Eliot.

The Brothers hadn't told us about this.

Luckily, at the library I found a book called *The Myth of T.S. Eliot* in which an Anglican minister criticised Eliot for taking most of his poetry references from the "Roman Catholic" Church and — I couldn't believe it — concluded that, had it not been for his friends and relatives, "Eliot would surely have died a Catholic".

Her mother said this was nonsense.

And she didn't like it when I mentioned how Henry the Eighth, who had started her church, was a lapsed Catholic.

She soon put me straight on that.

But, even so, I think it turned her against me.

When my girlfriend and I both passed Senior, her mother allowed us a joint celebration at their house. But during the afternoon she called me aside next to their tennis court shed and said she was sorry that the family would not be seeing me again.

I was a nice boy, but this was her decision.

When I protested she said it had nothing to do with my religion. It was because, by passing Senior, I would now get into journalism like Jack.

"I made a rule when my daughter was born that she would not be allowed to go out with two types of men," she said.

"Men on motorbikes, or journalists."

I said she was judging all journalists too harshly because her husband spent so much time at work as one of the top journalists on a Brisbane paper.

36

"No I'm not judging it on him. I'm making the judgment based on every journalist I have ever met," she said.

Straight away I decided that there was a simple answer.

I would forget journalism.

The only real appeal journalism held was that I had seen Jack sleeping in every morning, and getting paid to go to interstate rugby league matches and GPS swimming and athletics.

Thus I annoyed Jack by not going into the paper for my interview about a cadetship. Instead, I took the job my girlfriend's mother arranged at Mobilgas, even though one of the regulars who had his dinner in our cake shop warned me not to take it because the world would soon run out of oil. "Unemployment is already 1.5 per cent, and it could get worse," he added.

I didn't care what job I got, so long as I still had my redheaded girlfriend.

The trouble was Mobilgas wanted me to start work immediately, so I missed spending the Christmas holidays down the old Gold Coast near my girlfriend. At school I used to hitch down and sleep on the beach in the sand hills near her house, or I rode my bike from Surfers to her place at Nobbys when our family had a holiday in an old house behind "The Walk" in Surfers.

But now all that was over.

Workers, I was surprised to learn, only got holidays once a year: and then only a couple of weeks.

I could hardly believe schoolkids got five times as many holidays as workers.

My girlfriend was supposed to come up from the coast for the Australian tennis championships at Milton in January 1960, to watch my mate Kenny Fletcher from Annerley play, like she did the previous year. But she wrote from Nobbys Beach to say her mother wouldn't let her come.

"If I had my way I would be with you right now," she wrote.

When she finally did come back to Brisbane it was February, and University was already about to start.

We went to the Freshers' Ball at Cloudland, me in Jack's dinner suit — which was a bit too big — and her in a strapless mauve frock with a layered net skirt: something her mother made especially. In that dress, with her tanned shoulders meeting red hair, she glided around the ballroom among the thousands of students as if followed everywhere by a spotlight.

We drove to the Ball in Fred's Zephyr Six — our first outing in a car.

We got our photo taken together holding hands.

I was floating around the dance floor, with her once again so light in my arms, when an older student rushed up and handed me a brown paper bag saying: "Hold this for a minute would you Dad?"

The bag was shaped like a book, but felt harder.

I felt it would be rude to look inside, even though my girlfriend was telling me to get rid of it.

We were near one of the semi-circular alcoves that practically surrounded the sprung dance floor, and a small crowd of eyes watched as a police sergeant appeared in front of the two of us.

"Hand it over sonny."

"What?" I asked.

"Don't play smart-boy academics with me," he said. "I don't need a University degree to know what's in that bag."

The sergeant whipped the paper bag out of my hand and pulled out, to my astonishment, a bottle of Bundaberg Rum.

Apparently this bad boy had been drinking alcohol at the ball, and you weren't allowed to drink at dances in Brisbane.

Not even at adult dances.

It was against the law.

Then I noticed that there were police running everywhere, with students laughing at them.

It was a raid.

I recognised it from *The Untouchables* on TV.

I had never had a drink in my life. I was against drinking.

I was even against University students, because I knew from my mate Jim — who was studying first year Engineering — that they enjoyed themselves while I went to work. Jim said they had decadent parties called "smokos", and I didn't even smoke.

Although I was enrolled at night at the University I didn't feel a part of it. When Jim's mother proudly made us each an embroidered Queensland University pocket so Jim and I could each get a matching maroon University jacket I never wore it.

These students even pulled pranks on people.

Jack said they tricked up the Brisbane *Telegraph* by sending them a false article about the terrible diseases you could catch from cats. The paper published it under the heading: "Is your cat a killer?"

Yet here was a police sergeant — who thought I was a University student — arresting me for drinking rum from a bottle at a Ball.

As he took my name and address, and the crowd of students watched, I knew my girlfriend must think what an idiot I was to be the only one in the giant ballroom to be caught. I felt sure I would be arrested, but the policeman merely ordered me out of the Ball ... and I took my girlfriend, in her beautiful layered mauve net dress, home.

Still, my girlfriend didn't complain. She said it was an unfortunate incident and not to worry about it.

The following month she took me to a student concert called a "Uni Revue".

Instead of having singing or ballet or tap-dancing, there were a couple of older male students making disparaging remarks about everything, including the Catholic Church, nuns, and even the Pope's nose. There mustn't have been any other Catholics there, because everyone else in the crowded temporary wooden dance hall called "The Hut" was falling off the forms laughing.

But I wasn't going to let these two get away with this blasphemy.

I cupped my hands in front of my face, and started booing as loudly as I could. Everyone started looking at us: but I wasn't going to stop now. I was doing pretty well interrupting them, until this smart-alec Uni student on the stage boomed into the microphone:

"Someone forgot to let Bessy out to be milked today. Will someone let her out."

The entire hall broke up laughing.

At me.

My girlfriend and I left in disgrace.

Failure is worse, much worse, when it is inevitable. And not only was I headed inexorably for failure at University, and in my first job, but, much worse, I now realised I faced the loss of my life's love.

I started to see, as I always suspected, how badly life could go against you.

At Mobilgas — in between the pleasure of writing out her name on any blank paper in front of me — I started making an ink mark in my notepad for each horrible thing that could happen in life, without writing down what the marks were for.

Death of mother; death of father; death of brother; death of sister; loss of girlfriend; ear operation .... until, after 19 such marks, I wrote in my notebook: "There would be about 20 very sorrowful weeks in our life."

I didn't know then that sorrow is measured in years, not weeks.

There was hardly any time to see my girlfriend now. She lived on the other side of the city near the University, and I could feel she had found a whole new life among the sandstone buildings of the beautiful riverside campus while I was at work Monday to Friday. Her lectures and tutorials were limited to three hours a day and she talked of how she was going to start, of all things, a University weightlifting club. I just laughed at this: a seven-stone three-pound girl starting a weightlifting club? But secretly I was worried about all the male students who would come to lift the weights.

Even as I caught the bus to the University on Tuesday and

Thursday evenings, I appreciated the irony that each time I headed there, my love was leaving.

Her mother only allowed us a maximum of two meetings per week, which meant an awfully long time without her. It wasn't even an improvement on when we were at school, because then we used to meet every morning in Adelaide Street for ten minutes.

I wanted to see her every day again, but I couldn't.

I wanted to marry her, but I couldn't. On my wages we would never be able to afford a house. Anyway, even if I had the money, her mother had proclaimed that there was no way she was going to allow her daughter to marry until she had finished University. And that would be three years, if she passed every year.

Gone were the days of meeting clandestinely in town. Gone were the days of marching in army cadet uniform with my cornet down Queen Street. No longer could I invite her to watch me play for the school's First XV in my special red-and-black jersey with a big red leather number one on the back, and, as Lord Byron wrote, "see the bright eyes of the dear one discover, she thought that I was not unworthy to love her".

I was the complete nobody all over again, just like when I had first arrived at Terrace with Jim five years before.

It made me hate the University where all the rich well-dressed A grade kids in their white shirts and ties, who had been perfect prefects at school, were learning to become the class who judge.

I found my job embarrassing.

When I went out with my girlfriend, older students in their mid 20s would ask where I was working and then would say: "Are you a cadet executive?"

"No," I had to say, "I'm a mail clerk."

These older students seemed to hang around me and my girlfriend just a little too much.

I had good cause to worry too, because my girlfriend's mother now had a new rule: she insisted that her daughter also go out with other boys at the University, particularly one of them who, my girlfriend said, her mother adored.

I could put up with seeing my red-headed girlfriend rarely. I could even stand my boring job. I could stagger on from day to day. But I couldn't stand to think of her going out with other boys. Particularly Protestant boys who were unencumbered with the constraints of the confessional.

She confided in me about these occasional compulsory outings, which made it worse — when it should have made it better.

Jim rang one day to tell me that he saw my girlfriend walking around University in the company of some boy who was so well off that he had gold initials carved into a pigskin briefcase. Jim noted these initials down and read them out over the phone.

One night, when she said she was going out with another boy to a dance at the Uni, I watched through a window of the Hut to see her dancing with him. And when they left at the end of the night — so she would know how crazy about her I was — I let her see me watching from the bushes.

We started disagreeing on everything.

She said Catholic doctors were dangerous for women having babies because they would let the mother die in order to keep the baby alive. So, naturally — being a Catholic — I said the Catholic doctors were right not to kill the baby to save the mother.

Her mother sent her to a modelling course and I said there was no way she should ever model underwear. But she thought I was being a prude.

When she told me one of the students had set a new record of seven minutes in a Jaguar from the City Hall to the Uni I insisted it was impossible — even though there were no traffic lights on the journey.

I condemned the Uni Commem procession as disgusting, having seen it go through town — one of the trucks featuring a lavatory with a bloke sitting on it. And when she said she had learned at University that Catholics had the highest failure rate because they had been pushed through school I argued with her: even though I could see my education had not prepared me well for University. But it had got me there against all the odds.

Not only had I done no Uni assignments because none of the lecturers cared if I did them or not, but I got into long arguments with my English tutor, Cecil Hadgraft. I told him that as well as poetry and novels we should study pictures like my favourite Alan Ladd flic *Shane* because more people saw films than read books. When he described my favourite schoolboy poem "Horatius Defends the Bridge" as doggerel, I refused to accept what he said. I kept the argument going, saying that my opinion might just be the right one, until Mr Hadgraft said:

"You know, Hugh, some people think they're poached eggs — and no one can tell them any differently."

Everyone in the class, ever mindful of their marks, laughed dutifully.

I worked all the overtime I could get at Mobilgas wrapping up posters for garages, and saved five of the six shillings nightly overtime meal allowance by having a pie for dinner. Though I really wanted to buy a sports car, like a Goggomobil or a Renault Floride, I banked nearly all my wages and planned to brick in under the front verandah of our old house at 40 Ekibin Road, Annerley, so my girlfriend — who was being invited out by Architecture students — and I could get married and live there.

I even started to alter my language, calling petrol "gas", something they asked you to do if you wanted to get ahead at Mobilgas. And I impressed a manager who sent me up to City Hall to pay a one pound parking ticket for his new lolly-pink Holden by noticing that the ticket had his registration number wrong — so he didn't have to pay.

I tried to remember the good times with my girlfriend.

How she was the first person to praise up my distinctive raspy Lunn voice, instead of running it down.

How, like me, she liked to go to the cricket at the Gabba. I read and re-read her letters, including the first one ever to Greenbank army camp when I was in the school cadets

43

which had given me such a thrill because it had been signed "fondest regards".

And each night I prayed for a solution.

But I knew there was none.

Though we had known each other for 18 months, our parents had never met. This was strange, but I had not tried to bring it about, knowing what Olive might think of her chain-smoking mother, and what her mother — who always asked if I would like to use the bathroom (instead of the lavatory) — might make of Fred and Olive and our unpainted, untidy house with its lavatory enclosed by roofing iron under the house. And the long grass in the yard which Fred didn't like us to mow.

Fred continually said things other people found strange, like "I never knew you died until I was 30." Plus he was getting more deaf every year, but wouldn't admit it. Unless everyone at the dinner table shouted he would go "Pss,pss,pss,pss" and accuse everyone of whispering. And if you said he couldn't hear he would invariably say:

"I can hear you perfectly, I just can't understand what you're saying."

The worst part was that I could now see that Fred was no foreigner, as I had thought as a child. His voice was the same as mine. His thumb was dead straight just like mine. Even Fred's feet were mimics of mine. And both of us cut the tops of our socks with scissors because we couldn't stand elastic cutting off our circulation.

I could understand now what Fred meant when he used to say that if someone reached out and twisted his nose, he would wait to see if they did it again "to see if they meant it".

I could see that any outsider visiting our house would see me in him. On top of that, Fred still kissed us when we arrived or left home, even though Jack was now 21 and grown up with a groovy white Wolseley car. No one else's father did that. And Fred always said: "I will have to nurse you until you're 40", which was pretty embarrassing.

Olive was very presentable, but I knew that once this An-

glican woman had said her usual Anglican grace before
meals "For what we are about to receive may the Lord make
us truly grateful", instead of the Catholic "Bless us Oh
Lord and these Thy gifts which of Thy bounty we are about
to receive through Christ Our Lord, Amen", Olive would
have justified Ned Kelly, the IRA, and the ALP just for
openers. She was always ready for a fight.

Thus it shouldn't have come as a surprise.

But it did.

A big one. A total one.

On May 18, 1960, at five to three in the afternoon I was
called to the phone hanging on the back wall at Mobilgas.

It was my girlfriend saying haltingly that she had to speak
to me.

I thought she was ringing to arrange our weekend night
out. But then she said those words:

"I don't feel the same way about you anymore. I don't
want to see you anymore."

I went numb.

Loud bells rang in my ears.

No one could help me now.

Not the wisdom of Fred, not the strength of Jim, not the
fight of Jack, not the piety of Saint Anthony, nor the love of
Olive.

Not even St Jude, help of the hopeless, who had helped
me pass Scholarship.

I was surprised how calm I was as I hung up.

Things didn't seem to be bad enough.

My life had just ended forever, and yet here I was walking
around in Mobilgas where everything continued at 100 desks
exactly as before, but as if in slow motion.

I thought of running, but walked back to the copy desk.

Then my body started trembling involuntarily, and I left
the building by the fire stairs.

I went straight to her house, but she wasn't home.

Her mother explained that her daughter's decision was
for the best and that I should force myself to watch television to get my mind off things. She called me a taxi and the

driver, upset by my crying, pulled up near Boggo Road jail and told me not to try to hold back the tears.

He said girls often gave blokes the flick. It happened to lots of people. It had happened to him. It was something I would have to face. It would hurt, but "in two or three years, take it from me, you will be right as rain".

This bit of information made me worse.

I couldn't face years of such suffering.

We had planned to marry. I wanted six children. I already had names for the first two. I couldn't imagine life without her: her smile, her kiss, her red hair, our long talks on the phone, and the haunting memory of that day before school when she looked up at me in my army cadet uniform and said: "Crumbs, I'm in love with you, aren't I."

It was her going to University that did it.

All of those 22-year-old student doctors and dentists and lawyers who had been creeping around white-anting me when we went to their "Varsity five plus two" dances.

Them and their smokos.

The chemist in the Piccadilly arcade near Mobilgas the next day examined the cracked bloody scabs that had formed on the back of my hands and asked:

"Have you had a shock?"

I denied I had.

Mr Hawes, the old man who wrapped the parcels for Mobilgas in the basement, told me lots of people lost their girlfriends.

But I didn't know of anybody.

Everyone I knew seemed to have met a girl and married for life: like Fred and Olive, and grandma and grandpa, and all my aunties and uncles.

I thought of running away and becoming a priest or brother, but the Church and the saints had failed me. The one thing priests and brothers and saints knew nothing about was girls.

Yet the Church insisted I stay alive and not "sin against hope" by despairing.

And my family had failed me.

46

Fred continued making pies as if nothing had happened, saying: "You will get all that sort of thing, if you live long enough." He told me the best lesson he ever learned was when my grandfather Hugh told him to jump off a fence, and he would catch him. "When I landed in the mud your grandfather told me not to depend on others," Fred said: "And I don't."

Jack was too busy being a reporter and driving to Ipswich in his Wolseley to see his girlfriend. But he did say, wrongly, that it was her loss. That it was good really. "Now there is no excuse not to follow up on that job as a cadet reporter."

Gay, when she heard what had happened, said she was afraid I might do something to myself. She said I could go to the dances with her: as if that was any help.

Sheryl was too young to understand.

Olive was in hospital in Esk with clots in her leg and too ill to be moved home to Brisbane. The doctor had drawn a biro mark near the top of her thigh which, he said, the line of clots must not pass. Yet they were already three clots past: you could see the bumps in her leg.

For the first time in my life I was on my own, though Olive wrote from hospital a long letter saying how sorry she was, and telling me to always remember that she loved me and that: "There are more fish than them what is swimming about." It was the first time she had written me a letter since I bought her a mother-of-pearl knife and fork set from Prouds Jewellers with my first pay packet.

Over and over again I listened to the hit tune of Jim Reeves singing "Put your sweet lips a little closer to the phone, let's pretend that we're together all alone, I'll tell the man to turn the jukebox way down low; and you can tell your friend there with you — he'll have to go". And, later in the year, a new singer called Roy Orbison wrote a song just for me: "Only the Lonely .... know the way I feel tonight."

I slept in the lounge room because it was less lonely than my bedroom, and it was near the phone: in case she rang to say it was all a mistake.

I day-dreamed of riding out to the University on a white horse .... and moseying slowly over to impress her.

I dreamt of arriving on campus in an MG sports and wearing leather driving gloves. Of peeling them off, one finger at a time, as I deigned to chat with her: while standing with one foot of casual ownership on the front bumperbar.

And I worked out something about life: that the only people who know for certain that they don't want to see you are those you know really well.

All I could think of was poetry, my one contact with reality.

Hundreds of lines of poetry I had learned by heart at school raced non-stop through my brain: "Now you shall know the truth, no matter how bleak how black .... It is better to climb the ridge and stare on chasms of air .... than to run like a rat for cover when the truth comes storming by, better than huddling over the sinking coals of a lie." Or: "I am: yet what I am none cares or knows, My friends forsake me like a memory lost; I am the self-consumer of my woes. And e'en the dearest — that I loved the best — Is strange — nay, rather stranger than the rest."

I thought how terrible I had made her life in the three months since she went to University and hoped one day I would be able to tell her, as Francis Thompson, a Catholic poet, wrote: "All that I took from thee I did but take, not for thy harms, But just that thou might'st seek it in my arms."

A few months later, when I finally came to accept it was all over between us, I took my smallest photo of her and wrote on the back: "Where the treasure is, there the heart lies" — and sealed it away in a plain envelope.

# 4
# *Champion backhander*

The only thing that saved me from the sin of despair that long winter of 1960 was that my childhood friend Kenny Fletcher was around to cheer me up.

Ken, who lived halfway between Fred's cake shop and our house, was supposed to be away overseas all year, but he had been surprisingly dropped from the touring Australian Davis Cup team.

The previous year, aged 18, Ken was the youngest player with the squad that unexpectedly won back the Davis Cup in America. But, since then, Kenny had been having a bit of trouble with tennis officials.

Ken always seemed to be in some sort of bother with officials, even though the newspapers called him "happy-go-lucky Fletcher". I suspect they called Ken that because he was always so cheerful, even when he lost a tennis match: which was rare. Nothing seemed to be able to get him down. He was so confident, and knew so much for his age, that I called him "Uncle Ken", whereas everyone else just called him "Fletch".

While being dropped from the Australian team was a personal setback for Ken, it saved me. Had he made the team he would have been overseas from April until October playing tennis — and I wouldn't have had him around after my girlfriend gave me up.

When I broke the news that my slender, beautiful girlfriend had dropped me, Ken managed to bring an involuntary smile to my face. "I wouldn't worry about losing her. If she didn't have an Adam's apple, she wouldn't have a figure," he said.

Then, getting serious for a moment, Ken said I must forget her completely and start again "as if it never happened".

"It will be tough for a while, but you are whistling in the dark if you think she will ever come back," he said. "In my opinion, I would have to say that you have been rubbished. There's a whole world of girls out there. Why buy a book when you can join the library?"

Fletch listened to me for hour after hour each night. He insisted that, while I might not think so, I would find another girl I liked even more. One day he would take me with him overseas, and we would have the choice of all the girls in the world to give "the benefit of our excellent company".

At least it was something to look forward to.

Sometimes I even day-dreamed that I took up tennis and teamed up at doubles with Ken, touring the world and winning championships together.

Ken had brought back a portable radiogram with detachable small vinyl speakers from America, plus lots of 78 records. So, instead of spending my spare nights alone at home with Gay and Sheryl, I sat with Uncle Ken in the small back room of his home while his parents watched TV inside. The room featured a wall of windows overlooking the old ant-bed-and-chickenwire tennis court out the back where Ken had learned to play. There was just enough room for two cane chairs and the small cane table which held the radiogram.

This room itself cheered me up: it was the same room we used to play in with Ken's Hornby train set as kids.

Over and over again we played Chuck Berry's "Sweet Little Sixteen", Jerry Lee Lewis going berserk in "Whole Lotta Shakin' Goin' On" and Eddie Cochran's "Twenty Flight Rock" where, in order to get to rock with his girlfriend, he had to walk up 20 flights of stairs, but: "Get to the top, I'm too tired to rock."

There we sat listening to records until after midnight, two 18-year-olds, both spurned: one by his girl, the other by his country.

Although I was reluctant, Ken enrolled me in the city

gymnasium where he trained three nights a week so that he didn't fall too far behind the players who made the touring team. We met at the gym after work all that winter as Ken ran messages from Slazengers in Perry House instead of playing tennis at Wimbledon.

When we had finished lifting weights, throwing medicine balls, and holding each other's ankles while we did sit-ups, we would drop in, near exhaustion, to Christie's in Queen Street for a flavoured crushed ice — before walking up to North Quay to get a bus home.

Occasionally, Ken talked me into going to a dance or a party, but I found them a drag. I just knew that no girl could even remotely compare with my girlfriend.

It was difficult to bother dressing up in my dark blue yachting jacket with silver buttons when I didn't really want to go. But Ken, who looked flash in a blue and grey checked sports jacket he brought back from America, made sure I did. He said the more exercise I had, and the more outings I went on, the sooner I would get better.

Whenever Ken felt I should put more effort into these outings — to dress better, or adopt a more confident pose — he would turn and say: "Remember, we *are* gentlemen": and he would put the emphasis on "are".

Being Ken's friend was the one thing in life that made me feel important. And his positive attitude gave me hope.

"It's all down to kicking on from here well," he would say. "If you don't get a girl when we go overseas I'm a monkey's uncle."

Although he was a champion, Fletch was slight with no obvious muscles. In fact, I knew from playing with him since before we could both remember, that he wasn't even any stronger than me. Ken's face suited his earlier life as an altar boy at Mary Immaculate Church much more than the gladiator-world of championship tennis.

Uncle Ken's hair was fairer than mine, though he also combed it backwards in a cow's lick. His skin was pale and Ken's cherubic pink lips and clear blue eyes gave his small face an angelic look which contrasted markedly with the rough faces and dark, hairy bodies of most of the men he played against.

On any day in Annerley Junction Uncle Ken could be seen either heading off to play tennis, or returning home to change after a match.

He always looked the same, laughing away from under his white washing hat which went with his white shark-skin tennis shorts, white Dunlop Volley tennis shoes (always newly-stained white by his Protestant mother, Ethel), and white Fred Perry tennis shirt with its trade-mark green wreath.

Fletch was now so famous he was paid in US dollars to wear these Fred Perry shirts, and some other company paid him to wear their shorts. He had even been on television — the only time us Lunns had ever seen someone on TV we knew. Ken promised he would touch his tie-pin as a special message that he knew the Lunns were watching, and the whole family got excited every time he did it. Fred said Ken should go into politics if he could "wave and talk at the same time".

Ken was always telling jokes. He was so good at it that our whole family used to sit in the shop and listen to his stories, and Olive would get him to repeat them over and over — like the one about the elephant whose trunk was bitten off by a croc while he was drinking from a creek.

Ken, adopting an indignant pose, screwed up his nose, raised himself to his full height, looked down and said, with nose blocked: "Think you're bloody funny don't ya!"

Even Fred liked Ken's jokes, but he referred to Fletch as "Reilly" because he reckoned Ken had it easy playing tennis for a living. Fred didn't seem to realise that Ken liked him a lot. Despite all the famous people Fletch had met, Fred was his favourite. He often said: "You're so lucky. Your father is a lovely man." I liked this, especially since Ken at other times told me: "You are so much like your father."

As he walked through Annerley, Ken always held in his right hand a multi-coloured Slazenger "Challenge" tennis racquet — either by the handle or the throat. He used this for everything as he chatted in the street: pointing directions, swatting flies, clearing cobwebs, hailing buses, carrying parcels, knocking dust out of the grips in his shoes, waving to girls, and for gesturing when telling stories.

Every now and then he would hit the taut yellow cat-gut strings against the palm of his left hand while listening closely with his left ear, to hear if the pitch of the "ping" was just right.

I often wondered if this was the secret of his success with the racquet.

Ken had been cleaning up adults at tennis since he was a small boy. Once, when Ken was only eleven, one of the state's top-ranked players — a muscular 26-year-old — turned up to play Ken in the top grade of the Saturday afternoon Brisbane competition. He strutted on to the court with a beautiful, adoring girl hanging off his arm. His black hair was oiled back like Ken Rosewall's and under his arm he sported no less than three shining new black-and-white Spalding tennis racquets held in special wooden frames with butterfly nuts in each corner to keep them in good order. The racquets were strung with pure gut. His French short-sleeved jumper had a large green crocodile embroidered on the front. I was only ten, but I could see disaster coming as he put down his bulging Dunlop tennis bag, took out his Thermos flask of ginger ale, and proceeded to prance around and stretch his muscles as his girlfriend took a seat next to the court.

"Where's Fletcher?" he asked innocently. "I'm drawn against him at two o'clock."

"That's him down there. Down there playing on the swing," said Kenny's father, Mr Norm Fletcher.

"Don't give me that," said the Ken Rosewall look-alike, as he turned anxiously to his girlfriend for comfort. "That's only a kid. I'm not playing some kid who can't even see over the net."

I felt sorry for the 26-year-old as he dropped his bundle while his girl sat and watched. Kenny beat him 6-0, and then ran back down to play on the swing. As the Rosewall look-alike left, his swagger had gone, and his girl carried his tennis bag and held him up by the arm as they limped back to the Annerley tram stop.

These incredible victories gave Kenny a rich vein of confidence, but also led him into trouble with officials. Though he had a very strict father, Uncle Ken didn't take cheek from anybody, not even tennis umpires.

Perhaps this was because he was a master of back-answering.

If some boy said he was going to get him, Fletch would reply: "You and what army?" When Ken's tennis doubles partner Frankie Gorman said he had a headache before an important final, Ken shot back: "What else would you expect a head like that to do?"

That same day, when a Milton tennis official told Kenny and Frankie their doubles match had been tranferred away from Milton to a court that was "only two miles as the crow flies", Ken — who thought he and Frankie were too important to be moved — raised his nose in the air and replied: "Yes, but one usually can't catch a crow."

Ken didn't like this QLTA official, invariably referring to him as "the dunny man". I was worried the official might hear about this. But Kenny said: "Well anyway, it's true but. He used to work for Hunter Brothers: the dunny cart people."

Ken would even argue with his elders.

An ageing American tennis official at the Queensland championships tried to explain away Australia's tennis dominance by saying American parents made sure their children went to university. Whereas Australian tennis players left school early and just played tennis.

Ken interrupted.

"Yes, that's true what you say," Ken said to the American official, "except that your players go off to university to get degrees in *Ballroom Dancing*."

I don't know where Kenny got this confidence from.

His father Norman was a train driver and his mother Ethel a housewife. The three of them lived in a tiny wooden house on Ipswich Road with cabinets covered by Ken's tennis trophies which Ethel carefully dusted every afternoon.

I felt sorry for Ken's parents. When he was overseas with the Davis Cup team in 1959 they were so lonely they came to watch me play football for my school, Gregory Terrace. Yet they didn't follow football at all.

Ken even reckoned he was a better tennis player than the red-haired boy from Rockhampton everyone was predicting would be a world champion, a bloke called Rod Laver. In my last year at school Ken had asked me to come and see him play against the Big Red Rooster, as he called Laver, saying he was going to clean the champ up: "deal out stick" was the way Ken put it.

That day Fletch took his special precaution of not stepping on any patches in the footpath, or cracks in the road, as he crossed to the Safety Zone to catch the tram. It was a close match on Milton's grass centre court, but Laver — who was a couple of years older — won. I thought this was a disaster, but Kenny was the same as ever when he plonked himself down in a chair next to me.

"Come day, go day, God send Sunday," he said.

While he could put up with losing to Laver he didn't like losing to anyone else.

I read in the papers how he upset officials in Melbourne when he took his shoes off and threw them into the grandstand, and played in his socks. They didn't seem to understand that Fletch had a sore toe. Ken was always having trouble with tinea and calluses because he spent most of his life in sandshoes.

This incident caused a Melbourne paper to label Ken "Bad-boy Fletcher". But some of the other young Aussie players were worse: one tipped a bottle of sarsaparilla over his opponent during the 10-minute break at two sets to one at Milton.

Frankie Gorman was even more outlandish.

While Fletch belted the occasional ball away when he was angry, Frankie made front page news by hitting tennis balls from the centre court into a backyard several houses from

Milton Stadium. The next day, when things went bad for him again, Frankie picked up all six balls and addressed the crowd:

"You thought those yesterday were good, well watch this."

He whacked the lot out of sight.

That was what Ken admired so much about Frankie Gorman: he was funnier on court than Ken himself. Because, unlike some of the other young Aussies, they laughed as they went crook.

Ken had also been in trouble in Adelaide when he and some other tennis players went for a row on the Torrens.

"It just developed into a total war," Ken wrote to me from the Grosvenor Hotel. "People sat along the bank watching, and the bloke who owned the boats was yelling that he was going to get the water police. Laver and Frankie and Jimmy Shepherd and me all ended up in the drink. You should have seen us soaking wet and muddy walking back to the hotel. Every bugger was staring at us."

Ken was dropped from the touring team because during the Australian championships in Brisbane in January 1960 his racquet slipped from his grasp and sailed high over a Milton fence during a match with South Australia's best player. Ken was expected to win, but was losing to this man, who was a decade older.

Unfortunately, a lot of southern reporters were standing next to the court at the time, and the racquet whipped through the air above their heads.

They couldn't believe it.

That afternoon the headlines in the *Tele* said: "Fletcher in tantrums again".

Although I didn't realise he knew who I was, Davis Cup coach Harry Hopman was so angry when he saw the paper that he waved it at me under the Milton stands and said: "Have you seen this?"

But Mr Hopman stuck up for Ken. In the *Courier-Mail* the next morning he wrote that this story on Ken was proof of "the old adage 'give a dog a bad name'." He said the real story of the match was that Ken had played "some of the finest tennis I have seen to come back and win the match: showing he has the best forehand in the world."

But it didn't help.

Poor Kenneth Norman Joseph Fletcher — as he sometimes liked to refer to himself by his full name — was dropped from the touring team.

Yet even this didn't dampen Ken's enthusiasm for life.

"How did you sleep after hearing the news?" I asked him the next day.

"Like a little bay horse," Fletch said.

But, in the weeks that followed — after the other players had flown out — whenever Ken talked about his 1959 world trip I could see he was having a bad trot.

Ken recalled how he had spent 52 hours on a plane to reach Zurich in Switzerland, then caught a train for three hours to Lugano where he played his first overseas match: beating Kurt Neilsen who had just been a Wimbledon finalist.

A week later in Paris, Ken went for a walk with Sydney player Martin Mulligan. The first words of English these two 18-year-old Christian Brothers boys heard from a foreigner were from a big black woman who yelled out as they wandered past:

"I say honey, come over here and suck my arse."

Fletch talked longingly of his days in Rome, Paris, Mexico, London, New York, and all the free Davis Cup uniforms — right down to green and gold towels.

"I never had so much fun in all my life," he said, as we sat in the cool of the dirt with our backs against the round black timber stumps under his house, looking out at the silver trams going past on Ipswich Road.

"My portable gramophone lured most of the players around to my room. The room was wrecked so many times."

His hotel rooms had their own bathrooms *inside*, and their own TV sets, yet TV had only just arrived that year in Brisbane.

"We lived like kings," Ken would say.

He said I wouldn't believe the Wimbledon dressing sheds. He was given his own locker, which was especially designed to hold tennis racquets. Combs, tortoiseshell hair brushes, and soap were provided, free — and two men were paid to run baths for the players. A huge luxury car with a chauffeur in a cap picked him up every morning.

Ken wrote me letters from overseas which he always signed Uncle Kenneth Norman Joseph. On the back of the envelope — after he had played the French championships — he put his name as Monsieur Fletcher, because he liked the way the umpires announced his name in French so that "Flesh-ure" rhymed with Monsieur.

The only day he tried to get to Wimbledon on his own he got lost: "I ended up in the mulga and less thirty shillings so I certainly got the rough end of the pineapple," he wrote.

Ken even bought a dinner suit to attend functions in London because occasionally someone from the Royal Family turned up. "I looked a real square in the penguin suit," he said.

Despite the naughtiness of the world, Ken still went to mass and confession and communion. Occasionally in the city he'd pop into St Stephen's Cathedral "to pay a visit", as us Catholics all did.

But it was more difficult for him to be good.

Thus in every letter Ken always said "say a prayer for me".

None of this stopped him from writing about girls: "You've got no idea how easy it is to get onto a sort over here, if you want to," he wrote from the Kensington Palace Hotel. "You wanted to know if I was still holy. Well you don't stay holy too long when you are away. I am not a sex wreck, but I can easily understand how even the saints were tempted."

And when we talked about girls as we sat in the back room of the house after his parents had gone to bed, Ken explained to me that "sex is all in the mind".

I wondered what he meant by this until he added "If only I could get my hand on my mind".

I hated working for Mobilgas so much that the hope that shone from Ken was muted. The only thing I liked about Mobilgas was their symbol, the Flying Red Horse.

The Flying Red Horse seemed to embody every quality that a petrol would want to possess: not just horsepower, but red-hot, flying horse power.

Speed and power, plus beauty and fantasy.

So I couldn't understand why Mobilgas never seemed to use the Flying Red Horse in their advertisements. Instead they used a former pop song and changed the words to: "Mobilgas. Mobilgas. You get that smooth and even power with Mobilgas .... I didn't need a shove 'cause I just fell in love with that power-packed Mobilgas."

Desperate to get off the mail desk, I wrote an advertisement for them, incorporating the Flying Red Horse.

Because of my interest in poetry, I wrote it as a poem. Plus I made sure it included the two things — engine ping and pre-ignition — that all the gas companies talked about in their ads.

If you want sting
instead of ping,
If you want thrust
that you can trust,
If you want good-condition
instead of pre-ignition,
If you want power,
then you'll end'our
To strive for drive —
with Mobilgas of course,
At the sign of the Flying Red Horse

I blushed badly when I showed it to an assistant manager as I cleared his OUT basket.

To my relief, he said he quite liked it.

However, he said, it needed some editing.

Having apparently never heard of poetic licence, he said

"end'our" was the wrong word and changed it to endeavour: which neither rhymed nor scanned.

Obviously not knowing that lines in poetry had to scan, he said it wasn't good English to say "at the sign of the Flying Red Horse" it should be "obtainable at", otherwise people wouldn't know what the advertisement was advocating.

He made sting "stin-n-n-ng" and ping "pin-n-n-g", and then insisted it was a rule that the phrase "Mobilgas Service Station" had to be inserted in all company advertising.

The ad was almost unrecognisable by the time it was published in the company magazine, ending:

> If you want power,
> then you will endeavour
> To strive for drive —
> with Mobilgas of course,
> Obtainable at your friendly local Mobil Service Station
> beneath the sign of the famous Flying Red Horse.

This was not the only writing I was doing.

Now that I had nothing to do with my weekends, Jack got me to cover some Brisbane A-grade rugby league matches that long winter of 1960. Naturally, I didn't know how to write the story. So when I got to the *Courier* Jack would interview me about what had happened, and type the story.

Jack also got me to play football for the *Courier-Mail* rugby league team, so I got to know the reporters.

He had a lot of faith in me.

Jack said he not only thought I could handle the reporter's job, but said it was just the job for me.

Then one Wednesday arvo the Editor-in-Chief of the *Courier-Mail* and *Sunday Mail*, Mr T.C. Bray, called me at Mobilgas.

I couldn't believe someone so important would ring me up. I ran around the corner and up the stairs to his office, but I was in too much of a hurry and, as I opened the door into his room, the handle hooked inside my blue yachting jacket. As I stepped forward, I found I made no progress as he waited, hand outstretched. But "TC", as all the reporters called him among themselves, didn't appear to notice.

He was a small, neat, handsome man with a little silver moustache and a nasal voice and, as I sat down, he looked up and asked almost sternly why I had never proceeded with my previous application eight months earlier.

I told him about my girlfriend, her mother, and her rule about motorcyclists and journalists.

Mr Bray seemed to enjoy this story immensely.

He asked which part of the paper I read first, and I had to admit it was the sports page at the back. But I quickly added that Fred's favourite was the weekly comic about Radish, the hopeless racehorse.

Mr Bray emphasised over and over again that being a journalist was a tough life, involving all sorts of hours. I said I had seen poor Jack staggering out of the house at four in the morning to write radio news bulletins for the paper. And I told him the Lunn household motto was the same as Brisbane's only all-night garage, Barnes Auto: "We never sleep".

I expected Mr Bray to ask why I didn't get an A for Senior English, which Jack said was a usual requirement, but instead he asked me how much I was earning at Mobilgas.

"Well a First Year cadet earns less than that. But we can't have you losing money by coming to us — so we will pay you a pound a week more," he said.

Not only had I got the job, but I had already negotiated a wage rise.

# 5
# *Jim's left-hand man*

Six months after arriving at the *Courier-Mail* I was devastated to hear I had been transferred out of Sport into Finance.

If there was one aspect of life I definitely knew absolutely nothing about, it was money.

Not only had I recently failed Accountancy I, not to mention English I, at University, but no one at Annerley Junction who came into our cake shop had ever even mentioned stocks and shares. My teachers at school — being nuns and Christian Brothers — had talked of life as if it didn't involve money at all. To them the best way of getting something was not to save up for it, but to study hard or pray for it: preferably with a rosary.

With this sort of background I knew it was dangerous to put me into Finance.

By now — after working on Markets, General, and in Sport — I knew just enough to know that newspapers didn't want their readers advised that the best investment strategy was to rack up some plenary indulgences.

The Finance Editor, Mr Norm Hunter, tried to explain away my concerns.

Mr Hunter, an athletic reddish-haired very quiet man, said the stock market was where people invested their spare money in companies. I found this hard to understand. Whenever Fred said he was going to "invest a pound", I knew he meant he was going to back a racehorse. Fred felt companies were part of the "isms and osms" of society and therefore the less said about them the better.

For the life of me, I couldn't see why these companies existed.

They were treated as if they were real people.

These companies had names. They had addresses. They owned land and buildings. They had money in the bank. They even owned parts of other companies which owned part of them. Mr Hunter said they had reputations, could sue and be sued, and paid tax to the government like people.

Companies even owned houses, and cars.

The only difference I could see between them and a human being was that if a company went broke, no one had to pay the debts because the company had Pty. Ltd. after its name.

Which, I supposed, was why people wanted to own one.

Still, I really couldn't understand why we allowed most of the buildings and land in Queensland to be owned by companies which, so far as I could see, were just pieces of paper kept in long rows of grey four-drawer filing cabinets down at the Companies Registry.

Even more mysterious: why did ordinary people buy tiny parts of these bits of paper on the Stock Exchange? They had no control over these companies whatsoever. At least with horse racing, as Fred always said, you could "make your own mistakes".

I had always thought that if people had spare money they should put it in their bank passbook: preferably a steel-grey Commonwealth Bank passbook which Fred and Olive always used. Fred said: "You can't trust anyone with your money, not even me."

When I asked Fred about the Stock Exchange he said he had never thought of investing money there. "I've never made a lot of money because I've always had my head down and my bum up," he said. When I asked how other people got the spare money to invest in shares he quoted his old man Hugh as saying:

"Some were born with silver spoons and others with spurs to ride us."

Luckily, the cadet who taught me the Finance job, John Weinthal, understood these things.

John had also taught me the Markets, and he seemed to know lots, particularly about motor cars, which he test drove for magazines. He took me with him on some hairy drives and I always wondered how he could drive so fast while wearing thick glasses. He carried a small cardboard box of eggs on the front seat, and once we got out in the country, he would drop one egg out the window onto the bitumen, measure off a few miles, then drop a couple more. Then he would wind the car up and time it as we sped past these markers — to see how fast we covered the measured stretches.

John said it was necessary to give the cars a fast workover so he could write how gutsy they were.

He was so confident that he seemed to drive flat out everywhere while sitting at the wheel as if he were at home in the lounge. Because of his interest in cars he was very good friends with Bill Tuckey, who was the paper's motoring writer.

John didn't worry when the Finance Editor went out. He just lit up another unfiltered cigarette and took over the tiny Finance office, which was behind one of the numerous green-painted timber corridor doors on the editorial floor, next to Social.

The Finance office had a small window made of glass you couldn't see through. The office was just big enough for the three of us — if we manoeuvred carefully around the chairs and piles of old newspapers which took up most of the room. As we worked, I found myself wishing I was more like John as he discarded stories he didn't like: until he told me his father had recently died at his own birthday party.

John explained that the Stock Exchange was the place where people who owned shares in a company could sell them, or buy more, at a price determined by the number of shares available, and the demand for them. Our job was to publish how much people sold each share for the previous day, and also to list how many shares were sold.

We also had to work out the "yield" for each share.

"It's simple," said John. "To get the yield all we do is divide today's price of each share by their par value, and multiply by the most recent dividend paid."

I didn't know what he was talking about. So I just learned the formula and applied it to each share.

It all seemed dodgy to me.

How did people know if the company was worth as much as it said when the shares were issued?

What if the people running the company took most of the money for themselves?

What if the people who held the other shares wouldn't back you up if you complained?

Mr Hunter explained that each company had to issue an Annual Report so shareholders and their expert stockbrokers could see what was going on. It was part of our job to watch that they did this. Some companies did badly, others did very well, he said. That was why investors had to choose wisely which ones they put their money into. That was part of the skill.

Mr Hunter didn't seem to mind that I obviously knew nothing about stocks and shares.

"You'll pick it up quickly Hugh," he said. "Jack did."

There it went again: I wished people would stop comparing me with Jack. Apparently Jack took to stocks and shares like he had taken to reading and schoolwork. There had even been talk of making him a permanent assistant to the Finance Editor, but the Political Roundsman got him instead.

I could see that Mr Hunter needed an assistant.

This tiny Finance room had to look after two whole pages by itself, with finance stories pouring in from Sydney and Melbourne, via the telex room, onto Mr Hunter's desk. Yet he was often out at the Stock Exchange, or studying annual reports, or attending the daily afternoon conference the Editor had with all of his department heads to see what was going into the next day's paper.

But, luckily for me, John was there.

All I had to do was walk around the corner to the Stock Exchange building, collect the stock and share prices and sales figures from the front counter, and work out the yields. I didn't need to know anything about finance at all. All I had to do was a couple of hundred simple sums a day.

No algebra, no trigonometry, no calculus — just multiplication and division.

It was an easy mechanical task away from the glare and glamour of the General Reporters' Room. I had a friendly boss and a friend in John, who was the first person I had shared a desk with since nine years of sitting next to Dima Egoroff at school.

Now that I was at the *Courier-Mail* and had no girlfriend I had more time for Jim .... particularly because cadet reporters invariably worked weekends. This gave me two days off during the week to do things. Also Uncle Ken — having done his penance by staying home in 1960 — had headed off with the 1961 Australian tennis team to tour the world for the second time. Ken and Jim didn't seem to understand each other, so I saw them separately.

The only problem with seeing Jim was that, while I liked him, it always seemed to turn into a dangerous thing to do.

In his spare time when not at University, Jim was re-stumping under his mother's house at Kangaroo Point. He had perched the house on some thin steel pipes and bricks while he removed the wooden stumps which had held the house up for more than 50 years. A particularly long black stump was giving him some trouble, so Jim got me to help him lift the 12-foot long, thick, heavy, black, ironbark stump out of the ground.

It was a good three feet in, so we both bent down as low as we could get to lift it out on the count of three, counting on our experience of winning three-legged races together at school.

Jim pulled so fast and so hard that suddenly the stump was well out of the ground, except that, because Jim had lifted his side further and faster, it tipped towards me. The only way I could now stop the stump from landing on me was to hold on tight and go with it. For a few seconds I staggered around Egoroff's backyard with this giant stump in my arms, a stump which — like life — I could neither control nor put down.

Luckily, Jim caught us both.

From then on Jim reckoned I was accident-prone, and insisted on lifting out all the stumps by himself. As he did each one he asked me to "undig" the holes. This was Jim's Russian way of saying to fill the holes in, in the same funny way he called his underpants "U-pants".

As he pulled out stumps, he told me (while carefully avoiding mention of my former girlfriend) a weightlifting club had finally started up at the Uni.

"You should of have seen them," said Jim.

"Without word of a lie, they were all struggling to lift this tiny weight with both hands and Lord and behold I came along and went 'zick'...." — and Jim made a little clicking noise with his mouth and held his thick right arm above his head, moving slightly unsteadily as if the weight were held above him in just one hand.

Then Jim dropped his mouth and gaped in awe, as if he were them looking at him.

"Cutting a long story short, they couldn't believe I lifted one hundred pounds with one hand," Jim said.

I believed him though.

Jim, I noticed, had grown arms like a gorilla in the 15 months since I left school. And no wonder: according to Jim his father's grandmother was so strong that she had once been a Cossack wrestler in the Ukraine.

One of the reasons for his bigger muscles was that Jim now spent all his spare time repairing refrigerators to pay his Uni fees. This meant picking refrigerators up and also delivering them, after we'd push-started Jim's ancient International truck.

I drew the line when we arrived with a refrigerator for a flat at West End.

They hadn't told Jim that the flat was up two flights of

rotting, narrow, wooden stairs which had been tacked onto the side of one of Brisbane's oldest houses.

I said not only couldn't I help him carry the refrigerator up those stairs, but I wouldn't.

This would have upset most people who needed help, but Jim didn't mind. He looked at me disdainfully, pulling his head backwards to exaggerate the distance between us and screwing up his nose so that his mouth twisted slightly sideways:

"I don't want to insult you Lunn, you spastic, but you are too weak. You should eat more," he said.

Jim was always saying food saved him from getting sick. When I occasionally got chesty with bronchitis he said it was because I didn't eat enough.

I stood firm, though I was worried he might grab me as he sometimes did to emphasise my weakness compared with him.

"What are you going to do?" I asked.

"Cutting a long story short, in any case I will carry it up myself," Jim said.

And he did.

No trouble at all.

"I don't know what to do with my strength Lunn. I'm getting stronger," said Jim. He said his favourite animal was the hippopotamus "because he is tough and everybody is scared of him".

Even driving around with Jim was dangerous.

He correctly christened his old red International truck "the bare essentials".

It was a strange contraption. There was no tray on the back — it was just a cabin and a chassis. There were no windows, no doors, and the floor had completely rusted out. Every few miles Jim had to get out and use a spanner to let the air out of the brakes to stop them seizing up.

Because there was no petrol tank, Jim had a five-gallon drum of petrol balanced on the seat between us, with a plastic tube running out from it to the engine.

To stop the truck, Jim pulled the plastic tube out of the can.

I didn't mind push-starting his truck, but I hated driving around sitting next to the drum of petrol.

"Petrol is not as dangerous as everyone thinks Lunn," said Jim. "What I am trying to say to you is this. Without word of a lie I have shot bullets through a can of petrol and Lord and behold nothing happened."

It wasn't just the petrol I was worried about.

Since Jim had got his driving licence a strange aspect of his personality had become evident: he had changed from a youth with an easy approach to life to a young man who had to get where he was going immediately, no matter what. He became like Toad of Toad Hall in *Wind in the Willows*: his eyes lighting up as soon as he touched the steering wheel, his foot driving the truck as fast as it would go — while unable to brook any criticism from his friend and passenger.

Still, I put up with it because Jim was always up to something interesting, and we had a wealth of awful shared experience behind us: including taking the oath of allegiance to the Queen to become Kangaroo Point telegram boys one Christmas holidays.

Jim knew all the best places to get a lot of food quickly. He knew the location of every Greek fish-and-chip shop in Brisbane, because he got jobs repairing their shop refrigerators, and the Greeks always stocked the long red saveloys he liked so much.

In town there was a Chinese restaurant looking down Adelaide Street from the T-junction in George Street where Jim always ordered his favourite, combination short soup, which overflowed with noodles and little flour-and-water pouches of meat.

Jim had now forgotten his plan to build and sell fridges with doors that opened and shut on voice commands — which had won him the Queensland schoolboys science competition three years before — and, instead, wanted to go into mass production of these pouches of meat. People always needed a quick tasty feed to keep their strength up, he

said. He even had a name for these things: "Boberoffs" ...
a combination of the name of the bloke who introduced him
to them (Bob) and his own surname, Egoroff.

Jim was also very interested in "unstable solutions".
Whenever he talked of his experiments with these solutions
he became as excitable and frenetic as he used to get when he
was making Hydrogen at home. His room still bore the ceil-
ing scars from the time his Hydrogen experiment blew up.

Now that he was at University, instead of milk bottles
filled with bubbling substances, Jim had beakers and pi-
pettes and algebraic equations all over the desk in his room.
He said unstable solutions were not only good for synthesis-
ing aromatic esters, and thus making artifical flavours like
banana from chemicals, but one could also make explosives.

"You bastard boy, Lunn," said Jim one day when I arrived, "you should of have had helped me."

He was shaking a solution very slowly to precipitate aspi-
rin. He needed some more chemicals, so we headed off in his
truck. But it broke down at Stones Corner and I couldn't
push it far in the heat.

"Have you been eating today, Lunn," Jim shouted sarcastically from the rusty-red cabin through the missing rear
window.

As had to happen sooner or later, a copper came along
and told Jim his truck was unroadworthy. Jim was sum-
monsed to appear at police headquarters to show cause why
his licence should not be suspended.

An angry Sergeant read the policeman's report out to us.

"You had no brakes," the Sergeant said.

"That's not logical," replied Jim. "We were broken
down because the truck wouldn't go, not because it
wouldn't stop. If we had of have needed brakes we wouldn't
have been there to be caught."

"This report says 'the foot brake travelled to within a
quarter of an inch of the floor'," said the Sergeant. "That's
illegal."

He had us there, I thought.

"Bugger-me-dead that's not right," said Jim. "How

could he say that? The truck has no floor, the floor has rusted away."

"Well according to this report your truck is un-roadworthy anyway. It hasn't even got windscreen wipers or side rear-vision mirrors," said the Sergeant dourly.

"Of course it doesn't," said Jim. "Look, I'll give you all the dope. All jokes aside, there are no wipers because there is no windscreen to get wet. And I couldn't of have had side rear-vision mirrors on the doors, because there are no doors."

The Sergeant let us off with a warning because he said we were only 19, and we kept the truck. But it didn't help, because a few weeks later we wiped it out.

Jim was doing me a favour.

To keep Olive happy I had decided to clean up under our house and the back yard, including getting rid of the chicken-wire cricket nets which were now falling down and covered with vines. Jack was never at home to play cricket now. He spent so much time at his girlfriend Lyn Turner's home at Ipswich that Fred now called him "Jackie Turner".

Jim liked to help Mum, he was always doing things for her like fixing the washing-machine. So he helped me load all the rubbish of childhood high onto his truck — though I kept the penny money-box with a secret opening that Jim had given me for my birthday a decade earlier — and we headed along Ipswich Road bound for the Fairfield dump.

As we turned right, a Holden utility just kept coming faster and faster up Ipswich Road.

"Get going. Get going," I said, as the Holden sped straight into our side and knocked the truck and all its rubbish over into the gutter outside the newsagency at Chardon's Corner.

Jim blamed me for telling him to get going.

I blamed the bloke in the car for continuing to drive as if no one was in front of him.

And the police blamed Jim.

That was the end of the truck. "It has been killed," Jim said matter-of-factly.

71

Jim needed a vehicle to repair refrigerators. Otherwise it would be back behind the counter at Astor TV for him, where he had worked for the first year out of school.

Then his fortunes changed. He was just thinking of getting a milk run and giving up University for a while when he won a lot of money in — of all things — a word game competition.

Although Jim had passed Senior English, it was really only his second language. While he could rattle off Russian tongue-twisters, he had his own way of using English. Whenever he phoned me up he invariably said: "It's Jim out here Lunn." When we met some girls down the Gold Coast who couldn't quite get my first name right, Jim explained by pointing: "This is I, that's you. It's me, he's Hugh."

We went to town for some combination short soup and Jim had a smile as white, and as wide, as a refrigerator. He would now be able to stay at University and buy himself a car to replace the old truck. And he said he would let me drive his car if I needed some wheels to take a girl out or something.

I said this was unnecessary.

"You bastard boy Lunn," Jim said. "You are one of my left-hand men. What does it profit a man to let his grass grow and then get lost in it?"

Then Jim added proudly:

"I made that up myself. Honestly I did."

Jim said he was going to get the coolest chariot money could buy, something with excellent engineering and design specifications: in other words a machine that was mean, fast, and, of course, very powerful.

We went to a second-hand car yard at the Gabba and Jim immediately fell in love with the biggest jalopy I had ever seen.

It was a huge light green car with sharp fins rising upwards and outwards like small rear wings from each side of the boot at the back. The roofline was so sleek that there were no central door pillars. Down each side was a cream strip which widened then narrowed between strips of chrome. The dashboard was chockers with instruments: each one set in large round circles of chrome, the tops of which jutted up sharply over the top of the dash like headlight covers. Best of all, it had white-walled tyres and four headlights instead of two.

It was twice the size of a Customline, and its looks far more snazzy.

When the salesman opened the snooker-table-sized bonnet, the engine itself was as big as Fred's Zephyr Six: boot and all.

This car was called a Plymouth Belvedere which, the salesman said, had been fully imported from America a few years before. It had so many horsepower that he couldn't quite remember the figure.

Jim took the Belvedere for a test drive.

I never imagined a heap like this could take off so fast. Instead of a gear lever it had inch-long slender black buttons on a silver background to the right of the dashboard between the steering wheel and door. These were numbered one to four and "R" for reverse. To change gears you just pushed whichever button you were after. Jim pushed the top left one in to engage first gear and, as he stood on the accelerator, my head went straight back over the top of the wide low two-tone green front seat, and the squealing tyres left a swirl of smoke trailing way behind us like a whirly-whirly in a dusty playground.

We were still accelerating when Jim had to apply the brakes for the Gabba Fiveways.

It was definitely no bomb.

The salesman offered to let us have a test drive by ourselves because he said he had some urgent work to do back at the office, but Jim said there was no need for any further tests: "In any case I will have it."

I noticed Jim signed the papers using his original Russian initial of "D" for Dimitri. I asked him why he didn't use "J", since now everybody called him Jim.

"Dimitri is my real name," he said.

"But why then have you had everyone calling you Jim for the last seven years?" I asked.

"Are you an idiot or what Lunn?" he said. "In Australia everyone shortens long names. So my name would of have been made 'Dim'. That wouldn't of have sounded too hot, so I chose Jim."

In the big Plymouth we idled sedately up Main Street, Kangaroo Point, both with elbows out the window to catch the cool air as Jim alternated between flat out and dead slow to better contrast the power of the car.

But even this car wasn't powerful enough for Jim. He took it to a mechanic and had the head shaved, bigger valves installed, and added a new four-barrel Holley carburettor. After that, using special high octane petrol, the tyres squealed and smoked every time Jim took off.

It was how you knew when Jim arrived, or left.

On my first go cruising Brisbane behind the wheel of the Belvedere I found it difficult to control. There were two thick, hand-shaped white handgrips on either side of the steering wheel which made me feel I was master of the car. But once this mass of green metal started moving swiftly forward it became difficult to change direction. The steering wheel had to be turned many more times than the Zephyr's to turn a corner, but once it had been spun a few times the Belvedere would suddenly spurt off in the new direction. This made it the perfect car for driving girls around in. Every curve in the road would become a COD corner — Come Over Darling.

No one else on the road stood a chance as I flashed across the Story Bridge and up Queen Street, hoping someone I knew would see me.

For the first time since I was at school with Jim I started to feel on top of things. I was suddenly in command and raring to go: ready to give this betsy a kick in the guts at a moment's notice.

Out along Coronation Drive towards the University I burned off some squares in their Holdens.

I was herbing along so quickly that I even imagined I could get to the University from the City Hall in less than seven minutes.

# 6
# *The Doctrine of the Five Fs*

Despite my longing for a girlfriend, girls had been out of the question for me since my girlfriend gave me up.

I no longer had any confidence in myself. So I became self-conscious when talking to girls. So much so that one day when I ran into a beautiful girl called Jocelyn England in Queen Street, a girl Ken had been out with, not only did I blush but — after a couple of minutes — the left side of my face started to twitch involuntarily.

I didn't know how to stop this from happening, and it was getting worse. So I smiled, pointed at a tram and jumped aboard as if in a hurry. It didn't matter that the tram was going to Chermside in north Brisbane. I got off in the Valley and caught another tram back.

I ran into a similar problem when a buxom older girl reporter from the *Courier-Mail*'s Social department came and asked me to pose with her for a photo.

She had written a fashion story that men were now wearing ties made of the same material as their girlfriends' dresses, to show everyone they were a pair. So she needed a photo of a loving couple dressed in the same material to go with the story.

To get this photo we had to stand next to each other for several minutes, with her so close in front of me that I could feel her large satin breath-taking softness through her frilly blouse as it came into contact with my white shirt.

It was one of the many times in my life that I wished I wasn't wearing a singlet.

For the purposes of the photo she had to stand against me and smile up into my eyes, like a girlfriend, while holding the special tie — which was made of white material with black spots, the same as her skirt. As we posed together and locked eyes my whole body began to change, as if I was again going under chloroform for an ear operation. Then my face began to twitch and I came spinning rapidly back to reality. So I smiled hard.

Still she looked up into my eyes, acting out her role perfectly, as if nothing was happening.

The photographer was mucking around, as they always did, doing everything possible except press the button to take the bloody picture. I had to do something to get my mind off the girl, so I started talking loudly to the photographer on every subject that might get my thoughts elsewhere.

"Slasher Mackay has just got to be the best cricketer in the country!" I said loudly. "Think of his unusual batting style which has caused the English press to say 'Mackay doesn't hit the ball, he squirts it'."

"Rod Laver must be a good show at Wimbledon this July," I shouted even louder, secretly hoping that Kenny Fletcher would beat him there.

But the photographer wouldn't talk.

"Queensland will definitely win the Sheffield Shield next year," I said, stabbing the air violently with an index finger.

It worked.

"That'll be the day," the photographer said. "They'd have to raffle it."

As I thought about this I realised the twitch had gone. He took the photo, the buxom girl left without saying goodbye, and I was never asked by Social to model for a picture again.

What they didn't know was that I was still suffering, even though it had been more than a year since my girlfriend gave me up: a year of seeing her photo in the social pages, or spotting her from a distance at events like the rugby Test at the Exhibition ground when she arrived with some drip. And her looking like a film starlet in a full-length fawn coat and red-blonde hair, longer now, down below the shoulders.

I tried not to see her or hear about her, but people couldn't wait to tell me who she was going out with. It was funny, I thought, when I saw her in the distance one day: we had been such great friends. Yet now I was the only person in Brisbane who couldn't just go up and say hello.

It was all so irreversible.

I didn't talk about her at all, now that I was 20 years old: at least not since a boy called Greg Petrie who was in Jack's class at school — whom I much admired because of his football and cricket ability — came up to me at a dance and said: "Stop telling everyone about this girl giving you up. Start being yourself and people will think better of you."

I was impressed.

Not by the unsolicited advice, but by the fact that he cared what people thought of me even though I barely knew him.

The day after this happened at a dance at the O'Connor Boathouse, I made the mistake of asking an embittered older journalist on his way back from a session at the pub what he thought it was best to do: should one not talk about a girl at all after she gave you up?

His answer shocked and also disgusted me.

With girls, he said, it was best — now that I was out of school — that I learnt what the Christian Brothers would not have taught me.

He called it "the doctrine of the five fs".

"Find them, feel them, finger them, fuck them, and forget them," he said.

I laughed nervously with him, so as not to seem a spoilsport, but I was disturbed by this new faith, even though I didn't for a moment plan to become a follower. I believed girls were pure: you met them, you kissed them, you fell in love with them, you married them, and you had a family with them.

The old journalist laughed when I said this.

"You are lucky you didn't marry at your age," he said. "Fifty years is one hell of a long time to be married. You wouldn't be going to all those journo parties if you had."

Now that I had been on the paper for nearly a year, I had

77

started to go to these parties which started at midnight when most reporters had finished work for the day.

Since Fred was asleep, I could take his Zephyr.

I was a bit scared of these shindigs after hearing about some of the ones Jack had been to over the years: like the one where a drunk reporter woke up after the party and discovered he was in Mt Isa, 1,000 miles away. Or the infamous party where the "nudie cuties" from Brisbane's Theatre Royal turned up and danced for, and with, the journalists. Or the fights that reportedly sometimes broke out once they all got drunk.

The only drink I had ever had was a skol of vodka with Jim at his house. But I didn't know where to put my hands — in my pockets, behind my head, or under folded arms — so I held a cold glass of beer and sipped gingerly: always remembering the frightening scene the night Jack came home drunk.

Olive's voice echoed off the walls of our wooden house in the darkness as if she wanted everyone to hear: "You're drunk."

This was said with such vehemence that I stayed in my room until late the next day. Gay said Mum was particularly upset because her sister, Aunty Vera, was there to see Jack "in this condition". Mum always said she had eyes in the back of her head.

I also knew that you had to be tough to survive some of these booze-ups, otherwise Jack wouldn't have developed such a stern answer to anyone who said anything he didn't like: "Drop Dead."

Many of these all-night bashes were held at the Annerley home of a red-haired cadet called Peter Thompson, whose parents and sister didn't seem to mind the noise.

Peter Thompson was also 20, but he knew infinitely more about journalism than I did. He had written sports reports for the paper while he was still at Brisbane Grammar School and he read the paper every day. Thus he had lots of opinions on stories and how they were written, and what stories should have been in the paper but weren't.

When Mr Bray wrote a feature about his overseas trip Peter gave a lecture at a party, saying how well written it was, and pointing out the occasional two and three word sentences which, he said, gave the writing punch.

Peter had started eight months ahead of me, joining the *Courier* at the same time I joined Mobilgas. But he was much further ahead than that. He had already had features published, and had even worked as a sub-editor because he had taught himself the many different type-faces the paper used for its headlines.

Even Jack reckoned Peter was a budding top journalist.

Peter seemed to like me because I was Jack's brother. He would corner me at parties over a glass of beer and in his quiet, though enthusiastic, voice would emphasise what a serious business journalism was. He thought journalism was much more important than other people did, and he was always backed up in this view by his schoolmate, Bob Macklin, who Peter had talked into joining the paper after Bob spent a year as a jackeroo out west.

I liked Peter. But I was a bit annoyed by Bob Macklin. He was so confident with girls, and was doing so well at journalism, yet he had joined the paper four months after me.

Macklin and Thompson had already had a joint by-lined feature published — something about the lack of racist feelings among primary school children. I wasn't too sure what they wrote, because I didn't bother reading the paper each day like you were supposed to.

Even on your days off, Peter reckoned.

I found the paper pretty boring. Particularly page four, which was the foreign news page. This page was full of headlines about countries I knew nothing about. The headlines were mainly about "Reds". But Peter believed that reading page four was the key to journalistic success.

"Dad, if you know what is happening overseas you will be way ahead of everyone else in Australian journalism," he often semi-whispered over his glass of beer at his kitchen table, before smiling slightly and taking a swig.

I always seemed to end up in the kitchen at these parties.

Perhaps this was because at first I felt very much on the outer.

I didn't smoke or drink and had no opinions on what was wrong with the paper.

I wasn't even interested in getting knocked back by any of the girls who seemed to arrive from everywhere: the Library, the copy desk, the artists, the *Tele*, and even the hospitals. When they were short of girls, the older reporters would just ring up a hospital and invite a dozen nurses "to a journalists' party".

Amazingly, the nurses would turn up.

When the journalists sang the songs they always sang at parties at about three in the morning I just listened. Bruce Wilson always led a song all the journalists who had done French at school seemed to know.

There was another song which seemed blasphemous to me because the chorus was: "Yes by Jesus Christ I am". And they always sang the one to an old hit tune I knew from my tap-dancing days: "Binga Banga Bonga I don't want to leave the Congo." The *Courier* reporters had their own words which included reference to a Brisbane hotel called "the Nundah" where some of them drank on days off.

It began:

Chunda, Chunda, Chunda,
I don't want to leave the Nundah —
I refuse to go;
Splita, splata, splutter —
I'm so happy in the gutter,
I don't want to know.

One of the journalists was famous for having auctioned his underpants just for fun at one of these dos. There were occasional loud arguments, but most of the night was made up of groups of quiet drinkers earnestly discussing newspapers and great stories that had been written by them — and bad stories that had been written by other, less-talented journalists, who weren't at the party.

Gary Evans placed his huge frame on a table and recited

"The Man from Ironbark" right through without a mistake, to loud applause.

Having no party acts myself (Jack and I kept our tap-dancing ability to ourselves), one night I sat listening to records in a corner. Luckily I did because I discovered a beautiful singer I had never heard of on the wireless, Joan Baez. She sang what was called folk music and I played her hauntingly pure voice singing "Mary Hamilton" all night.

Jim sometimes turned up at these parties. He drank only the occasional straight vodka, so he was usually quiet, unless someone wanted an arm wrestle.

With a coat on, Jim's massive dark forearms were not obvious, so there would always be some mug who would think he could beat him. Yet Jim's body was as hard as a windowsill. And, had they watched him closely, they would have seen Jim cracking with one hand the walnuts he was eating.

Jim's patter would always be the same. After he and his opponent had strained mightily for several minutes before a hushed crowd of males in suits, Jim would suddenly look up and, sounding deliberately bored, say: "Come on, start pushing."

Jim now occasionally allowed himself a swear word: "Bugger me dead, mate. You're not even trying."

The only person Jim had ever had any trouble with in an arm wrestle was a bearded bloke from Uni who turned up in a dark suit, with a live pet rat in one of the coat pockets. But then this man turned out to be a Russian too.

Jim said the fact that his opponent was Russian had nothing to do with it: it was the thought of the rat, he said, that had weakened him slightly.

One night some medical students arrived at a party with a bloke with a dark cow's lick hairstyle who they said was the University's champion arm wrestler. He would do Jim like a dinner — they would bet on it — and everyone gathered in the Auchenflower house for the fray.

Jim and this student sat opposite each other with their elbows on a solid wooden table in the kitchen. As they rolled up their sleeves, both groups of supporters gasped audibly as they saw the size of the arm of the person they hadn't backed. The calluses on the palms of both right hands stood up like warts.

Jim must have been a bit worried, because he resorted to one of his old ploys.

He announced to the disbelieving audience that he would wrestle this supposed University champion "using two fingers" — and Jim raised two fingers above his resting arm, as if giving a scout salute. Jim knew the student would never accept that, and he didn't. But the damage had been done.

They both joined hands. For a few minutes there was no evidence of a struggle as the arm muscles touched. It appeared neither was trying, until the plates on the timber kitchen dresser at the other end of the room started to rattle. Then vibrate violently. The tea cups on the dresser's hooks swayed. But still the Uni champ smiled at his supporters.

Jim, of course, couldn't help but talk.

Whenever Jim was going to insult someone he always began: "I don't want to insult you, but ...." So he said: "I don't want to insult you mate, but, if you're not going to push, I'm not going to sit here holding hands all night with you."

With that, the timber in the Queensland house gave a groan and, just for a moment, I worried for Jim's sake. It seemed to me that there was just the hint of give in his arm, and I began to worry if he might be in more trouble than Flash Gordon.

Then, suddenly, as if he lost all strength at one go, the other fellow's arm fell over.

To celebrate, Jim drank half a glass of vodka.

Jim was pleased with himself because it was his second win of the night. Earlier, Jim — on being introduced to a pretty French girl called Dominique — kissed her hand and pretended he could barely speak English by putting on a heavy accent and carefully mis-pronouncing the few words he did use.

"Dimitri," she said. "You must learn zee Anglaise better."

Soon she was sitting on Jim's lap getting him to pronounce "I like you" after her, and shaping his lips with her fingers.

"Arrh Louuuke yaah," said Jim.

"Non. Non. I like you," said Dominique.

"Arr Lukie yowah," said Jim, as Dominique played with his mouth.

"Like another drink Jim?" I asked.

"It's OK mate I'm pretty busy with this sheila at the moment," said Jim.

The French girl leapt off his lap: "I spit on you. I swear at you. You egotist," she said.

It was after one of these parties that Bob Macklin pulled me aside at work and, in his infectiously happy smiling way of talking seriously, told me I had to be prepared to take the plunge "and be a small fish in a big sea".

I wasn't sure what he was getting at but, at the next do, I surprised myself by announcing that I could put Fred's Zephyr into first gear while doing 35 m.p.h.

No one believed me. But I had been practising what Jack called "double de-clutching".

This was done by putting the clutch in, pushing the column gear stick into neutral, letting the clutch out, revving like mad with the right foot and — just as the revs started to die — pulling the gear lever down into first while re-depressing the clutch.

Then, as the clutch was let out, the engine roared and bounced as the car suddenly found itself travelling at speeds it could never reach in first gear.

Everyone went on to the road outside in Fairfield as I zoomed down the bitumen.

I revved until the Zephyr's donk screamed, dropped the clutch, and sent the engine roaring as the car protested violently at doing 40 m.p.h. in first gear.

Peter Thompson, who as yet didn't drive, was much more impressed with this than anything I had ever written for the paper. At the next party he took bets that I could do it, and got me to do it again.

The next week Fred broke an axle and the garage asked him what he had been doing to the Zephyr.

"We've never seen axles like that before. It is as if some giant has come along and twisted them," the mechanic said. Fred told me this story while eyeing me suspiciously. But I had had too much practice lying to teachers to crack that easily.

Remembering that Fred often drove the Zephyr without using second gear — because he said it was unnecessary — I replied: "You were warned Dad not to keep changing directly from first to third."

Bob Macklin must have been impressed too because, one night shortly afterwards, he invited me to accompany him to a nightclub after work.

We went up a dark stairway opposite the Treasury Building in Queen Street, paid a cover charge, and sat at one of the small round tables in a large room filled with smoke and men. We ordered a couple of cappuccinos just before a beautiful woman danced suddenly out between the tables and started to take her clothes off.

I couldn't believe it.

Bob's face was covered with a bigger-than-usual grin as I marvelled at the texture and shape of the female form, a thought which seemed to place a large weight on the centre of my chest.

No wonder, I thought, Brother Campbell told us "look not upon a maiden lest her beauty be a stumbling block to thee". Particularly when she removed her brassiere to reveal her bosom. I was surprised how far apart breasts were; how round; how obviously soft; and how they could move independently in what we had learned in Senior Physics was called "simple harmonic motion".

These breasts were not what I had imagined girls had under their clothes.

They dropped slightly with their considerable weight and

then curved ever upwards and outwards to two stuck-on patches of silver paper in the middle at the front.

No wonder breasts were considered sinful and were kept covered.

She came so close to us I could have reached out and touched them.

I marvelled that she hadn't covered her belly button with a patch of silver paper too, seeing as the *Courier-Mail* and the *Telegraph* employed artists who painted out the belly-buttons of bikini girls before publishing their photos: so as not to offend or excite readers.

# 7
# *Tarzan takes a holiday*

Jack had much less to do with my life now because, aged 22, he had married his girlfriend, Lyn Turner, and had moved out of our Annerley house to a rented flat on Milton Road just past the Elite picture theatre.

He nearly ended up missing his own wedding.

Jack was so hot on the trail of some scoop that he forgot to ask the Chief-of-Staff to give him his wedding day off. So Jack was rostered on General reporting for the *Sunday Mail* on his wedding day. The only way out was to find a reporter who not only had Saturday off, but who was willing to swap it for the Wednesday.

This wasn't going to be easy.

Saturdays off were rare. Almost all *Courier-Mail* reporters were rostered to work on Saturdays because the *Sunday Mail* was a much bigger paper with much earlier deadlines. And, unlike the *Courier* which had no Brisbane opposition, it was involved in a neck-to-neck race with another paper, the *Sunday Truth*, which was very popular because it was a small paper with big headlines and lots of stories on sex and murder.

Both of these papers tried to beat each other out on a Saturday night to catch the city theatre crowds first with all the latest news. At six o'clock on Saturday nights editors and sub-editors kept running in and out of doors urging reporters on by yelling out "the *Truth*'s on the street! the *Truth*'s on the street!" Thus, no reporter who happened to be lucky enough to score a Saturday off would want to give it away just because someone else was getting married.

Also, Jack's options were strictly limited.

He couldn't just swap a day off with anybody. It had to be someone of similar experience who the Chief-of-Staff thought could handle Jack's job.

So Jack couldn't swap with me, even though I was rostered off for that Saturday. Besides, I had to be there, as I was to be Best Man.

Jack was such a big star now that he sometimes appeared on television on *Meet the Press*. If he was on, the whole family — except Fred who was at the shop — gathered around our Bush Simpson TV set on a Sunday night to watch Jack and a couple of other reporters pin someone down with questions. By now, Jack was obviously so important that Olive didn't even bother skiting about him any more. She said his success was "there for everyone to see". Jack even got his photo on the front page of the *Courier* inspecting a head-on collision at Wynnum.

Jack got out from under at the last minute and arranged a swap for his wedding.

A priest who was a friend of Kenny Fletcher's married them — after giving Lyn lessons in Catholicism and making her promise to bring up the kids as Catholics because she was a Protestant. But at least, being a friend of Ken's, he married them in front of the main altar. Usually such mixed marriages could only take place at a side altar.

Practically everyone was crying at the wedding because suddenly our family was splitting up forever.

Olive was holding back her tears, but I could tell she was particularly upset because Jack was her first baby, the one she won the bonniest baby in Brisbane with in 1939, the baby she came through the whole of World War II with, the one she always said had "gumption", her highest praise. Jack was the one she fed barley water to improve his constitution, the little boy Fred had always said he would have to nurse until Jack was 40.

Gay, who was 18, always bawled at such sad occasions, and my youngest sister Sheryl was very, very quiet. But she had to be.

Mum had caught her smoking and gave her what for.

While I felt unhappy to see this sign of the Lunn family changing, I couldn't help seeing that this wedding also had a bright side. I would have a room to myself at home; Jack wouldn't be there to urge me to write more stories or to study for my Uni exams; and I could sleep in as long as I liked.

Jack always complained I was sleeping my life away.

He never seemed to appreciate my explanation that I didn't want to go to bed because I was enjoying myself so much when I was awake; and I was enjoying being asleep so much that I didn't want to get up.

However, as I handed over the tiny gold wedding ring to Father Carroll, I also knew I would miss the stories Jack told at the dinner table about his job. One of the ones we liked to hear him tell over and over was the one about the spelling mistake he made in a radio news bulletin.

These bulletins were read at 4BK on the floor above the Literary Department, and Jack had lots of hair-raising stories about running upstairs with part of a story for the announcer, and then dashing back down to write the rest quickly so he could get back upstairs before the announcer ran out of story to read.

Sometimes, he said, the announcer would have to slow right down as he neared the end, speeding up again when he heard Jack pounding up the stairs.

This need for speed, Jack told the family around our oval silky oak dining table in the breakfast room, caused some mistakes in typing. One of these proved almost disastrous when Jack hit the ''s'' instead of the ''w'' — which were next to each other on the typewriter keyboard.

If the radio announcer had time, he would quickly read through a story aloud for practice before going to air, and as he did so with this story the announcer nearly fell over as he heard himself read aloud in front of a stunned Jack:

''President Eisenhower said from the Shitehouse yesterday ...''

Fred loved this story even though he always said ''you have to show due respect''. But he said this in a way which suggested he saw it as something you did — not out of respect — but to make people think you had respect.

Once, as Jack ran up the stairs with a breaking story, he stopped to make a last-second alteration. Jack put the sheet of copypaper up against the wall and changed a word. "Then I couldn't get the story back off the wall. The wall had just been painted," Jack said. Eventually, he peeled it off and handed the announcer a story dripping with green paint.

Jack got a special note from Mr Bray another day because he had insisted the radio announcer interrupt a record to broadcast a news-flash that a man with a gun had attempted to hijack an aircraft over Brisbane.

He was doing so well that the Editor of *Sunday Truth* offered him a job: not just upping Jack to a C grading, but saying he would be "in on the ground floor" — whatever that meant — if he changed papers. But Jack preferred to stay with the *Courier*, which Olive said was the right thing to do. Olive read the *Truth* from cover to cover every Sunday. But she said she didn't want one of her sons writing for it.

Jack had also been writing politics, and Mum's two brothers couldn't believe that he had travelled all over Queensland in a car with one of the top Labor Party politicians in Australia: a Mr Gough Whitlam, from Sydney.

Uncle Cyril and Uncle Les, and Mum too, all liked the Labor Party best: although Olive always told us that the best way to vote was: "put the lion in and the tiger out".

Uncle Les was a life member of the ALP and Uncle Cyril was so much for the Labor Party that he reckoned the *Courier-Mail* was against them, but Jack said this wasn't right. Uncle Les was always telling jokes against Prime Minister "Pig iron Bob" Menzies, and I don't think Mum's two brothers really forgave her for letting us work for what they called "the Tory press".

At least not until they heard that Jack had had lunch with Gough Whitlam in Sydney on his honeymoon.

Jack and Lyn were honeymooning in a tent at a north Sydney camping ground: the same tent with the cowboy and the indian on the sides that the family had used on its epic drive to Melbourne in the Zephyr seven years before .... except that this time Jack didn't have the rest of the family to help him. So he forgot to take the tent pegs and had to borrow some from a nearby house.

Jack arranged to meet Mr Whitlam at a posh Sydney restaurant. When Mr Whitlam asked where he and Lyn were honeymooning, Jack said as casually as he could:

"Oh, we're staying on the North Shore, Gough."

With Jack away for six weeks, at least I knew the Chief-of-Staff could not mix us up again for a while. This had happened twice since I had returned to the General Reporters' Room.

A particularly vague Chief-of-Staff — who once called Cliff Dawson into his office, gave him no stories to do, and then said "that'll be all" — came over to my desk and said he was sending me up the north coast with Chief Photographer, Al Pascoe.

I should have realised they would never send a First-Year cadet with the Chief Photographer. Or at least I should have guessed no one would give a First-Year cadet such a vague instruction as "dig up a couple of good stories".

As we drove through the countryside up around Nambour I finally thought of a story and began making notes on how the farmers seemed to be doing very well because the grass was long, and thick, and green. But Al cautioned that this wasn't much of a story, because he couldn't take a photo to go with it. On our way back, empty-handed, Al pulled up at a burnt-out refrigerated truck on the Bruce Highway, and said "here's our story". The paper ran the photo on the front page next day, with my story underneath re-written by the Pictorial Editor into what they called "block-lines".

Jack told me later that a few hours after we left, the Chief-of-Staff asked him why he was still in the office and not up the north coast with Al Pascoe.

A few days later another Chief-of-Staff must have mixed us up again.

When you were on General reporting, the Chief-of-Staff would often casually inquire, as you sat across the other side of his desk taking notes, if you had read a particular story in that day's paper: or even a certain letter-to-the-editor. Since I never bothered reading the paper, unless Jack had something in, it was lucky that Jack had warned me to always — no matter what — say I had read the story.

On this day I was surprised to be one of the first people called in to be briefed.

"Did you see that para in the paper this morning that one of our top PMG officials retires this week after 50 years in the job?"

"Yes," I lied, adding unnecessarily: "Interesting story wasn't it?"

"I don't know how you can call one para interesting, Colonel," the COS replied, looking at me with one eyebrow raised.

I said nothing.

"Anyway, I want you to find out just how interesting that para was. They're expecting you and a photographer at the Gabba Post Office for the interview at three. That'll be all, Colonel."

Interview?

Why were they sending me on an interview? I didn't interview people. I just wrote down what people told me.

The trouble with going out on a job in Brisbane with photographers was that they carried cameras as big as footballs with giant silver flashlights on top. This attracted unnecessary attention wherever you went, probably because people always wanted to get their photo in the paper.

So when photographer Norm Lye and myself walked in to the Gabba Post Office the place went quiet, and all work ceased.

An official was in such a hurry to greet "the Press" he tripped over. He ushered us behind the counter, offered drinks, and introduced us to an old man in a suit who was sitting down smoking a pipe.

Norm Lye, who Jack said was a great photographer to go

on jobs with because he was experienced, seemed to wash his hands of the whole affair by taking up residence sitting on someone's desk several yards away, his elbow leaning on his giant camera. So I was forced to say something to the man.

"We're from the *Courier-Mail*. They sent us here to interview you."

"Yes," he said.

He sucked on the pipe and stared at me.

I pulled out a brand new blue-grey soft-covered Quill notebook and a pencil, both supplied to reporters for just such interviews. Actually it was only half a notebook, because the *Courier* cut the notebooks lengthways down the middle either to save money or because it was quicker to write quotes down in a long, narrow pad.

I folded back the thin grey "Qu" cover to reveal a virgin white page covered with equidistant thick horizontal blue lines and poised my pencil carefully over the paper as the man watched and smoked.

I knew enough about reporting to check his name — even though it was in the paper that morning — and to ask him to spell it out so I didn't get into trouble with the subs. I also knew enough to ask his age.

"You don't need to know that sonny," he said.

"Yes, reporters get the age of every person they write about so that readers will know if the person is 18 or 80," I said, quoting Jack.

"Well I wouldn't be retiring if I was 18," he said.

By that time about 30 prying PMG employees had gathered closely around. They all tittered.

"I've never seen a reporter interview anyone before!" a woman said to the girl next to her.

Having also extracted his title in the PMG (I had to be careful not to call the Post Master General's office "the Public Money Grabbers" like Olive always did), I looked at the sea of faces.

What did I do now? What else to ask?

"When do you retire?" I said.

"Today," he said, blowing smoke in my face.

I carefully wrote "today" in the notebook which didn't look anything like the crumpled notebooks Bill Tuckey and Jack used. It looked too new. Probably because so far I had filled only three lines of the first page.

I looked up again hoping the crotchety old man would say something.

But he just sucked his pipe.

Silent minutes passed as my mind raced, and the crowd craned forward.

How long before all of these people would realise I wasn't pausing for effect — but rather didn't know what I was doing?

I realised that very soon I was going to have to announce "I'm sorry, but I can't think of any questions. My mind has gone blank."

There was nothing else for it, unless, of course, I said I was sick.

Maybe a headache?

That was it. I'd ask for a Vincent's APC and say I had a really bad headache.

Then I heard a noise from behind.

It was a voice starting up.

"You must have seen a lot of changes in the PMG over the last 50 years?" the voice said. I swung around and it was Norm Lye, the photographer.

Norm was still sitting on the desk with his camera now resting heavily on his thighs, and he winked encouragingly.

"I certainly have," said the old man, as I madly wrote down that he had seen "unlimited changes".

But once he had listed those I was stuck again.

"Are young men in the PMG as good today as they were when you started?" said Norm from behind me, and once again the 60 prying eyes darted from me to him.

"There has been no change in the standard of young men. Don't let anyone fall for that story that modern youth are no good. I won't hear of it," the old man said.

Norm had saved the day, and I had a new respect for the knowledge of photographers.

In fact, now that I had been a journalist for almost a year, I had learnt a lot of things.

I had learnt that there was an unwritten law in newspaper offices to always approach a reporter from in front of his typewriter, never from behind. One day I just happened to be surreptitiously watching how an A-grade reporter wrote his story — sucked in, I guess, by the huge pile of newspaper clippings covering his desk — when, without warning, he swung around nearly knocking me over as he leapt up out of his chair and swore.

"Listen, son," he said, fixing me with small black eyes. "Let me give you a piece of advice. Never, ever, read another reporter's story until he is happy it is finished. And it isn't finished when it is still in the typewriter. It isn't finished until he puts it in the subs basket!"

And he sat down and started typing furiously again.

One General reporter who taught me a lot was a D-grade called Rosemary Merson. When she had nothing else to do Rosemary used to ask cadets what they were writing and then would help improve the story. She saved me from the wrath of the subs one day by warning: "beware of 'first' claims because someone will always come along who did it three decades ago".

When I was struggling to write a story about a glut of cheap apples Rosemary suggested I ring the *Courier-Mail*'s doctor "Doctor Brisben" and get him to recommend that now was the time to take to heart the old "apple a day keeps the doctor away" trick.

I had seen this "Doctor Brisben" quoted in the *Courier* a lot, so I was surprised to find out that was not his real name.

Dr Brisben was some sort of medical specialist up on Wickham Terrace who the paper paid to give opinions to reporters under this made-up name. It sounded a bit dodgy to me: interviewing a fake name, a person I had never seen, over the telephone, and then quoting him in the paper.

But I did it.

The only trouble was that this doctor refused to say apples were any good for you. I even tried to pin him down on orange juice in the end, but he said that oranges only put an extra strain on your kidneys. Anyway the story didn't get in because the Test cricket from England was what they called at the paper "the splash" — the story in big type at the top of page one.

Egg-eating contests were all the go in Brisbane and I had to cover people trying to eat them by the score at Coles in Queen Street. Some ate them scrambled, some fried, some poached, but the winner drank them raw.

I didn't like the whole thing, it almost made me sick, but Rosemary helped me get the story in the paper by using made-up words like "eggciting", "eggsperts", and "eggceptional". The newspaper seemed to like plays on words like that, and footnotes (or, if it was a story about dogs — "paw-notes").

Though the first time I tried using a footnote at the bottom of a story it turned out to be the wrong thing to do.

A young man from Sydney had made headlines by going native in north Queensland. He didn't shave, wore a loin cloth and, locals said, ate wild pigs, mangoes, coconuts, fish, and even birds to survive. His name was Michael Fomenko and all the newspapers in Australia — including ours — had christened him "Tarzan Fomenko". Photos of him semi-nude and bearded in the jungle had been published, but he wouldn't talk to reporters because he said he wanted to be left alone.

The Chief-of-Staff called me in and said he had heard Tarzan was travelling with a Catholic priest who was taking him back to Sydney on a train. I was to go to South Brisbane railway station and see if I could get a story.

He must have thought I had no chance, because he didn't send a photographer.

This time when I hit South Brisbane station I was determined to do better than my first visit for the migrant train. This time I wasn't carrying a *Courier-Mail* half-notebook: instead I had a copy of the *Tele* rolled casually in my left fist for jotted notes — a trick Kev O'Donohue taught me when he took me with him on an interview one day. Kev said notebooks frightened people. Best to make the occasional scribbled word on the edge of the *Tele*.

And this time if I saw someone, anyone, I was going to "buttonhole" them, as Jack called making sure they stopped and talked to you.

I saw a priest in black suit with a wild-looking long-haired, bearded man in shirt and trousers already disappearing into a carriage on the interstate train which was due out in two minutes.

I raced along the concrete platform and jumped up the stairs and raced through the train to find them.

The pair were sitting together.

After hesitating briefly I approached the priest, calling him "Father" and letting him know, first up, that I was a Catholic boy who had attended St Joseph's College, Gregory Terrace, and had played fullback for the First XV.

I suspected Catholics would stick together, and it worked.

The priest invited me to sit down, but said I couldn't interview Tarzan as he wasn't interested in talking to the Press.

The train jolted.

Tarzan, the priest said, speaking for the hynotic-eyed man on his right, just didn't want publicity and wanted desperately to be left alone. The priest said Mr Fomenko, as I called him, just needed some help and understanding.

There was no story here.

Mr Fomenko merely wanted to visit his mother in Sydney for some White Russian celebrations with his family, before returning back north to the jungle.

This was too good to be true!

My best mate, I told Tarzan, was a White Russian like him. Did he know him? His name was Dimitri (Jim) Egoroff, and he was a bit of a Tarzan too.

Strong, incredibly strong, those White Russians, I said.

Silence.

A loud train whistle blew.

Tarzan Fomenko fixed me with the gaze of eyes that were just a little too clear.

"All I can tell you," he said very slowly, "is that I am the sort of person who likes jacaranda trees and things like that."

Then the priest, annoyed that Tarzan had spoken to me, ushered me off the train saying it was about to go.

Back at the office I was very excited to have the story and spent hours working and re-working it in triplicate on copypaper until I had a 20-word intro complete with "yesterday" in the first paragraph. This was essential, Jack said, to make the story news.

"Queensland's Tarzan, Michael Fomenko, has come out of the jungle and yesty was on his way by train to Sydney." (Top reporters, I had noted, wrote yesterday "yesty" to save time.) Then I wrote that Tarzan was accompanied by a priest, and how the priest said Tarzan was planning to see his mother, a White Russian in Sydney. I added that the priest said Tarzan would be returning later to the jungle.

After a dozen trim, taut paragraphs, I triumphantly added a footnote:

FOOTNOTE: Tarzan says he is "the sort of person who likes jacaranda trees and things like that".

I was sitting contentedly with my feet up on a desk in the green General Reporters' Room, listening to Rosemary Merson saying that any story with "may" in the intro was no good because just about everything possible in the world "may" happen, when an old silver-haired copy boy called Boyd — who still used hair oil — appeared in front of me.

Boyd seemed to like me a lot, so I wondered why he had such a grim look on his face.

"The Chief Sub says he wants to see you straight away," said Boyd, with a streak of sympathy running through the sentence.

Shit.

I knew immediately that I had done something wrong.

The last time the Chief Sub, Kev Kavanagh, had wanted to see me I had placed a small tick over the spelling of a surname: something we were taught to do if the spelling was unusual to show we had double-checked it. But Mr Kavanagh had somehow found out I was wrong despite my double-check.

"Look I can understand a cadet making an error on a name. But don't go around ticking *wrong* names or we will all be in trouble," he said: and he showed me how he triple-checked the name against the electoral rolls in the library.

Kev Kavanagh had also got me for calling the "Chamber of Manufactures" the "Chamber of Manufacturers", which seemed much more logical to me. He had warned me a few times that if I didn't know something not to write it down: "when in doubt, leave it out," he repeated twice, as if hoping I would learn it off by heart.

When I entered the Subs Room no one looked up from around the large oval table, except Kev Kavanagh. This was a bad sign for starters.

The GPO framed him as a backdrop through the windows, as he slowly got to his feet.

Mr Kavanagh was a short, serious-faced man with thick curly hair, bushy black eyebrows, and dark eyes — a man who rarely looked up from his work checking stories.

He had my Tarzan story in one hand and his heavy black-rimmed glasses in the other: though all stories were typed double-space on the same copy paper I recognised it, instantly, from across a crowded room.

Where had I gone wrong?

I had triple-checked the name, but hadn't taken the risk of ticking it.

The first para had 20 words.

I had fully backgrounded the story with who he was.

I had gone through the list of six "musts" Peter Thompson told me about: "how, when, where, who, what, and why."

I had made sure there was a mix of direct and indirect speech.

Instead of staying at his seat, Mr Kavanagh motioned me gravely over to a long line of newspapers on a bench against the far wall. These were the month's papers piled on top of each other for ready reference. They were tied together by rope, and a piece of wood stopped the rope from tearing through the papers. These files were on sloping benches to make them easier to read while standing in front.

Kev Kavanagh leant on the thick *Brisbane Telegraph* pile and held my story out in front of me on the thinner *Courier* pile.

I could feel my cheeks burning. My heart pounding.

He seemed to be struggling to think of what to say.

"Can't you see," he said finally, "that you have a very good story here?"

Well this was promising.

"Tarzan has lived in the jungle for years," he said. "Everyone in Australia has heard of him. Everyone's seen Fomenko's picture in his dugout canoe in the jungle. He never talks to anyone. Then today, of all people, he talks to you. Not only that, but he explains to you — to Hughie Lunn — why he is like he is. He explains that he lives like he does because he loves things like jacaranda trees." He paused. "That's not a footnote, Hughie. That's a great story."

I didn't know whether to be happy or devastated.

I said I would re-do it.

"No. I'll fix it up," Mr Kavanagh said, obviously not trusting me.

The next morning I raced down the stairs three at a time — more excited than I had been in my whole life — and opened my free copy of the paper in the front yard after fishing it out of Fred's long wet grass.

There was my story with old jungle photos all over the top of page three — the second most important page in the paper, Jack said.

The bold black headline said: *Tarzan speaks: "I love trees"*.

Then underneath it said "By a Staff Reporter".

That was me.

99

# 8
# Desperately seeking Sallyanne

There was rarely a moment when I didn't know there was something missing in my life — a girl.

Not just any girl, but *the* girl.

One like I had before: a friend like no other person could or would be.

I knew such a girl was hard to come by.

None of my mates, not even Kenny Fletcher who had lots of girls interested in him, had yet met one they wanted to marry. And it worried me that I might never again team up with a girl as one another's best.

I wasn't really interested in finding a passion pet. I wanted a girl — not to race off — but to love. Otherwise what was the point of trying to succeed?

Journalists joked about going out with Mrs Palm and her five daughters. "At least you don't have to get out of bed at 2 o'clock in the morning and drive them home," an A-grade reporter called out across the General Reporters' Room.

Kenny Fletcher, as usual, had the funniest way of putting it. He said that having impure thoughts did have its advantages: "You get to meet a better class of girl." I guessed he was talking about Brigitte Bardot or Marilyn Monroe. But Ken said all his impure thoughts had "long since turned to wishful thinking".

I still wasn't sure of the exact mechanics of making love, but at least I knew more than a country girl the court reporters told me about.

This girl had appeared in court as a witness against a sex offender, and the barrister wanted to establish whether or not the man had had "an erection". However, after several goes at re-framing the question, it became obvious that the girl didn't know that this word had a sexual, as well as a building industry, meaning.

So the barrister tried a different tack.

"In which direction was the man's penis pointing at the time of the incident?" he asked.

"Towards Dirranbandi," said the girl.

When I told Uncle Ken this story he said we shouldn't laugh. He and I, he said, knew so little about sex that if we ever did flash on to a girl who was ready, willing and able, like in the Doris Day song, "we'd as likely put it under her arm and yell out 'Paper, *Tele*, city final'," like the paper-sellers in Queen Street.

Girls were mysterious.

Our newspaper contained many sexy ads for their underclothing. Myers sold "Jezebel" bras which, apparently, stopped girls from looking drack.

"You are younger, more alluring. Suddenly you are shapely in your *five-way* contour bra," said the ads, accompanied by intimate sketches. Step-ins and "active life girdles" were "instant magic for your figure and your morale .... the prettiest way to look your slimmest".

Bits of lace and satin bras could be seen when girls in the office bent over. The outline of small bits of metal — shaped like an eight — pushed through tight skirts high on the thigh.

Was this where suspender met stocking?

The seam of the stocking was always dead straight up the back of the leg, as far as I could see.

My worries about getting a girlfriend at least no longer stemmed from losing my girlfriend eighteen months before. At school Brother Campbell had warned us that a fight with a girlfriend would put us through "insomnia, indigestion, indignation, and indifference". I had now visited them all.

So much so that I knew nothing could ever hurt me again.

What I needed, now that was behind me, was to win on to another bird.

To cheer myself up I had an especial look at the wedding

photos in the paper every Monday morning. These photos made me realise that every week lots of people must fall in love.

However, as month after month went by without meeting anyone, it seemed less and less likely that my photo would ever appear in these pages. Thus I slowly developed my own sayings out of those that others said. "So far, so bad," I would say. Or my favourite, "as one door slams in your face, another door slams in your face."

I now had seen just how wrong things could go in a relationship, even one that went as far as marriage.

One day at the races I saw the wife of a top *Courier* reporter stumbling around and giggling with a handsome, wide-shouldered, older man. I followed them out into the car park where they got into a brand new Holden Special and drove off.

I wrote down the registration number and gave it to the reporter, who didn't seemed very pleased that I had helped him.

A month later a Brisbane solicitor called me to his city office. He said the reporter and a friend had followed that car and had caught the wife and this man together in the dark, parked near a rubbish tip. He wanted a full signed statement from me on what I had seen at the races.

"Prior association is the most important evidence in a case like this," the solicitor said. "If the judge believes the couple had been seen in public together then he will believe the testimony of the husband and friend about what was going on near the rubbish tip."

I was surprised how full the court room was when I got there. It seemed to overflow with lawyers in black robes and people sitting down the back — including the wife, half a dozen seats away from the man I had seen her with. I could see that he had the right build for his job as a professional wrestler.

One of the lawyers asked me to describe *exactly* what I had seen at the racetrack that day.

"I saw the reporter's wife was drunk with another man," I said.

The judge intervened.

"You can't say that. That is a conclusion. Just describe what she was doing."

"Well she looked drunk to me," I said, and I saw the wrestler sitting down the back roll his hands together as if he was twisting someone's neck. He was looking straight at me.

In the end I had to put it like this to satisfy the court: "She was red-faced, giggling, swaying and hiccupping, and carrying her shoes."

Every time I went to say what another person at the scene had said to me, I was stopped.

It was very frustrating. Didn't the court want the truth as I saw it?

Then the judge asked if I could see the gentleman in question anywhere in the court.

Remembering the neck-wringing gesture, I hesitated for a moment — and then pointed him out.

Now it was the defence lawyer's turn to cross-examine me. The barrister stood up in gown and wig, holding the top edge of his gown with a fist, and looked hard at my eyes.

I had been warned they would go for me.

The lawyer for our side said their only hope was to discredit my evidence. And, if they couldn't do that, they would have to discredit my character. To show that I could not be trusted.

It was a sordid business I was in.

The defence was claiming the wife had found a used prophylactic under the lounge chair when she got home one night. What then would they throw at me?

I was so worried I was shaking.

"If it please Your Honour I have a certain line of questioning I wish to pursue with this witness. It will take quite some time, so I think we should adjourn until after lunch," the barrister said.

For two hours I wandered the streets of Brisbane wondering what it was that he had on me.

Cheating at school? Failing both Uni exams? Losing my girl?

When the court re-opened, the defence lawyer stood up and, to my surprise, said: "No further questions." I thought the judge should have chastised him for worrying me and wasting the court's time. But that was it. The reporter got his divorce, but never even thanked me.

Occasionally I met girls through University.

One night at an English lecture a bloke called Chris Lovelock, who owned a Dragon-class sailing boat, said he needed a deckhand, so I volunteered, even though I had never been on a sailing boat in my life.

Chris was a pretty smooth operator, and, when I got on board, he had two other deckhands: both University girls. One, Kathy O'Sullivan, was in the Young Liberals.

Out in the middle of Moreton Bay, Chris and I were splicing the main brace — which, I had just learned, meant drinking rum — when I saw an abandoned timber dinghy floating past.

"Captain, a ship, a ship. Prepare to go aboard," I shouted. "Hand me a rope."

One of the girls passed me a rolled-up rope and I leapt overboard into the dinghy.

The dinghy was totally water-logged and sank beneath my weight and I was suddenly up to my neck in deep water in Moreton Bay: still wearing my corduroy coat and blue canvas hat.

Only then did I realise that the rolled-up rope wasn't attached to the boat.

Heck, I couldn't see land in any direction.

Chris and the girls were finding it difficult to manoeuvre the large sailing boat around. He had to teach them what he had taught me — how to pull the ropes to turn around, or "go about" as Chris called it.

When they finally came past where I was, the boat was going flat out. Having bumped into a few large jelly-fish, and knowing that several world shark-fishing records were held in Moreton Bay, I leapt up out of the water like a porpoise and grabbed hold of one of the wires that supported the mast of the speeding boat. Weighed down by my wet coat, I slowly hauled myself up onto the narrow edge of the boat — and lay there to recover, while they wondered why I didn't get in.

It was cold in the wet clothes but, luckily, Kathy had a spare pair of dry slacks and I tried these on. They fitted like a pair of short green ballet tights, and I felt like Errol Flynn as I danced out onto the deck. I was particularly pleased, not just because I had been saved from the sharks. I would now be able to tell Fletch I had got inside a girl's pants.

Ken was just back from his second world tour. He had again detoured to visit Lourdes, the scene of many Catholic miracles, not only because he was a good Catholic, but because he wanted to win Wimbledon one day: and Ken looked to prayer to help him.

Fletch was nice enough to remember me while he was at Lourdes, and brought me back a blessed gold ring with the Virgin Mary's profile on the top. I liked it, but I didn't wear it — in case some smart-alec made a derisory comment.

It was bad enough having people ask why I wore a singlet.

On weekends, though there were miles and miles of beaches, everyone went to Surfers Paradise because the lifesavers had a DJ who played all the hits and read out greetings to people on the beach over loud-speakers on poles stuck in the sand. So you could lie on the beach listening to the Everly Brothers singing "Walk Right Back" or Elvis doing "Wooden Heart".

Once, after I queued up to get sprayed with Mutton Bird oil by Oscar on the beach at Surfers, some girls Ken and I had been trying to win on to walked past.

They asked what I was doing.

"Just sun-baking," I said, excited by their sudden interest.

"But, Hugh, you're going puce," one said.

Olive wrongly thought my lack of confidence was because of my scarred left ear from the time I set my mosquito net on fire when I was five.

One night at our cake shop she accused me of "slouching around" — her biggest criticism.

"You know Hughie, you were lucky with your ear. Because you have pink skin it doesn't show out livid like it would with dark skin, like Jim's. It just looks like a cauliflower ear. It makes you look like a footballer or a pug."

Good try Mum.

What Olive didn't know was that I was more worried about my nose than my ear. My nose seemed to be allergic to just about everything. Every time I talked to a girl I had to pull out a handkerchief and blow my nose.

Olive never had to make excuses like that for Jack or Gay.

Gay, who was nearly two years younger than me, had now left All Hallows Convent after a "finishing year" and was a secretary at Greenslopes Repatriation Hospital.

She had turned into quite a good sort, what Jim would call "a pretty little girl" — I guess all girls seemed little to him.

Gay had white blonde hair and big blue eyes, so someone at the hospital asked her to enter the Miss Wool Princess contest. She made it through to the finals and was to appear on television on Channel Nine's *In Brisbane Tonight*. Sheryl — who was now at All Hallows — was thrilled that Gay might win a beauty contest because it would make her famous at school. But Fred said such things were "only good for women and kids". Olive said Gay was fortunate that she had inherited her fine Duncan skin.

Somewhat surprisingly, Jim was more excited than anyone. He polished up the green Belvedere and insisted on driving Gay and me up to the top of Mt Coot-tha to Channel Nine for the show. "Cutting a long story short Lunn, we have to make Gay look important. There are a lot of pretty little girls in the final," Jim said.

When the compere, Brian Muir, interviewed Gay, things were going swimmingly at first. Though she could screech louder than anyone in the family, Gay could also put on the dog — and she sounded very sophisticated as she spoke about her job, and how she went into major operations and took notes dictated by the surgeons.

Even though she was my sister, I could see Gay was the best sort in the contest and came over really well on TV. She was smart because she had especially bought a beige-and-white checked woollen suit with a huge white collar which lit up her small pale face beneath a triumphant hairstyle. Somehow Gay had got all her blonde hair off her shoulders and piled up on top of her head. She had also bought a new pair of shoes.

Fred had given her his ultimate compliment, saying as he arrived home wearing a sugar-bag fitted on his head as he always did when it rained: "You look like you're off to the Royal Ball". Women, he added as an aside, "love to wear their money on their backs".

Unlike me, Gay had always been successful at whatever she tried. She had been a top ballet and tap dancer, acrobat, fast runner, and was near the top of her class in shorthand and typing. She even had boys running after her. Because Greenslopes Hospital was only a couple of miles away across Ekibin Creek and up around behind the quarry, Gay used to walk home from work — and a doctor had started picking her up in his Hillman Minx and dropping her home. He had even asked her out.

Gay was doing really well in the TV interview — she didn't even sound nervous. But then the compere asked: "Now, Gay, you could well be our new Wool Princess. What is Australia's biggest export?"

"Gee, that's a hard one," said Gay, trying to cast her mind back to Social Studies classes at primary school.

Jim was distraught next to me.

"I can't believe it Lunn," he said. "She must say it. It is too obvious."

Of course it was.

"Uhm, coal?" said Gay, "no .... wheat."

That was the end of all our dreams of Annerley Junction's first beauty queen.

On the way back down the mountain Jim berated her for

the mistake, but Gay just said: "I wasn't thinking. I was trying to make sure I got my best side to the camera."

To try to make myself more appealing I bought a tailored suit in a shiny dark green material I picked out myself at Rothwells tailors, at the smarter end of Queen Street. I did this because Fred said his father had always told him that to get ahead your clothing should be as costly as your purse will allow.

Two tailors spent hours measuring me up and testing the suit at various stages of manufacture.

But it didn't work.

The two tailors tried too hard to improve my figure by sticking large shoulderpads in the coat, and I came out looking like I was wearing false shoulders. I only ever wore that suit once, and then went back to wearing the grey suit. Though I did wear the pearl tie-pin I bought to replace my brass grip.

It didn't really matter, because my only outings were to *Courier-Mail* parties.

I had tried going to Cloudland with my smoker schoolmate, Rod. But he and his friends always went drinking beer until the hotels shut before going to the dance.

Olive said they were getting "Dutch courage".

Because I sipped only a shandy, or a double sarsaparilla, I didn't find this much fun. They said they needed a drink because when you went up to ask a girl for a dance at Cloudland the whole alcove of girls watched.

Rod — who also didn't have a steady girl — was not sympathetic to my complaints about having a bad trot with women. Whenever I whinged he would always say: "Such is life without a wife" — and one of his older married mates would invariably add: "and Hell on earth with one."

One night I thought I had finally made it when I went stag to the O'Connor Boathouse before hotel closing time. If you could get there before ten the girls greatly out-numbered the boys, and this night I got to dance "the creep" above the muddy river in the arms of a pretty brunette.

I thought I was doing well, but after a while I noticed her

pulling faces and rolling her eyes to her girlfriend over my shoulder. Feeling like a real dill, I told her she had tickets on herself — and left her in the middle of the dance floor.

Going to a University "Varsity Five plus two" dance with Kenny Fletcher further convinced me I was no social satellite.

The fox trot and the quick step were the main dances, and they were way beyond me. The hall overflowed with young men studying at Uni, and there were far fewer girls than at Cloudland. I found myself standing like a deadbeat in a corner wishing I was cruising with Jim and stopping for a waffle and ice cream at Christies, or listening to Peter Thompson or Kev O'Donohue talk about newspapers.

It seemed to me that there were just too many young men around who were killer-dillers with girls for me to have any chance. They were invariably drinkers: so I attributed at least part of their success to what Brother Campbell told us Ogden Nash wrote: "Candy is dandy, but liquor is quicker."

These killer-dillers were so successful that they even labelled girls who lived at Wynnum or Mt Gravatt "GIs" — Geographically Impossible.

They were doing so well that they could reject girls who lived too far away, and they talked tough. "You can hit me, but don't shit me," they would say. They called girls "bed babies". And, while I practised saying "hello beautiful" into a mirror as if I was doing a line for girl, they could get away with outrageous greetings like: "Hello darling, how's your bum?"

Ken was the equal of any of these guys — though, like me, he didn't drink.

While I worried about how to properly pronounce a word like "vase", Ken would look at a girl and turn to me and say in front of her: "Perfection, son, perfection." Or, at the beach he'd say: "If I had ten bob I'd buy the rest of those shorts for you." But Ken was a tennis star. So much so that he had been invited to dinner by Prime Minister Menzies in

Melbourne on his return from overseas: although Ken told me the evening was pretty boring.

"By the end of that dinner old chap I felt like I was on the centre court and had just lost the fifth set 66-64," he said.

Fletch didn't even worry that most of these young men chasing girls at dances were at Uni becoming professionals — the sort of guys girls seemed to want. "Easy to see you've had a University education," he would say to anyone who made a mistake.

I knew what sex maniacs these University types were.

Carved into the desks I sat at for night lectures were sayings like: "Man is an animal that eats roots shoots and leaves," and "I'd rather be a stinking med than a greasy engineer," both of which had to be explained to me.

They even played dirty jokes on the police. Only recently they had hung a large sign outside the CIB headquarters, an old stone building next to Queen's Park: "DICKS HANG OUT HERE".

Much as I hated going to Uni lectures, it was better than going to dances. It kept me busy, and it led to meeting the most beautiful girl I had ever seen or imagined.

In 1961 I had repeated English I, and changed from Accountancy to another University subject: Journalism A.

As usual there were so many people in white shirts, ties and dark trousers, or dresses and high-heeled shoes, doing English I at night in the biggest lecture theatre — B9 — that I couldn't get in the door, until people started dropping out after the first month.

No one cared if you were listening or not.

Jack told me he did well because, instead of taking notes, he paid attention to the lecturers and absorbed what they were saying.

When I did this instead of going home to watch Eliot Ness and his Untouchables on TV I found the lectures interesting. Like the night Cecil Hadgraft showed us the power of words by tapping a student on the arm with a toothpick and saying he had "belaboured her with a hunk of wood". He explained how people saw things differently if they were involved: "I'm firm; you're stubborn; he's a pig-headed fool". And later Andy Thompson bent and picked up his chair and moved it to explain what Shakespeare meant in a sonnet when he wrote: "Bending with the remover to remove".

In our textbook *Seven Centuries of Poetry* there were some inspirational new poems I could apply to myself to cheer me up, especially "Invictus":

In the foul clutch of circumstance
I have not winced nor cried aloud.
Under the bludgeonings of chance,
My head is bloody, but unbowed.

Journalism A was even more interesting because experienced journalists gave the Uni lectures. Only cadet reporters could do the course, so these were held at the *Courier-Mail* to save everyone traipsing out to St Lucia. This meant *Tele* cadets had to walk down Queen Street from their building. No lecturers came from the *Sunday Truth* — which didn't surprise me because of its reputation. If you wanted to insult anyone at a party one way was to say: "You wouldn't know it was Sunday, unless the *Truth* came out!"

Heading for one of these lectures, I was cutting through the Library area between General and Social when I was knocked backwards by what I saw.

In that small room among piles of old newspapers on sloping benches I saw at last what I had once read about in a poem by Andrew Marvel: "An hundred years should go to praise thine eyes, and on thy forehead gaze".

There, chatting by bundles of torn, twisting, browning newspapers was a slender prim dark-haired girl with pale skin, big brown liquid eyes like Judy Garland's, dark eyelashes, red lips, and a button nose. Not only did she walk in beauty, but all that was best of dark and light really did meet in her aspect, and her eyes. Now I knew why someone had written that hit tune "Beautiful, Beautiful Brown Eyes ... I'll never love blue eyes again".

Her voice was fast and feminine with a beguiling rushed

111

hesitation in the gush of starting sentences. Her pronunciation was perfect, better than any elocution teacher's: like listening to a bird. Yet she wasn't putting on the dog. And when she talked, a natural beauty spot on her top lip quivered.

I was so excited I ran around the building until I found someone who knew who she was.

Her name was Sallyanne Kerr, a cadet reporter from the *Tele*. She was here for the University Journalism lectures.

The same ones I was going to!

She was the best thing that had happened to me.

She proved what I had started to disbelieve: that such beauty did exist outside poetry books.

I decided to try to get to know her.

It wasn't that I had much chance of winning on, but I knew I had no chance without a car.

One day when Jim and I were cruising I saw a car that was a real bobby-dazzler: a strawberry-coloured sports car called a Sunbeam Alpine. It was a demonstrator, but as I walked towards it I knew — like I had known when I first met my red-headed girlfriend — that this was the wheels for me.

I went for a test drive with Jim's muscular bulk barely fitting side-on in the little space behind the two seats. Being uncomfortable, Jim kept complaining that the car didn't seem to have much horsepower, and there was no wireless or heater.

As usual with these things, Jim was right.

But, boy, would this buggy impress girls.

This car almost touched the bitumen at the front, and angled upwards to the back to sharp rear fins which stuck out above and behind the back bumpers. It had chrome spoked wheels held in place by three-pronged silver spinners which reminded me of the blades on the chariot wheels in *Ben Hur*. There was a black top you could pull up if it rained or fold away neatly behind three special interlocking panels. On the dashboard everything was controlled by flat black toggle switches which flicked down for on, and up for off.

The upholstery was bright red, with blue piping around the edge of the seats. The tiny boot lid was topped by two large silver hinges.

On the front was a round yellow-and-blue badge.

As I drove along, weaving past the occasional ordinary sedan or truck, above the speed limit of 30 mph, it was just like the day-dreams I had after my girlfriend gave me up.

It was as if life was evening things up, except that this time I didn't have the leather driving gloves.

Not yet.

We whipped silently along the Brisbane River below Hamilton Hill, bathing in the reflected glow from the strawberry red duco. I could tell that those twitching days were behind me now. The only problem I had was that the wind was blowing my cow's lick hair-do forward into my eyes — rather than jauntily backwards, as I had always imagined.

As I looked out over the sloping red nose, I felt a surge of confidence in myself.

Had God and Saint Anthony relented and decided to let me enjoy this life?

Olive didn't want to hand over my insurance money — one hundred pounds which had come due when I turned 20. She had paid this off weekly for each of us since we were babies. But, just as he had when he unexpectedly bought us a new bike as kids, Fred stepped in and pulled the money out of his wallet saying: "Olive, you can't put an old head on young shoulders."

Suddenly it was mine and — though Jim was unhappy that it only had four cylinders — he was glad that I had joined him as a king of the road: and I noted that the scar down the middle of his nose was far less noticeable than when we had first met at primary school more than a decade before.

I decided to make a grand appearance in the car at the next journos party.

This meant not driving in to work for a couple of weeks.

Because the Alpine was so low it fitted much further under the house than Fred's Zephyr, which he parked be-

113

tween the house stumps. So I drove the Alpine up under the house far enough for the Zephyr to park behind. It gave me pleasure just to go and look at it under the house before leaving for work: its polished paintwork contrasting starkly with the dirt floor and the surrounding vertical black timber battens.

Not using the car was no great inconvenience. I was used to catching the tram in to the *Courier-Mail*. The tram trip was a relaxing, cool ride where you could sit and think. It went right down Queen Street and, if I was lucky, it would stop right outside the newspaper building waiting for cars on the tram line to turn right into Creek Street. As the frustrated tram driver dinged his bell at the drivers, I could jump out and run straight in the front door. Or I caught a rough bus ride to North Quay and then walked downhill nearly four blocks to work, though you couldn't walk down Queen Street without running into someone you knew.

To get to the Gold Coast for a surf, I only had to go out to the loading dock after work and jump in the back of one of our trucks and ride the papers on a fast trip to Surfers.

Jim was always available. We took in *Doctor in the House*, plus a huge feed, at one of Brisbane's five drive-ins, which were always full despite the arrival of TV. Particularly when they put on a midnight show with the double-bill of *High Noon* and *Stalag 17*.

It was at the next journos shindig that — armed with my new-found confidence — I talked to the prettiest cadet reporter on the *Courier*, Tina Cleary.

She wrote a column for the Social pages called "Tina's Party Line".

There was no sign of any twitch this time as I sidled up next to her and said: "Just what *is* your party line, Tina?"

Kenny Fletcher would have liked that, I thought. It was almost as good as Ken's own line when a girl told him she couldn't dance with him because she was going out with a doctor. "That's funny," Fletch said, "I can perform a few operations myself."

Tina blinked her long dark eyelashes and smiled.

I was out to delight this girl, even though I knew in my heart of hearts that girls this sophisticated and pretty became the wives of richer, smarter, older men. Nevertheless, I was so keen that I bummed a fag from Peter Thompson. Since girls didn't smoke, it seemed the thing to do.

For the first time in my life, I lit up and blew smoke out of the left side of my mouth like Paul Newman, and downed the rest of a glass of beer from my other hand.

I felt good and, as we talked, I noted that she was so nice it was just like talking to a mate. Around us the blokes were singing along to "Running Bear".

As the ash grew longer on my cigarette I held my left hand out over an ashtray and — with the cigarette held between thumb and middle finger — I tapped it lightly with my forefinger several times (as I had seen the Count do) and watched the cold, lifeless ash crumble slowly off the end. Meanwhile I talked in sophisticated phrases to reporters around me: "Take it easy, greasy" or "Take it on the lamb, Sam".

When someone asked when I started smoking I replied: "When men were men, and women were glad of it."

"You know you really shouldn't smoke," Tina said, just as I sucked in another deep draw. "It looks ridiculous on you."

Well what was I supposed to do? Now that it was decided that I didn't look sophisticated enough, what was I to do with a gob-full of smoke?

Swallow it?

I had come a real gutser.

Every handsome Hollywood actor sucked continually on a cigarette while talking to girls through clouds of smoke. Yet this girl thought that, of all the people in the world who smoked, I was the one who looked ridiculous.

What to do with the half-smoked cigarette?

I guess I could have blown the smoke into her face for insulting me. But she was too nice for that. So I stubbed the cigarette out, while blowing all the smoke down towards the floor. It was as I did this that I realised — in a rash moment of inspiration — that there was indeed still one way left to show her I was more desirable than she thought.

We were only a few streets from home, so I suggested that she come with me if she wanted a pleasant surprise.

When we got to 40 Ekibin Road I took her up under the house, though she was reluctant to continue through the dirt in the dark in her high-heeled white shoes. When we were next to the Alpine, I triumphantly turned on our lavatory light from behind the roofing-iron walls which touched neither the ground nor the floor above. The light beamed out through all the openings onto the strawberry red car, looking like a lost Christmas present.

Tina never said a thing.

She just reached out and touched the duco gently with the tips of long, slender fingers and slowly circled the car without looking up into the glare of the lavatory light.

As she did so, she traced tiny trails in two weeks of dust and I was reminded of a stanza of poetry we had learned by heart at school: "Full many a gem of purest ray serene, the dark unfathomed caves of ocean bear; full many a flower was born to blush unseen, and waste its sweetness on the desert air."

I got the keys and drove Tina slowly back through Annerley in the dark with the hood down. The breeze swirled softly around our heads. The first night on the road, I thought, and already I had the prettiest girl at the *Courier* alone by my side.

But when we got back to the party Tina went off and talked to Peter Thompson all evening and ignored me.

The car hadn't had any effect whatsoever.

# 9
# *Jim chases an ambulance*

People occasionally came in to the newspaper to seek help, and one night an acting Chief-of-Staff sent me out into the foyer to see a man who had come to make a complaint.

I put on my suitcoat, grabbed a half-notebook — since here was a person who *wanted* to speak to a reporter — and dashed out. I was surprised to see an Aboriginal man sitting in army uniform on the long varnished wood seat left for visitors. Despite my four years in the army cadets at school, I didn't even know Aborigines were in the Australian army.

I told him who I was and pulled out the notebook and took down his name, his age, his address, and his rank.

Then I held the notebook in front of him and asked if the details, including the spelling, were correct — a new technique for getting it right that I had invented myself.

No more stupid mistakes from me.

The soldier said he was upset because a city hotel had refused to serve him — an Australian soldier — a drink. He said he believed this was done because he was Aboriginal. That seemed obvious enough to me, but Jack said a reporter's job was to report what people said, and not to jump to conclusions. So I interviewed him at length.

After he left, I wrote a ten-paragraph story which took me until late in the evening.

I handed in the story and the acting Chief-of-Staff called me in and asked if the man was a full-blood Aborigine, or a half-caste.

How would I know?

I could see by his reaction that I was in trouble. So I stuck up for myself. It didn't have anything to do with me, I said.

"It has everything to do with you," he said, because it was a point of law that the publican couldn't serve a full-blood Aborigine. I had better ring up the army to try to find him, or at least to establish the soldier's true racial background.

I was in a real panic now. I felt the heat of embarrassment once more running through my cheeks.

No one had ever taught me about things like this. All that time learning calculus and Latin. Yet all I knew about the Aborigines was that they fought Captain Cook, were wiped out in Tasmania, and were friends with my grandfather.

At first the army officer I spoke to at Enoggera barracks was very helpful. But he got annoyed when I asked about the soldier's race. He asked what right we had to that sort of information?

I had to tell the Chief-of-Staff that I could neither find the man, nor establish if he had any white blood in him. The Chief was furious and thrust my story hard on to the vicious-looking portable steel spike with lead bottom on his desk — something everyone at the *Courier-Mail* did with stories which they were patently not going to use.

These stories were, as they so truly said, "spiked".

He told me I had blown a good story.

I tried unsuccessfully to point out that I had looked up the word Aboriginal in the paper's Bible — the blue Style Book — and all it said was:

"*Abo. — Not to be used in either text or headlines, except in deliberately quoted speech. Is as derogatory and contemptuous as Dago.*"

But he wasn't interested in my excuses.

I had even looked up the entry for "Coloured races" which merely warned reporters to avoid the use of "black races" or "yellow races".

"'Native peoples' or 'coloured races', and sometimes 'negroes', serve the same purpose," the Style Book said. And it added a further warning: "Never 'niggers', please, unless there is strong reason for using it in direct quotation. Certain latitude must, of course, be applied to this rule. 'His grandfather was speared by the blacks,' for example, remains good — and we do not suggest banning 'nigger-brown' as a colour definition.''

There was nothing in the Style Book to say the law was not the same for everybody, or that it changed depending on how black you were. This I could see was a hard part of journalism: knowing the law. Yet I knew nothing about the law. This soon became a major problem because — now that I was well and truly a second-year cadet — the paper decided it was time I got some experience in court.

For once I started at the top.

At the Supreme Court a couple of old *Courier-Mail* and *Telegraph* reporters showed me around their little Press Room in the two-storey stone building at the North Quay end of Adelaide Street. I liked the little semi-circular stone balconies off every room, including the Press Room.

The Chief Reporter, Jim Delaney, showed me how to make a strong cup of tea.

Once I had mastered this, Jim got me to sit in with him on a very boring murder trial appeal. It was before no less than three judges in wigs and black robes.

After a few hours Jim went off to check another court case.

I was finding it hard to stay awake. My head got heavier and heavier as I sat alone at the varnished wood Press Bench, with decades of reporters' initials carved into it.

I blinked hard.

I slapped my face.

Then I rested for a moment on my folded arms.

The next thing I knew, a man in a black uniform was banging a long stick on the floor in front of me. As I came to, the judge in the middle warned I might be next in the dock charged with Contempt of Court.

Later an experienced reporter warned me that judges had tremendous powers. He told me to get out of their way if they came walking down a corridor or I could be arrested for hindering their progress. I should step aside, and bow my head, he said, just as we had to do on entering or leaving the courtroom.

I knew I was Mr No One, but I could hardly believe I had to go around bowing to people. We didn't even have to do that to the Brothers or nuns when we were at school. Or Priests. Or even Archbishop Duhig. When I told Fred about this that night at the shop, he said sarcastically: "I told you we all have to show due respect and pay attention. As my old man said there are 'those born with spurs to ride us'."

I never liked judges after that. But I noticed that they seemed to like the press.

About once a week a judge would appear in the Press Room to tip off reporters that he would be making a statement worth reporting in some case later that day. When they did this they wore ordinary clothes, and I noticed how much less important they looked without their wigs and gowns and wide high desks. I was never let loose on these stories, so I don't know if the judges did as they said. But I sat in on a lot of cases.

I was surprised to find that often I felt sorry for the accused.

Like the short, pudgy, middle-aged man with glasses who had been a law-abiding person all his life — he probably had to be to survive — who wandered into the grounds of a motel at Kangaroo Point to see what was going on. The next thing he was pleading guilty to being on a property without lawful excuse.

One day a well-spoken young man in a suit appeared in the dock charged with something called "carnal knowledge" of a girl under seventeen.

She looked much older to me, and I was relieved when the judge said: "But did you really know for sure and certain that the girl wasn't seventeen?"

Here was the out.

If only the Christian Brothers had asked us that sort of question when we were in trouble at school, I thought, we would never have got the cuts. It made me think the judge was a Catholic. The only way a Catholic could commit a mortal sin was if you "knowingly and willingly consented to something which you believed to be a mortal sin".

"Yes, she told me she was fourteen," the young man said.

"Well, now I have to give you six months jail," answered the judge: somewhat reluctantly, I thought.

After a few weeks of courts I was at last on to a scoop which Jack would be proud of.

During the swearing-in of a jury for a major trial the two opposing lawyers kept standing up and rejecting people they didn't want. They did this to a dozen different men right at the last moment, just as they were about to place their hands on the Bible. The juror then had to leave.

About the only thing I knew about the law was that people had the right to be tried by "twelve good men and true", as Olive always said.

So I knew lawyers couldn't start picking and choosing the jury that they wanted.

I saw the headline in my mind's eye: JURY FIXED BY LAWYERS.

But when I told the older court reporters back in the Press Room, they said that was how our justice system worked. There were complex legal reasons for it, which I didn't understand. Far more important for me, they said, to concentrate on getting everything in the story right, like the plea and the age of the accused.

Later, Jim Delaney emphasised the need to check everything in a court story before filing it. But then he mixed me up by saying not to get into the habit of checking too much or I would never get enough done.

"How do I know when I'm checking too much?" I asked him.

"When you start checking the carbon copy with the original to see if it comes through the same," he said.

It was lucky Jim Delaney had given me these warnings because the next thing I knew I was on my own: down in the assignment book the Chief-of-Staff filled in every night. I had to cover the Bankruptcy Court which, I found out when I got there, had something to do with things called "Seque-stration Orders".

The Bankruptcy Court was blocks away from the other courts on its own in the middle of a government building next to Anzac Park. It was run by two men who chatted happily in between cases in the large windowless courtroom which seemed weighed down by heavy dark varnished forms and tables and a similar large desk at the front. This desk was where one of them, called the Registrar, sat once the court opened.

These two men had the same initials, except one was T.J. and the other J.T., and I had been warned to make sure I got them the right way around: "Every sub in the building knows which is which," John Weinthal said. He also told me a person before the court was a "debtor" until declared a bankrupt.

As the person in financial trouble arrived, one of the men — J.T. — always sat up behind the high bench in a black gown but no wig. The other, the Official Receiver, stood in front of him in a dark suit, with the debtor seated on a stand facing both of them, and me — often the only other person in the room — taking notes from the side.

The man standing in the front — T.J. — would ask a series of questions.

What are your assets? What liabilities do you have? How much a week could you pay back?

Then T.J. would reach dramatically under the table and pull out a large cardboard box overflowing with ledgers and financial documents — which always looked like the same boxful to my untrained eye — and would drop them heavily on the table and wave his palm significantly above them as if to include everything in the box in the conversation, and ask the long litany of questions he posed to every debtor:

Have you put any money away in the last six months? Have you made any gifts to relatives or children? Have you spent any large amounts of money? ....

Usually the person said "no" to all of these questions and J. T. declared the debtor bankrupt. Then J.T. would come down from his bench for a chat with T.J. before returning for the next businessman to appear.

One day a debtor, when asked if he had any assets, surprised all three of us.

"Yes, I have contingent assets of 200,000 pounds!" he said as I fought to stay awake beneath the quiet drone of the dark courtroom.

I sat up immediately. This seemed like a good story to me.

If Peter Thompson reckoned a dog biting a man wasn't a story because it was common, but a man biting a dog was a good story .... then how much better to have a bankrupt with assets of 200,000 pounds?

The man said he had invented a device which zapped rats with light waves. It would eliminate them from Australia, but large commercial industrial interests were keeping it off the market.

"Why would they do that?" asked T.J.

"Because rats are big business," said the man.

I took two notebooks full of notes as he explained his invention — and the mating habits of rats — so quickly that I couldn't keep up.

I cursed my non-attendance at cadet shorthand classes before work.

It was after 4 p.m. when I hit the office worried and excited, grabbed a typewriter and started writing. I knew reporters with good stories were supposed to put in a "summary" of the story for the 5 p.m. conference — which all the section editors attended to decide what would go into the next day's paper. And, approximately, where.

But there was no time to try for fancy writing now.

By nine o'clock — five hours later — I had had no dinner, and was near despair.

I couldn't do it. I had been backwards and forwards through my notebooks until I knew them off by heart: but I couldn't turn the Sequestration Order by the Official Receiver against a bankrupt inventor with contingent assets of 200,000 pounds into a simple, interesting story.

I didn't want to ask Jack or any senior reporters, or any

other cadets for that matter, for help — because I didn't want anybody to know that I couldn't do it.

Luckily for me, Peter Thompson — who was doing so well he was now working on the subs desk full-time — just happened to be walking past my desk.

"Hi Dad, how's it going?" he said.

Remembering our long talks at parties about stories and newspapers, I confided that, while I was definitely on to this good story, I was having a little trouble getting a strong lead. "That's it old chap," Peter said, "you're on to it. 'A man appeared in the Bankruptcy Court yesty saying he had "contingent assets" of 200,000 pounds'. What a story Daddy-o."

After I had quickly written down what he said, Peter stayed and helped me structure the story with a series of direct and indirect quotes. He made it seem easy, and, within half an hour, the story was done. When I got the paper in the garden just after dawn the next morning it appeared exactly as written: the first time this had happened to me.

Following this success I was assigned to the Coroner's Court and then the Land Court, where at least I had been before. It was a boring case with two barristers arguing on and on and on about the value of a large chunk of land in central Brisbane which no ordinary person could ever afford. So I decided to go for a walk down Queen Street, get a hair-cut, and then wander slowly back to the office.

Just as I was about to leave, a woman crept into the court, doing the usual bow to the bench, and said I was wanted on the phone. The Chief-of-Staff told me to get up to the Magistrates Court. Someone was sick.

I hadn't realised the paper would ring a courtroom and move a reporter somewhere else. It was a close shave.

The Press Room at the Magistrates Court was similar to the Supreme Court and the one at City Hall. A couple of old reporters in their 40s or 50s or 60s watched over a dozen courtrooms from an untidy Press Room with desks covered in copy and carbon paper, phone books for the whole state, silver pins, newspaper clippings, old stories, typewriter ribbons, torn notebooks, transcipts, cups with mouldy tea in the bottom, big black phones, newspapers, and the occasional discarded, broken typewriter.

Operating from here I sat in on traffic offences, and was surprised at the way the cases were lined up by the score with fines handed out one after the other — no matter what was said in defence.

Those motorists represented by a lawyer seemed to get hit harder than those who attended themselves.

It seemed to me these magistrates were much tougher than the judges, and this was soon confirmed.

A man who had appeared in the Magistrates Court charged with abduction, because he took a 16-year-old girl over the border into New South Wales where she was legal, had elected to be tried by a judge.

When he wasn't sent to prison, a magistrate burst into the reporters' room with the *Tele* story waving it around.

"I would have given him nine months in jail. I didn't like his attitude," the magistrate said to a reporter he had known for years. "He was a real bodgie-type."

I thought this was a good story, but the reporter told me it was not said in a court room. It was a friendly conversation, and was therefore not to be reported.

A few days later I got the shock of my life when I was told to cover a drunk driving case.

I didn't know much about court reporting, but I knew covering these cases was a dangerous job. The only reporter who had been sacked in my time at the *Courier* was one who got the guilty and not-guilty drunk motorists the wrong way around in the list the paper published every day.

This full list was published to deter people from driving when drunk and, as the court reporters told me, to show we reported "without fear or favour".

"Even if it's one of our Editors the result must be published," I was told.

But I knew that writing such cases without favour could be harder to do than people might think. Another cadet reporter told me that when he had this job recently a woman

125

who had been found guilty of being drunk whilst in charge of a motor vehicle offered to do "anything he wanted" if he kept her name out of the paper.

So imagine my surprise when I walked in to cover my first drunk driving case — and the accused was a good-looking woman.

Coppers in uniform said that the woman — who had pleaded not guilty — had been bleary-eyed, slurred her speech, and had been unable to walk along a straight line when picked up late at night in the city. This was the standard way of proving a motorist was drunk, and very few ever beat the "unable-to-walk-a-straight-line" charge. Another test was to make the motorist stand with feet together and eyes shut and touch the tip of the nose with a forefinger.

It was alright to drive after drinking a lot, but not if you were too drunk to walk straight.

The woman said she didn't like to talk about it, but she had always had a natural limp, which had prevented her from walking the police line.

She asked the magistrate if she might demonstrate this for him, and proceeded to limp on both legs back and forth across the courtroom. As she passed the obviously sympathetic magistrate for the third time, the woman looked up at him and said her eyes had been red — as they were now — because she was so upset at being vilified in public by being forced to limp around while being looked at.

That was also why it had been difficult for her to talk.

She beat the charge.

I was glad really, because I knew that the cops did pick on people.

Jim had been having a lot of trouble with them ever since he got the Belvedere. He had been booked several times and, on each occasion, Jim was completely innocent.

Or so he said.

Jim said the reason the coppers noticed him was that his car stood out because of its large rear fins. And no driver in the world — no matter how careful — could possibly drive such a powerful car within the speed limit. And, I must admit, every time I drove the Belvedere Jim caught me out exceeding the 30 mph city limit.

Once, Jim beat a charge in court when he defended himself and argued it was an act of God that his tail-light had failed just before the policeman arrived behind him.

"Your Worship, I was very glad the policeman pointed it out to me," Jim said.

Jim was an expert at making excuses. He had developed the art since that day as a 15-year-old when he hadn't learnt a theorem for the Christian Brother we nicknamed "Basher", and later, when we got to know him better, "Charlie". When Charlie asked Jim to recite the theorem, Jim got up from his seat next to mine and tried to stall for as long as he could. Of course Charlie knew what Jim was up to. Deliberately and slowly he put his hand into his briefcase on his teacher's desk and said menacingly: "I'm coming Egg, I'm coming."

At this, Jim became flustered: "I could have known it. I should have known it. I would have known it."

"I'm coming Egg ..." said Charlie, pulling out the strap.

Thus when Jim was charged with failing to keep left, he successfully argued in court that he had had to move to the centre of the road because he was planning to turn right: "In any case, you can't turn right from the left side of the road can you?" Jim said to the magistrate.

The very next day the same copper stopped Jim again, this time next to the Brisbane River on Coronation Drive.

"What would you like to book me for today?" asked Jim.

"Speeding," said the copper.

"But I saw you in my mirror so I made sure I wasn't speeding," said Jim.

The copper said nothing, but wrote out the ticket. However, he mis-spelled Jim's surname, and Jim got off by arguing in court that the policeman had charged the wrong man.

Not content with this victory, however, Jim added: "I suggest, Your Worship, that the standard of entry to the police force should be raised above the Scholarship level to Junior so that this sort of thing does not continue to happen."

The magistrate interrupted: "I think you have said enough for today."

As Jim left the courtroom, the arresting policeman walked past and whispered: "I'll get you, you little shit."

After that the police were really after Jim.

A mate of Jim's told me he was pulled up while driving Jim's Belvedere home from Uni one night. The copper asked if he was the owner.

"No, as it turns out, I am not," said this priestly fellow. "But I can give you the name and address of the owner if you like."

"Just a minute and I'll give that to you," said the policeman. And he reeled off Jim's full name and address.

I was with Jim the day they finally got him. It was my weekday off. After we'd cruised around doing nothing except talking about girls, Jim parked the Belvedere in Adelaide Street and we headed off to the Primitif coffee lounge in Piccadilly Arcade.

We hadn't gone ten yards when Jim remembered that we hadn't put a sixpence in the parking meter.

As we walked back, a copper on a huge motorcycle pulled up, got off, and took a long parking-ticket book from his black leather knee-high strapped boots. Jim immediately sped up and I got worried: I couldn't think of two more immovable objects colliding than a large motorcycle cop and Jim.

Jim stuck sixpence in the meter while explaining that he had forgotten to put the money in a moment earlier. But the copper started writing out a ticket as if we weren't present.

Jim walked right up next to him and I noted how each matched the other's size perfectly.

"You police are like spiders, you are biting me," Jim said.

The policeman spoke for the first time.

"What's your name and your address?" he said.

"I don't have to tell you for a parking ticket," said Jim, ever the bush lawyer.

"You're under arrest," said the policeman, shutting the pad. "I'm taking you in."

I was shocked.

Surely the copper was joking?

I offered to give him the name and address for both of us, but he said it was too late. The offence had been committed, and he put his hand on Jim's shoulder and told him he was under arrest and was being taken to the watchhouse.

Jim laughed and readily agreed to go.

He climbed onto the pillion seat on the motorbike and said: "Well come on. I might escape."

But the policeman said he wasn't allowed to take prisoners as pillion passengers.

"Then we'll use my car," said Jim. "Hop in."

The policeman got into the car with Jim but, as they were about to drive off with me in the back seat, he jumped out.

"No. You're under arrest, so you aren't allowed to drive."

So I got out too.

At this I hoped the copper might relent because of Jim's co-operative attitude.

"Then you drive," said Jim, throwing the bemused policeman the keys.

No, the policeman said, he didn't want to drive Jim's car. It was evidence in the case.

So, of course, I — who had only wanted a cup of coffee — ended up driving Jim to the watchhouse as the pair sat shoulder-to-shoulder together taking up the whole of the back seat. Jim was formally charged with failing to give his name and address to a policeman. It took a long time, because Jim was fingerprinted, and they even measured the scar down the middle of his nose for their records.

I was pretty disgusted, even though I knew Jim had been pushing his luck too far in the Belvedere.

Only recently he had passed an ambulance on Beaudesert Road very early one morning as it screamed along, siren blazing. Jim said he did it to show the ambulance drivers that they needed bigger, more powerful vehicles if they were to get to accident scenes quickly. But all he did was show he had made a bad error of judgment.

"Bugger-me-dead, I was terribly unlucky. When I passed the ambulance I found I was also passing two motorcycle cops," Jim said. "How unlucky could I get. The ambulance had a police escort."

As soon as Jim saw the motorbikes he swung right and cut back across suburbs. He was in his pyjamas with the car safely in the garage when some police arrived.

I went to see a lawyer who had given us a journalism lecture and told him how the parking meter policeman had arrested Jim. He looked up a law book and said if a Queensland policeman asked your name and address you had to give it to him or he could legally arrest you. And if he thought you were lying he could also arrest you.

"So he can just arrest you no matter what?" I asked the lawyer.

"Yes," he said.

It was this experience which saw me appear in the dock in the Magistrates Court myself just a few weeks later.

I had been to the cricket at the Gabba to watch the last couple of hours of a match, because that season of 1961-62 Queensland had an excellent chance of winning the Sheffield Shield for the first time. In fact we were leading the competition.

I parked the Alpine across the road from the press box and fed the parking meter, but still got a parking ticket.

I decided to take the case to court because of something Peter Thompson had written.

Peter made the front page of the *Courier* with a story about a policeman who revved his bike up during the unveiling of a plaque on Wickham Terrace by the Queensland Women's Historical Society — drowning out the ceremony. "The rudest policeman I have met" was the heading on his story, which won a state-wide prize for cadet reporters. It made me realise I should have written a story on what the policeman did to Jim.

So I decided to do a story on going to court over a parking meter ticket.

I was a much more nervous character than Jim and, when I arrived to appear in court, my whole body was on edge. But I kept reminding myself of my teacher, Brother Campbell's dictum: "To be brave is not to be without fear, but to overcome it."

One of the old court reporters said I should have seen him and he could have fixed it up.

That, I said, wasn't what I wanted.

I was surprised how many people were at the court. There was the copper to say he remembered writing out the ticket and placing it on my car; there was a man from the Treasury Department to say payment had not been received; there was a man from the Main Roads Department to say the car was registered in my name; there was the police sergeant who was prosecuting me; there was a shorthand typist; and, of course, the magistrate up on the bench.

Just before we walked in, the old police sergeant pulled me aside and said: "Listen son, why don't you just pay the fine and save yourself some money. I can tell you it will cost you a lot more. You have absolutely no chance of getting off a parking ticket."

I had been to the Library at Uni and had found that the Chief Justice in England had ruled in a similar case that, while ignorance of the law was no excuse, "a person has to have a reasonable chance of knowing the law exists".

I quoted this in court, and argued that — because the sign saying "no parking 4 to 6" was obscured — I had no chance of knowing the law.

When the policeman said he had been proceeding down Vulture Street and had seen a strawberry Alpine "parked between two signs saying 'no parking 4-6 p.m.'" I stood up after wiping my sweating palms on my handkerchief and asked: "And how far apart were these signs?"

He said he wasn't sure.

"I contend, Your Worship, that they were at least 100 yards apart, ten feet off the ground, and in letters less than an inch high and, anyway, totally obscured by trees. I suggest we adjourn the court to the site to inspect these signs."

The magistrate did not go along with this, but he seemed impressed when I said from the witness box to the sergeant cross-examining me: "I am here today because you said before we came in here that there was absolutely no chance to beat this law. And I believe there must be a chance for the innocent to beat any law. Or else we have no law."

After a few hours the magistrate, as was his job, found me guilty.

But he did add that there were mitigating circumstances, and he reduced the fine from one pound to seven shillings and sixpence which, with costs, meant I had to pay a total of two pounds: double the original fine.

I went back to the *Courier* determined to do a Peter Thompson.

I wrote a story which began: "This week I tried to beat Brisbane's parking meter bogey, and failed."

I knew that hundreds of people got parking meter fines every week, and that no one ever went to court because if anyone was ever allowed to win it would wreck the system of sticking tickets on cars without ever meeting the accused.

So I thought it was a good story.

I wrote how nerve-wracking it was to appear before His Worship; of the sweat in my palms; of the forces lined up against me from four different government departments; of how I had no chance anyway; and how — once the case started — I wished I had just paid the fine.

But the paper didn't run the story.

# 10
# *Touched by the sun*

Listening to the older journalists and editors give Uni Journalism lectures helped me realise what a wonderful job I had somehow stumbled on to: a job where we were, apparently, among the most important people in the land.

They told us we should not be afraid to be aggressive when seeking interviews with public figures and officials because journalists had a "right to know": on behalf of all the people who were busy doing other jobs.

I already had an inkling of this because I once heard one of our top reporters, Alan Underwood, yell into the telephone in the General Reporters' Room: "You will answer the question because I represent three-quarters of a million Queenslanders who want to know."

We were, the lecturers said, the people's only protection in a naughty world.

Mr Arthur Richards, who wrote a column in the paper and had won a national prize for feature writing, was one of the lecturers. I recognised him immediately because he was the only big-name writer on the paper outside of Sport. The other top news journalists got "By a Staff Reporter" on a story if it was considered particularly good. But in some cases Mr Richards even got his photo on his articles.

Now, smoking a pipe, Mr Richards sat in front of us — a lean, balding, grey-haired man with a soft voice — telling how, when he wrote his award-winning series of articles exposing how bad Queensland's free hospitals were, it wasn't the interviews, or the statistics, or the accusations, that gave his story impact.

No, it was the description of the sparrows sitting on the occupied hospital bed pecking up old crumbs.

This was an important difference between a writer and a non-writer: the writer would include what he saw.

Mr Richards said he loved writing so much that, even if the paper didn't pay him, he would still come in and write.

"But don't tell them that," he said, leaning forward on his seat so that his brown sports coat tightened across his neck, "they might stop paying me."

And we all laughed with him.

Mr Richards also told us about other important people on the paper.

He told how Mr Holmes — the eighty-years-plus white-haired man with the walking stick and tiny glasses who wrote the *Courier*'s daily editorials — needed a great store of knowledge on every subject to do the job. To emphasise this, he said Mr Holmes knew so much that he could quote the entire Bible off by heart.

I found this difficult to believe.

Mr Richards also told us about our cartoonist, Mr Ian Gall, who also wrote a "Nature Notes" column. He suggested we should look more closely at Mr Gall's sketches and we would often see birds flying in carrying words like "rhyme" or "reason" in their beaks to underline his message; or we would see buoys and beacons and seagulls — because of Mr Gall's interest in Brisbane's Moreton Bay.

His lectures were so interesting that, when he finished, he asked those who would like to be feature writers to put up their hands: and I noted that everyone else in the room — more than 20 *Courier* and *Tele* cadets — did so.

About every second week a different journalist gave his view of the job.

Mr Bob McDonald, the *Sunday Mail* Chief-of-Staff, told how an irate newspaper reader once went to the paper and the Editor shot him dead: "and that was the beginning of letters to the Editor". Mr Bray told us he had just sent *Courier-Mail* reporters to Mt Isa and Cairns — which was the same in terms of distance as a London paper sending reporters to Warsaw and Rome.

Subs told us that a small paper was called a tabloid and a big one a broadsheet and that the paper got 20 times as much news every day as it could fit in. That the most important thing was to get the paper out on time to catch trucks, trains and planes — even if it meant physically chiselling a mistake off the steel plates before running the presses. And that the *Tele* had banned "big" in headlines because it was such a convenient word that every sub overused it. Any boy under 21 was a "youth".

We learned that papers were aimed at an average education standard of a twelve-year-old so that almost everybody could read it. But articles for the more educated reader had to be carried, since the *Courier* had to cater for everyone in the state as the only state-wide morning paper.

We were shown how newspaper artists painted over the photographs before they went into the paper to remove background and emphasise the outline of the main subjects. It seemed a bit like cheating to me, but I didn't say anything.

One lecturer told us that some said television would eventually knock newspapers off because it could bring the news in pictures immediately.

"But I remember when radio started everyone said 'Oh we won't need newspapers anymore now'. All that happened was people got more interested in reading about the people and events they heard about on the wireless, and we sold a lot more newspapers!"

Armed with all this extra knowledge I not only began to feel I was someone, but I was now much better able to realise what was going on at the paper. For example, I was surprised to see that once when we missed a rape story even the Police Roundsman who was not working that day got into trouble.

One of the major things I noticed was that, while we cadets were required to spend a lot of afternoons and nights going to Uni lectures and shorthand classes, the older journalists didn't have to improve their minds. They spent all

135

their spare work time at the Royal Hotel. This pub was right next door, across a laneway called Isles Love Lane.

A constant stream of journalists shuffled back and forth every evening. Even on a Sunday night when hotels weren't allowed to open they seemed to disappear in that general direction, and re-appear an hour later either more aggressive or much happier.

The Royal Hotel didn't appeal to me.

Each time I walked past I could smell the thick musty stink of beer and, as the doors swung open and closed, I noted crowds of men pushed together around a high bar.

The place seemed like the Haunted House in Sideshow Alley at the Ekka to me.

It was said that downstairs under the Royal was a place where the tougher *Courier* journalists, and their friends, drank and fought. It must have had blood on the walls, I guessed, because the journalists called this place "the Blood Room".

So many journalists slipped out to this pub — including even Jack — that one night the Chief-of-Staff looked all around General, but I was the only one there. "Here I am Chief-of-Staff and no bloody staff to be chief of," he said.

Some of the cadets even drank there, but most didn't because you were supposed to be 21 to drink legally.

One of the advantages of having this pub next door was that older reporters were much more forthcoming late at night. One said that as a cadet he was sent to the airport to interview a famous man. He had never even heard of this bloke, so he couldn't think what to ask as the man rushed through the airport hanger to get to his chauffeur-driven car.

"What brings you to Brisbane?" the young journalist finally called out.

"Because I bloody well live here, now get out of my way," said the man.

Another told us his method of getting rid of readers who rang to complain about a story. "You're right," he would tell them. "You're so right. I'll sack him. Mind you, his wife and five children will suffer, but we can't have this sort of slipshod work." In the end, he reckoned, the complainant would be begging him to forget about the error.

Late in the evening other reporters would become sour after several trips to the Royal.

"Never agree to go off the record because you might walk around the corner and get the same piece of information from someone else — and then you won't be able to use it," Kev O'Donohue — who didn't give lectures — warned a group of us late one night as we waited for the paper to come up off the presses downstairs.

He also warned us never to become political writers.

"It's a dirty, dirty, dirty game. Stay away from it," he said.

Even though he was grey-haired, was often a boss, and didn't drive a car, Kev O'Donohue would go to the all-night parties after work. I finally felt I was someone when, one night, he asked me if I would take him to a party one of the Library girls was giving at a farm on the Coomera River, halfway to the Gold Coast.

It was as if I had suddenly been elevated in status one hundred times.

Not only was "K. O'D", as everyone on the paper called him, the top reporter but I particularly liked him because it was said that — when an Editor once told him he had to do what he was told "because you work for my paper" — Kev replied: "I only work here as long as I want to. And I don't want to work here any longer."

K. O'D was the President of our union, the Australian Journalists Association, which everyone referred to simply as the AJA. He was always campaigning to get everyone higher wages.

Once when reporters missed out on a national wage rise for all workers because the judge ruled we were "sui generis" (a race apart), Kev called everyone to a hall in Elizabeth Street and suggested we should all wear black armbands so people we interviewed would ask "why the black armband?" and we could tell them about this judge.

But the majority let him down and voted against it.

However Kev got his way the next time. A brewery offered to finance his dream of building an AJA Club: but only if the club refused to sell any other beer. Kev told a meeting that we should not be blackmailed into "a tied house".

"Better we don't have a club at all than for individuals not to have the right to choose what beer they want to drink," Kev said.

That was the end of the club.

On the way down to Coomera I asked him what a newspaper would do if there was a day when there were just no good stories around?

"Hughie, there is always the best news story of the day. So if there is nothing better then the best story of the day becomes the splash," he said.

K. O'D was a big help to me.

One day I had to cover a reunion lunch of retired reporters who had started out in journalism at the beginning of the century. I had no idea how I would get a story.

"Ask them what they consider the biggest story this century," Kev said, straight away, when I asked him.

All of these very old journalists quickly agreed on an answer. I thought it would have something to do with the two World Wars, or the Depression, or, most likely, a Catholic miracle.

"The sending of the first satellite into space," they all agreed.

I hadn't realised it was such big a story when the Russians did it with Sputnik while I was still at school. That must have been why everyone watched the sky at night. Satellites were so common nowadays that all I knew about them was the saying: "Next time you wish upon a star, make sure it's not just another satellite."

Perhaps because of Kev's influence, by the end of 1961 I found myself reading a lot of the paper every morning, though it was hard work. So hard, that I began to wonder why journalists weren't paid to read the paper each day, since it was part of the job.

In just one week the Russians exploded three experimental 20, 30, and 50 megaton nuclear bombs, sending a giant radioactive cloud sweeping over North America frightening everybody. One day a cricketer was killed by lightning while fielding at Chermside. The lightning knocked his cricket boots off and left a deep hole in the field. Then, on a day nothing much seemed to be happening, a company struck oil in Queensland for the first time at Moonie, and the shares reached six pounds each as everyone rushed to buy.

We were going to become an oil-rich state.

I started to see why Kev said there was always a best story every day. Large numbers of people were arrested at a giant Ban-the-Bomb demonstration in Britain, and then a few days later Mt Isa Mines — the second biggest mine in Australia — was crippled by a strike.

Everyone was very worried that the Reds might be behind these strikes and demonstrations, so I was pleased one morning to read a *Courier* headline that a military expert had told the RSL: "Brisbane is probably too small for an A-bomb attack."

Not everyone was convinced, because the Police Commissioner, Mr Bischof, warned the next day that "organisations with foreign ideology are trying to cash in on the plight of Brisbane's coloured people."

People were so worried about the Commos that one of the cadets told me he had been called before a newspaper executive and asked if he was a Communist after he had raved on about Lenin and Stalin one night at one of our parties just for fun.

So Fred was right after all: you did have to be careful what you said.

I noted as I read each day's paper that I was lucky I was not a big-time reporter, because they got some tough jobs. A bloke Jack and I knew was attacked and killed by a shark at Noosa, and our Police Roundsman, Winston Coates, was in such a hurry to get back with the story that he had a bad car accident — and had to dictate the story from his hospital bed. I thought it was a bit rough to ask him to do this. But Peter Thompson said it was the only way the paper could still get the full story at that late stage.

Our Industrial Reporter, Mal Crowley, was sent to Mt Isa to cover the strike. When Mal, a big man with prominent eyeballs, walked into the pub where all the union leaders drank, no one would talk to him. They said he represented "the Tory press" which was against their strike.

He had better hop it.

I would have been out of there like a shot out of a gun, but Mal bet the striking union leaders he could drink a glass of rum while standing on his head on the bar.

After he did this they said he could have all the interviews he wanted: and every day for months Mal had a story in the paper from the strike.

Bruce Wilson got sent to interview a woman who had opened an unusual shop in Rowe's Arcade: Brisbane's first shop devoted to selling provocative women's underwear. Bruce had to interview the woman owner while she was wearing just a piece of black mosquito net over her breasts. Lucky for him Bruce was incredibly suave, even though he was only a year older than me. He said on return to the General Reporter's Room as we all gathered around: "I couldn't look her in the eye."

Because cadets worked Saturdays and Sundays we had days off during the week when everyone else was working: so we tended to do things together. We played golf or tennis and were in the reporters' cricket and football teams.

We had a great cricket team and cleaned up the paper's office workers, and even Tattersalls Club. Bill Tuckey and Noel Vercoe were older reporters in their late twenties but they loved playing cricket and were very good — for their age. Bob Macklin was a top batsman and Bob Cronin and Bruce Postle, a photographer, were the fastest bowlers I had seen.

Jack was such a good spin bowler that he once bowled out almost the entire Lismore team by himself — but he didn't know that I had helped. I was our 12th man so I pretended I had nothing to do with the match and sat nonchalantly in their shed, telling each batsman as he prepared to go to the wicket: "Watch out for the left-arm spinner. He bowls Chinamen and has a vicious wrong-un."

The hardest part about beating the paper's office cricket team was they had a champion batsman called Ern Toovey who had played for Queensland. He could slog so well that he had once scored a century for Queensland before lunch. Jack and Toovey had an on-going battle between bat and ball. The only way to get Toovey out was to frustrate him from scoring too quickly.

Toovey was the best hooker of the ball any of us had seen. The one thing I prided myself on was my determination to stop any cricket ball, no matter how fast it was travelling. So myself, Thompson, and Macklin placed ourselves in a small arc on the boundary at square leg, and made a pact to let nothing past. We were all twenty-year-olds and, though we finished with blood on elbows and black ash-fill all over our whites, nothing did get past: unless it was a six.

Our most famous cricketer was a D-grade reporter called Mike Bingham who came up from Tasmania. Because he was from Tasmania we didn't know he could bowl, so Bill Tuckey didn't throw Bingham the ball against the Comps until the last over of the day. There was no chance of a result because they still had five wickets to fall.

Bingham bowled down three innocuous left-arm deliveries and, with five balls left for the day, I went and sat on the front of my car to be ready to leave. Incredibly, this Tasmanian reporter took the five remaining wickets with the last five balls of the day for us to win. Everyone agreed it was more remarkable than even the famous Brisbane Tie, and I wrote a poem for *House News*, the company's monthly newsletter, about how "Bingham could swing 'em" which ended: "Bingham, Bingham, Bingham, Bingham and Bingham".

Our sporting success was helped by the fact that all the male cadets seemed to have similar interests — perhaps because we were, with one or two exceptions, private school products: and even then almost all had attended one of Queensland's nine GPS schools. This seemed strange to me, because almost all of the older journalists were products of small state country-town primary schools.

And they knew a lot more than we did.

The trouble was that some of these cadet friends of mine — even though they had started six months after me — still seemed to be doing better than I was. Bob Cronin amazed me by writing a feature after only one year on the paper on something I had never even thought about: the effect Britain's proposed entry into the European Common Market might have on Australia. And Bob Howarth — after we had dinner at the Coronation Cafe in Elizabeth Street — took the beautiful waitress home. Bob had a good trick where he changed all his little bits of money into a big blue five-pound note so he could pull it out to pay for drinks in front of girls.

Another cadet told me he had showered with a girl he took out. This particular cadet broke the law every night and drank at the Royal, and it seemed to me more and more that this hotel was a passport to a lot of pleasures. It was such an amazing place that, for a while, a *Courier* journalist had a private pistol range under the hotel outside the Blood Room. But he had to stop using it after a stray bullet ricocheted through the floorboards into the public bar.

Since I was going to be 21 in a few months I accepted some invitations to pop next door for a drink. To me — brought up on the wide range of delicious soft drinks in Fred's cake shop — beer tasted like tar and smelt like ink. Not only had Jack been caught out by Olive, but my mate Rod got a clip over the ear when he vomited out the window of his bedroom all over the wall. He said he wasn't drunk, he was just calling out for three friends of his: "Geoorrrge, Heerrrb, and Arrrrcchie".

One day George, Herb and Archie got me too.

Bill Richards, Bob Macklin, Peter Thompson and myself played a round of golf in the morning at Victoria Park and then went to the Royal for a drink. I parked outside at a half-hour Queen Street parking meter, because I was only going to have one shandy, and walked down the long right-hand corridor that led to the private bar at the back where the journalists drank.

My other three cadet mates were having a beer so, not wanting to look like a sook, I ordered one too.

After two beers I felt strange, and realised I had broken the rule: never drink on an empty stomach. It was said at parties that the way to prevent drunkenness was to line your stomach with milk before drinking. So, saying I was going to the lavatory, I rushed out of the hotel and down to the Edward Street Milk Bar around the corner, and downed a glass of milk.

When I got back, there were two beers waiting for me instead of one. I was informed that I was "dragging the chain". It was my turn to shout.

That one glass of milk didn't seem to work.

I was getting worse.

So, after downing a few quickly — because they said you weren't allowed to sit on a beer — I raced back up the corridor, right into Queen Street, across Edward Street to the milk bar, and slammed a shilling on the stainless steel counter for another cold glass of milk.

I fed the parking meter on the way back.

I know I made at least one more trip to the milk bar that afternoon, because the girl behind the counter said if I kept mixing my drinks I'd get drunk.

That time I forgot about the parking meter.

As darkness fell I could vaguely hear the barmaid telling me to keep my voice down amid a sea of smiling faces.

I was just thinking of going next door to tell the Editor off when I felt a firm hand grip my right shoulder.

It was Jack.

"Come on, time to go home," he said.

I was incapable of arguing.

Jack drove me home in the Alpine, after removing several parking tickets, and said he was sorry to see this, because

Olive was going to give me hell: just like she had done to him.

Jack said he didn't want to witness it, so we crept up the back stairs and he somehow got me into bed without her seeing me.

But I just had to be sick.

Even though the house was revolving rapidly around, I made it down the stairs to under the cascara bean tree where the spinning became so great that I fell over, and couldn't get up.

Again Jack came after me.

But this time as he helped me up the stairs, Olive appeared from nowhere, filling the back door, to watch me vomiting all over the tank stand.

Always quick to act, she took over and hauled me off my feet and into my room. She lowered me to the bed, placed a cold wet towel over my face, put a bucket next to me, and poured some water into my mouth.

She turned — with anguish lining her soft face — towards Jack, who was waiting, eagerly I suspect, to witness the consequences of my foolishness.

"Poor Hughie," Olive said to Jack. "He's had a touch of the sun."

# 11
# The big flutter

The only day I hated going to work was Saturday. Not only because this was the one day of the week you expected to enjoy yourself, but the *Sunday Mail* had all different bosses from the *Courier*. And they gave me all the worst jobs.

It was as if they had no confidence in me.

I don't know what caused this, but it probably dated back to the time I deliberately tipped my typewriter off the desk on to the floor after more than twelve months of typing out the lawn bowls results.

Every First-Year male cadet was supposed to be assigned to do the lawn bowls results on Saturday at some stage a few months after arrival: once he had learned to type, and to get things right. Peter Thompson did them for a time. Even Jack did them. But I got stuck with bowls for 18 months — which meant all the other male cadets below me skipped the bowls results and went on to more interesting tasks.

It was even worse than it sounds.

Since most people didn't work Saturdays anymore, and with more retired people, more and more lawn bowls clubs had started up. So, by the time I got to do the results, there were suddenly 60 clubs to ring. There were so many of these bowlers that I considered starting a lawn bowls weekly newspaper because no paper ever wrote stories about bowlers: they just printed the results in the smallest type available, five point.

To speed things up, you rang around all the clubs early in the afternoon to get the events to be played that day, and the names of every player. Then you typed all this information up — with each club on a separate sheet of copy paper —

leaving spaces between the names for the scores. Then, when you rang back after five, you quickly wrote in all the scores with a biro.

Because everything was all typed up and ready to go, the theory was that this would be a very, very fast process.

But it wasn't like that at all.

On the first ring around the clubs early in the afternoon, a designated club official would be waiting. He would read out the events and the names clearly, concisely, and quietly over the phone. But, on the second call later in the day, the phone would be answered by anyone in the club bar, usually someone who had never heard of the *Sunday Mail*. Gurgling into the phone they would yell: "Who'd ya say it was?" drowned out by a background of tinkling glasses and shouted conversation.

Sometimes it took several people before I could get someone who could talk sense. Yet I had less than two hours to get more than 60 clubs done for the early Saturday night deadlines: about two minutes per club.

So that was why, late one Saturday, I calmly tipped the typewriter over the back of the desk onto the floor of the General Reporters' Room.

It hit with a much louder rattle than I expected.

Metal bits and ribbon spools leapt out of the top and rolled rapidly across the floor and under desks like cockroaches when the light is turned on.

The room went quiet.

So quiet that I could actually hear these tiny pieces of metal ending their short journeys against desk legs and walls.

The *Sunday Mail* Chief-of-Staff rushed out of his office and stood over the front of my desk looking down .... the only desk in the room without a typewriter sitting on it.

At that moment I didn't mind what he was going to say. I had had it completely with bowls results. I didn't even care if I got the sack.

But instead of being angry he was calm and helpful. When I told him how impossible the job had become since so many new clubs had started; how the system he relied on was donkeys years old; and how drunk all the bowlers were, he got a younger girl cadet to help me.

I thought that would end my stint on bowls, but the next week I was back — and alone again.

There was no getting away from it. The people on the *Sunday Mail* didn't think I was much of a reporter.

When a crop-duster crashed, I was instructed: "Have his wife rushing to his hospital bed to be with him." But she wasn't bothering to go to the country hospital to see him, so I didn't mention her in the story. Either she changed her mind later, or they thought she should have rushed to his side, because the paper the next day headlined: "Wife rushes to bedside".

When an Australian cricketer scored a century in a Test in England, someone had the brilliant idea that the *Sunday Mail* should ring his wife and write a story from the female point of view, on how thrilled she was that her husband had carved up the English attack overnight while we were all asleep.

"Why, what's he done this time?" she asked when I rang, unaware of the great news. "I'll tell you what. He won't be going over there again," she said as a baby cried in the background.

It didn't seem right to write a story on what she said. How would he feel to read his wife's reaction after scoring a century in a Test: the greatest thing any Australian could do for his country? So I didn't write the story. And I was smart enough also not to tell Jack, or Peter Thompson, or Bob Macklin.

I thought I had finally got off lawn bowls when Bob Macklin and myself were sent to the Mount Gravatt Show, and Dave Bentley was put on the bowls: something that should have happened to him many months before.

The Chief-of-Staff called Bob and me into his office and emphasised that he wanted every result and name from the Show that we could get into the paper: "from embroidery winners to best chook owner: don't forget, they all buy newspapers".

A Show official in a red blazer showed us to a small tin shed which contained pile after pile of long narrow cardboard result sheets in various colours, all held together by rubber bands. It was easy to see we could never do all of these results, but we could make a big hole in them. Being four months Bob's senior, I took off my jacket and hung it over a chair, unzipped our portable typewriter, grabbed a pile of copypaper and a stack of results, and suggested that he should read out the name of the best yellow-faced budgie while I typed.

But Macklin said he wasn't going to help.

"I don't care who is champion hack, or who owns the best visiting dog — I'm going to look for the real story."

I was left alone in the hot tin shed.

Outside thousands of people wandered around the showgrounds while, mindful of our instructions, I pursued the piles of result cards one after the other: working through the winners and place-getters in the wood-chopping pile, down into the jam results.

Scores of copypaper pages later, Bob strode in with the usual all-embracing smile over his actor's face: "Hugh, I've got a great story old pal, I'm gonna bust this Show wide open," he said with his flair for over-dramatising things.

"But Bob," I said, "we're supposed to be doing all these results. Remember what the Chief-of-Staff said?"

Macklin seemed surprised by my attitude.

"Do you realise, Hugh," he said with his radio announcer's voice (another quality he had that I lacked), "that the innocent little Mount Gravatt Agricultural Show has got the hottest stripper in town!"

"Listen Bob," I said, "I know it's a drag, but we've got to do all these results. That's what we were sent here for. Look, I haven't even touched the produce results or the best jars of honey yet."

"That!" Bob said, disdainfully throwing his arm at the coloured results card piles. "That's not journalism. If they

148

want that done, then they should send out clerks. Or copy girls. Or typists. Yes, that's a typist's job. Come on, and I'll show you the stripper.''

So I threw the green "best pumpkin" pile aside and followed Bob like an obedient cattle dog to the short row of sideshow tents.

Macklin was, as usual, right.

This dark-haired girl was much younger than the one in the nightclub. Much thinner. But, as she shed her red slacks, she revealed an aspect of girlhood I hadn't even thought of before. The other stripper looked and acted like I imagined a stripper would, with large amounts of female flesh to watch through the smoke and dark of the nightclub. But this stripper was so thin and young it was like watching a teenage girl at Mass taking her clothes off in front of everyone. In a nightclub, a girl could almost disappear behind something as flimsy as a pot plant, but here there was nowhere to hide. She was taking off her clothes confined in the heat and glare of a white tent.

Nor was this stripper being watched by a zoot-suited decadent nightclub crowd.

This tent was filled with suburban husbands in half-mast shorts who had merely meant to take their wives and kids to the Show for fairy floss and show jumping, but who had somehow been waylaid.

Macklin wrote his story and was praised up by older reporters, and no one mentioned the 2,000 winners and runners-up I got into the paper in just one afternoon: including "Best Vase of Sweet Peas".

The next week I was back on the bowls results again.

It was about this time that Fred's business started going downhill. The City Council forced him to remove the three alcoves Uncle Cyril had built where people for years had sat and eaten lunch and dinner, and, at exactly the same time, a large cakeshop chain opened a shop just two doors away.

Fred didn't think it would matter because he had so many loyal customers. He thought the cake chain was "whacky the noo" to open so close. But this new shop started selling everything at nearly half the price they charged in their other shops — and suddenly Fred lost most of the custom he had built up over the last 25 years at Annerley Junction. Then the landlord took part of Fred's shop frontage, yet upped the rent for a new lease.

Olive asked Fred if he would be changing his vote in the next Council election now this had happened. "You know I'm too smart to let people know how I will vote, duck," Fred said to Olive. "I've told you before it's dangerous to let others know what you're thinking. Let them try to guess."

Mum decided we would have to call it quits and move shop, but Fred insisted that things were still fair to middling. The customers, he said, would eventually come back if he kept the quality up.

Fred cooked less and less of everything each week, saying he was merely using his discretion. He got angry if you mentioned it, but now he sang his song of anger "Moonlight and Roses" much more often, and spent his time in the kitchen — after a lifetime of having too many customers — sitting on the flour bags looking up at the long, narrow mirror in the corner to see if anyone had come in to buy something.

But fewer and fewer people came.

Olive told Fred it was no use sitting around feeling sorry for himself. "Lend me your face to fight a bulldog," she told him. "Buck up and take that sour look off your face. Look at you. Come on Freddie stop moping about, get off your high horse and do something."

Finally, Fred asked Joe Noonan — a bachelor accountant who used to eat every night in the shop before we lost the alcoves — to have a look at his takings.

A week later, Joe announced gravely to a family meeting around the oven that for months now Fred — taking into account the dud cheques he had accepted from good customers — had been making just nine pounds a week. That was just over half of what I was earning. He said it was no use working seven days a week, night and day, for such reward.

150

So Olive went in search of another shop and a new start for the Lunns.

A millionaire called Mr Matthews, who came in for a pie occasionally, told Mum he owned a corner block of six shops way on the other side of the river. It used to do well until a big arcade of shops under one roof with lots of car parks around it — an American invention called a "Shopping Town" — had opened nearby at Chermside. A couple of his tenants had gone broke and some shops were vacant, but Fred's cakes and pies would soon lure the people back and everyone — including himself — would benefit. He would fit out the shop with all new stainless steel benches and an oven if Fred would move there.

Fred didn't want to go, and started buying more Golden Casket tickets than ever. But, of course, he never won anything.

"I guess the Missus is right. If I'm going to bring home the bacon we'll have to leave Annerley Junction after all these years. It's enough to drive a man to drink."

Olive was thrilled. "It's a long way out of town, but it's an expanding area or they wouldn't have built that shopping town there," she said.

Fred planned to move overnight after he finished work at Annerley so as not to miss a day. He had been a bit crook recently, so — remembering Olive's jibe when I was a boy that I was "laziness personified" — I said I wouldn't loaf around. I volunteered to help after work.

All night Fred and I worked together. We stacked his black oven trays on the back seat of the Zephyr and filled the boot with all the tiny instruments he used for cutting pie tops and pasties and weighing buns. The next trip we took two 120lb bags of flour and two 70lb bags of sugar and returned for the ply boxes of margarine. We started cooking at six o'clock the next morning and the shop opened as if we were still in the old Annerley shop.

Fred said my blood was worth bottling.

We didn't have to move everything, because Dad wanted to keep the old shop going, just in case the new one failed —

by bringing pies, buns and cakes each day in the Zephyr all the way from Chermside for Olive to sell to his most loyal customers at Annerley.

But it was chaos at the Annerley shop that day as Olive waited for me to bring Zephyr-loads of pies and buns on the 35-minute drive across the city. This went on for a few weeks — with Olive standing out the front telling customers "he should appear at any moment" and Fred spending more time "running the cutter", as he called it, than cooking. Finally Fred had to accept his fate, and "Lunns for Buns" disappeared forever from Annerley Junction.

The cake shop two doors up immediately put its prices back up to their chain levels — well above Fred's.

This now raised the ugly question: should we leave the family home at 40 Ekibin Road to save Fred the trip to Chermside and back every day, and to make it easier for Olive to go and help him. No longer could she just walk a few blocks up the road carrying her large green basket.

I was devastated by this suggestion. I couldn't imagine us leaving our home.

But Gay was very keen.

Gay wanted one of the brand new brick homes they were building on the northern outskirts of Brisbane because she said our house was old-fashioned, unpainted, untidy, and had no front fence — because I had knocked it down and hadn't put it back up. "It's alright for you," she said. "Boys are different. Girls have to bring their boyfriends home."

Big deal.

I couldn't see what she was complaining about.

Gay had already taken over Fred and Olive's front bedroom, kicking them out. She bought herself all modern powder-blue-and-white masonite furniture with leather-texture doors from Trittons at the Gabba to replace Olive's old dark timber stuff.

She had painted the bedroom and the lounge room using a chair on a table, and had got Mum to buy a new kitchen suite of orange laminex and vinyl-covered chrome chairs, plus a glass cabinet to display Gay's new set of coloured glasses, part of her glory box. Plus Olive and Gay had prevailed on Jim to line the bathroom walls with a new product called Marblelite and to tile the kitchen floor.

Gay had turned most of the house into a palace.

But just because she had doctors calling on her, didn't mean we had to leave our home.

Gay and Olive took us all to see a new brick home at Chermside not far from the shop. Gay was in love with it, and Olive said it would be practical to move there. But, luckily, Fred didn't like the small windows. He said he needed plenty of fresh air. Fred hated the carpets too — he said carpets stank and all floors should be bare boards, washed very occasionally with kero. But then he started to ruin his argument by going into his old spiel: "Furniture is unnecessary. All we need are a few kerosene tin boxes and some bully beef. Houses are too large. Twenty people could easily live in our house."

To shut Fred up I started backing him up, saying our Annerley house was far nicer. I said Gay only wanted a brick house in her efforts "to get a rich boyfriend".

To my surprise, Gay picked up a hunk of wood the builders had left lying around and threw it at me, hitting me in the elbow right on the funny bone.

It wasn't funny either that when I graduated from bowls slavery I ended up phoning through the horse-racing results every Saturday afternoon from various racetracks while everyone else listened to the rugby league or went to the Shield cricket.

Hundreds of horses raced each other in various classes like novice, transition, encourage and two-year-old and — even though all my life Fred had followed the gee-gees — I had never heard of any of them. Fred was always backing horses, whispering into the phone, getting telegrams and letters with tips he paid for, and rushing off to place bets while telling me to watch the buns didn't burn, saying: "I'm off to see the wizard."

It seemed to make him happy.

153

The racing job entailed writing down the order of the horses called by a racing writer at two points during the race, and phoning through to a copy-taker at the paper after each race the starting price for each horse and the tote payments: win, place and double; the placings; the jockeys and their weights (if they were overweight by how many pounds); the trainer of the winner; and the age of the first three horses, their owners, their barrier draw, and the distances separating them at the finish.

It wasn't a bad job really because it was out of the office and easy to do. The chief racing writer, Jim Vine, drove us there, and a couple of racetracks provided food and alcohol — if you wanted it — for the Press in a special room with a waiter.

Occasionally one of the writers got me to place a bet for him, and I noted he never seemed to win.

You had to know all the style so that, for example, a "br. g." was a brown gelding and a "ch. f." was a chestnut filly. And God help you if you so much as got the colour of a horse wrong.

There were usually eight races from midday to five o'clock and so you rarely stopped working, except for a bite to eat.

When the races were over, the racing writers would stay behind waiting for the stewards to report on complaints against jockeys and to interview trainers: and I had to hang around waiting for them.

I started writing little poems on copypaper while looking down on the crowd from the Press Box window. I never showed these to anybody. One was about the men who searched through the thousands of tickets at the end of the day in the ridiculous hope that they might somehow find a winning ticket accidentally discarded by a punter.

I called it "Fat Chance":

The punter in his plight is seeking
To win a world — a world of dream;
The bookie knows it's in his keeping
As he shouts the odds and stands supreme.

The punter in his mind intangible
Comes back to lose again today;
He has one destiny at the races
— to pay, pay, pay and pay.

The bookie on his stand, untouchable
Looks at this motley crowd with glee;
He know that racing is his fortune
He knows that this crowd is his key.

The race is on.
They cheer and shout,
They scream and hope,
But all to no avail.
Their horse has lost
Their hopes are tossed
They're doomed to weep and wail.

Slowly they leave,
kicking up the torn up tickets;
Some, in blissful hope,
Get on their knees and search
For a ticket which could fill their purse.

It's a sad sight,
It's a bad plight,
It's the racing game
And they'll be back again
— next week.

Every Saturday it was off to a different racetrack. The
sand at Albion Park; the grass at Doomben or nearby Eagle
Farm, and then broken-down Bundamba near Ipswich.

Personally, I couldn't see why they wasted money on all
these different racetracks and grandstands when each got
used only once a month. So much land was wasted, especially in the centre of the tracks.

A couple of weeks into the new year of 1962, my Saturday
racetrack experiences turned from work to pleasure.

Kenny Fletcher had returned from overseas, and after

playing all the state championships around Australia he was back in Brisbane for a couple of months.

Ken for some reason had taken to horseracing like a priest to prayer — saying it was "money for old rope". He had started backing horses when he was in Rocky with his coach, Arthur Liddle, selling Slazenger tennis racquets. There he met a tennis player from Millmerran called Mary Jones who told him: "Daddy thinks his horse Earlwood will win on Saturday."

Ken went to the races and Earlwood was 14 to 1. Although he was earning less than ten pounds a week he put ten pounds on Earlwood, no doubt expressing one of his favourite phrases like: "You might as well get killed for a sheep as a lamb" or "It's now or never." Unlike me, Ken wasn't concerned with tomorrow. When people asked him what he wanted to be after he finished playing tennis, he always replied: "A rich eccentric."

Earlwood won by half a head.

Fletch won 140 pounds.

However, he couldn't tell his father about it because Mr Fletcher would have gone crook. So Fletch just told his Mum, Ethel.

Ken got on so well with his mother that he would often announce when I was there that he was going to bash Ethel up, and she would immediately start laughing. Then he would wrestle her down onto the floor until she was laughing so much that she couldn't fight back.

Now that I could do the race results without even thinking, instead of sitting in the Press Box with the dour racing writers, I got to wander nonchalantly through the crowds with Ken. He seemed to know everybody important from the first day he arrived at the track — with a free member's pass, of course, on the lapel of his new white sports coat which had a slight black fleck running through it.

And, like a real punter, he wore a small grey pork-pie felt hat.

Actually, the hat didn't belong to Ken. This hat had been lent to him by his doubles partner, Frankie Gorman, who had since been killed in a car accident while Ken was overseas. Frankie had also toured overseas as a tennis player and he and Ken had won the Linton Cup junior tennis championship for Queensland — Frankie beating Bob Hewitt and Ken beating Martin Mulligan of NSW in the final. So they were great mates. Ken was sitting at the airport in Kuala Lumpur when he heard the bad news, and that was when he decided to wear Frankie's hat in his honour.

Ken knew more about the language of horses than I did, even though I enjoyed listening to the race callers on the radio because they said things like "one furlong from home and, from behind a wall of horses, he pulls to the extreme outside," or "You can put your glasses down, it's London to a brick on Lancaster."

I went to the races directly from the office, so my first sight of Ken would usually be him waving his racebook from a corner of the grandstand, calling me down to see him urgently. For a Christian Brothers boy who was an only child with strict parents, I don't know how he picked it all up. He always had the drum on some horse or other: either that it was a dead-set cert, or that it couldn't beat time with a stick. And he knew which horse was a roughie — which meant it wasn't much good.

Fletch talked about the ring, and welchers, and strappers, and horses that were in the red. These were horses Ken said we shouldn't back under any circumstances: "Odds on, look on," he would say gravely over his race book as he held it folded out in his hands like a Missal.

Nor did Ken like horses that had been heavily handicapped for a race with a large weight: "Weight stops a train but," he would always point out.

He didn't like backing the favourite either, not only because of the poor odds, but Ken said punters hated looking at a beaten favourite after a race: "it always looks so ugly".

This racetrack language overflowed into his everyday speech, even though tennis terms like ace or volley or serve never did. Thus, a pretty girl he didn't particularly like the look of would be described as having the look of a beaten favourite. And one who wasn't a good sort would be a roughie.

Ken also talked a language no one else in Brisbane understood, though I slowly learned the meaning of the unusual words and phrases he had picked up on two trips around the world. Ken could swear in most languages now, so rarely swore in English, which saved him from the wrath of his father, and confused the Australian tennis umpires. But his favourite terms were from the casinos he visited regularly overseas. If he thought we had better get our money on the next race he would say "*Faites vos jeux, mesdames et messieurs*", and if he said "*Rein ne va plus*" it would signal that the horses had jumped.

If he served an ace on the tennis court Fletch would call out loudly for a "*répétition*".

Ken liked casinos because he had had a huge win at one in Italy.

"The bank notes in Italy are so big but," Ken said as he imitated himself trying to stuff large bundles of lire into every pocket. "I couldn't believe it. I never imagined I would ever have so much money that I couldn't fit it all in my pockets."

But Fletch was lucky he won on that last bet, otherwise he would have been in trouble with Rod Laver, who had won Wimbledon that year for the first time.

By the time Ken's thirty-five-to-one shot finally came up on the spinning wheel he had lost everything: except for the money Laver had lent him to buy a Rolex watch for a Brisbane tennis official.

"So I put that money on for one last shot. It was hilarious," Ken said, "because the Rocket was sitting there saying he couldn't understand how I could take such a chance with my money. But what he didn't know was that by that stage it was HIS money that I was betting with!"

Although going to the races with Ken was fun, I noted that overall we were backing many more losers than winners.

158

I was starting to lose money betting on the horses like everyone else.

After a couple of months — though I didn't want Ken to think I was getting mingy — I decided to have no more bets. Fred said you could win on the horses but you had to have a system "and stick with it". And Ken didn't seem to have a system.

When I told him this he said not to worry, because today was the day we would win all our money back.

"With interest old son, with interest."

He motioned me closer and whispered: "I've got something up my sleeve, a few irons in the fire. It's all down to striking while the iron's hot, and kicking on from there well."

Fletch had become friendly with the famous Brisbane racing announcer, Vince Curry, and Vince had told him that he knew of an absolute certainty that would be running down south in the fifth.

A horse called Dhaulagiri.

Ken said the connections of this horse would let Vince know later in the afternoon if it was really going.

Vince would tell Ken.

And we would put all of our money on it.

I said I thought all the racehorses were really going, but Ken said many horses didn't try so that they could carry less weight and run at greater odds at some future date.

The trick was to know which horses were ridgy-didge "definite goers".

Ken said Dhaulagiri was a huge horse and "a dickiebird" had told him it had a turn of speed like nothing else this side of the black stump. Only a select group of one or two people — and us — knew about it.

As the fifth race approached, Ken waited in the milling crowd at the front of the main grandstand among the ladies in their matching hats and gloves, and hundreds of men in suits while I waited under the umbrellas in the betting ring — a large, hot, open, concreted area behind the main grandstand where the bookies listed their odds and took bets.

There were rows and rows of them with large leather bags over their shoulders, each standing next to a column of numbers that could be altered with a twist of the fingers. These were the odds for the horses, and punters walked up and down the rows looking for the best price for the horse they wanted to back.

But that was largely a waste of time. As soon as one bookie altered a price, all of the others seemed to know about it and altered theirs. It was an exciting place as punters shouted out and tried to pass money to get the best odds before the price fell or the race started. And the bookies called out the bets to a "penciller", who wrote them all down as the bookie scribbled an indecipherable message in thick pencil on the betting slips he passed out to the punters — after dropping their green pound notes into his bag.

Because Vince Curry had to be up in his race-calling studio at the back of the grandstand for a local race, it was arranged that he would signal "two to the Valley" to Ken just before the race if we should back Dhaulagiri.

"Two to the Valley" was the same as the Winston Churchill Victory sign, or the rude sign apparently used in other parts of Australia. But in Brisbane it was the most frequent sign when buying tickets on a tram, a journey which often ended at Brisbane's huge shopping centre of Fortitude Valley.

If he signalled Ken with this positive sign, Ken would signal me in the betting ring to place the bet.

There was — apparently — going to be very little time to make what Ken called "the plunge".

Since Ken thought Dhaulagiri — he was by now calling him "the mighty Dhaulagiri" — was such a certainty that you could put your house on, we gathered every last shilling from our wallets for the bet: over fifty pounds at least. The odds were shortening all the time — as Ken said they would as word spread among "the connections".

Still, the mighty Dhaulagiri hadn't yet gone near getting into the red.

I was a bit worried that we might lose the equivalent of

nearly three weeks' wages in one hit, but Ken was completely confident, as usual. Even though one of his favourite sayings was "don't count your chickens but", he was very sure when it came to gambling, tennis, or even dealing with ruffians: who Ken called "low-breeds".

Just before the race started, Ken got the "two-to-the-Valley" signal from Vince. He looked from a slight rise over to me and waved his racebook madly from side to side.

"Get the money on," he seemed to be mouthing.

I got two-to-one, so we stood to triple our money, just by knowing the right people.

When I showed Ken the small betting ticket covered in coloured type he said: "This is it well, old son. This is where we turn fifty pounds into a hundred and fifty at one hit!"

There was an announcement at the track: the horses were under starter's orders.

Everyone stopped where they were, like statues that listened.

The gates flew back, the race was on, and Dhaulagiri thrilled us both by immediately jumping to the front and grabbing "a rails run".

Because the race was at a southern track, like thousands of others we stood under the shade of the sloping grandstand, our heads cocked to the side listening anxiously to the loudspeakers above which blared the race call all over the ground.

Every time the announcer called the mighty Dhaulagiri's name we caught each other's eye, but said nothing, as our ears concentrated on the speakers.

"Big Dhaulagiri has been pulled to the extreme outside ....

"Down the back straight and the huge Dhaulagiri is slaughtering the field .....

"Dhaulagiri's already six lengths clear," said the caller, surprise echoing through his voice.

Ken, who was just slightly taller than me, raised his eyebrows.

"Round the corner and into the straight, and as they

straighten up for the home turn with two furlongs to go the mighty Dhaulagiri has raced to ten lengths clear!" shouted a clearly amazed announcer.

Ken leapt involuntarily up into the air. "Kick on, kick on," he said.

Lacking Ken's optimism, I clenched both sweating palms together in tight fists, hoping more for a win on Ken's behalf than mine, since it would give him such a thrill.

"The whips are out, and half-way down the straight the giant Dhaulagiri's still five lengths clear," called the voice on the loudspeaker ... and Ken gave a sidelong glance, and adjusted his checked sports coat with a tight right fist.

I suddenly remembered that I had heard a racing writer say the jockeys sometimes whip their own leg to make it look as though they are trying hard to win.

So was the use of the whip good news, or bad?

As the announcer returned from the rear of the twenty-horse field to the front I only heard his next sentence as a sort of echo from the speaker:

"Half a furlong from home ... and Big Dhaul's finished."

Ken and I stood looking at each other: Ken's top lip curled slightly upwards. There was a dazed look in the light blue eyes beneath the brim of Frankie's dark pork-pie hat.

"Big Dhaul's finished," said Fletch, as he symbolically tore up our losing ticket.

I thought Ken might do his nana, but he surprised me.

"I like that," he said. "Big Dhaul's finished! That sums it up very well. It's exactly how I've felt on court in the fifth set. It sums up life when things go wrong: 'Big Dhaul's finished!' He certainly gave us a run for our money but."

Ken could always be philosophical at such times.

"Well Hughie, come day, go day, God send Sunday," he said.

That night at Ken's place he laughed and laughed over and over again at our experience, and said that — whenever things went wrong in our lives over the next fifty years — all that one of us would have to do to bring joy to the occasion was to say "Big Dhaul's finished".

And he told me the latest joke about how we all got a belly button.

"When God finishes making all the babies he walks along the line sticking his forefinger into their tummies saying: *You're done, You're done, You're done.....*"

# 12
# *Head over heels for Sallyanne*

In February 1962 something happened which made me much more determined than ever to take out Sallyanne, the beautiful cadet reporter on the *Tele*. I found myself stuck in the Mater Hospital, suffering once again from earache.

It was the same problem I had operations for when I was seven and fourteen.

Now here I was, about to turn twenty-one, with my ears once again bulging with a build-up of wax attached to the ear drum. As usual, the doctor said the wax was as hard as cement. I was even put back in the same bed on the same side verandah at the Mater where I'd been seven years earlier.

As if hospital wasn't depressing enough, the doctor couldn't get all the wax out in the first operation because, he said, the blood filling up the ear made it too difficult. So I had to stay in hospital for a week so a specialist could have a go. This new doctor complained that, with my ear record, I should have kept a check on my ears because I was risking my hearing with these operations: and he wouldn't believe I had been to see an ear specialist just six months earlier.

I wrote an abusive letter to the specialist on Wickham Terrace before entering hospital — and was surprised to receive a two-page reply in which the ear specialist defended himself stoutly. I thought he would just ignore my letter.

While awaiting the operation I read some novels, which always seemed to contain descriptions of sex after 30 pages.

I also met some nurses.

One nurse, Deidre — who looked like a movie star — made me cups of Ovaltine late at night, but another ignored me until one day she saw me typing in bed on a portable typewriter. She started telling people I was "a writer" and from then on talked to me every day, until one night when things went wrong.

I awoke in the early hours with bad earache and got up to get a pill.

After midnight there was just one nurse in the all-male ward. The only light allowed flickered faintly from a kerosene lantern on a desk in the middle of the rows of iron white hospital beds, each with a chain and ring above the pillow so the patient could pull himself up.

Holding my sore left ear, I walked barefoot on the cool timber floor through the darkened ward in my flannelette blue pajamas towards the small table where the nurse was sitting doing her studies by the lantern light. The reflection of the flickering lantern shone upwards from the white papers, lighting her face from underneath.

She was a slight brunette, with small brown eyes and a starched, tight, white uniform which had worked up several inches above her knees revealing more closely-woven parts of brown stockings not normally spied. The uniform had two thicker bits of starched white material down both sides of the front and back, which made her look even thinner.

Her uniform seemed to glow at the edges in the flame light. And when the fire flickered, the white edges blurred. This made her white veil dance a little in the dark.

She was, I thought as I approached, like a white moth near a flame.

When I arrived at the side of the desk, she didn't look up. Her veil was held to her short hair by bobby pins and, unusually for nurses, she wore lipstick. As I stood and waited for her to look up she wrote intently, copying from a book into a pad. After a couple of seconds I carefully leaned across the lantern flame and tapped her — very lightly and nicely so as not to scare her — on the left shoulder.

She screamed.

She got a hell of a fright. She leapt into the air so suddenly

165

that she knocked the wooden chair over, breaking one of its arms. I just caught the lamp.

I thought she was going to run, so I grabbed her by the arm. It was much weaker and thinner than I expected.

She became even more terrified.

"It's only me. The writer. I've got earache," I said, squeezing the arm tightly to calm her down because she was sucking in big breaths and trembling next to me in the dead of night like a butterfly I had once captured to put in a bottle.

The terror in her face seemed exaggerated by the shadows from the lantern below us.

Suddenly, she was alright.

I was surprised how quickly she regained her nurse's efficient composure. She adjusted her uniform and gave me a tablet, but never came and talked to me again.

I didn't mind.

My spirits had been lifted beyond earache because a card had arrived at Ward Five from, of all people, Sallyanne, or "SAK" as I knew her in my mind — because of her habit of signing things just with her initials.

SAK had obviously gone to some trouble, I worked out, because it was a card with a newsboy selling papers with a front page splash reading "H-bomb Test Due" and the newsboy was yelling out "read all about it!" And, inside, the card asked: "Are you sure you want to get well?"

Then, in hand writing as bad as my own, was written: "I wondered why the *Courier-Mail* hadn't been up to standard lately — and then I heard. Best wishes, Sallyanne."

After the "then I heard" was a small cross. Was this a kiss? Or was it just the normal journalist's Pitman's shorthand version of a fullstop? I had to admit the latter was more likely. But could the kiss have been sub-conscious?

Now I realised that I simply must ask her out, no matter what the consequences.

For too long I had been hanging around on her periphery acting like I was just a nice bloke. Jim and I never ever discussed sex — like Ken and I did — but Jim had told me he

166

thought I was going to have to take some action with SAK. Typically, Jim resorted to physics or chemistry to describe what he was thinking: "Cutting a long story short, without word of a lie, you won't form a relationship with Sallyanne by just being with her. It won't happen by osmosis."

Jim was right, of course. It wasn't that I wanted to put the hard word on her. A brief touch of the lips would do me for life.

However, what if I mistook friendliness for something more? There was no doubt she always seemed to be happy to see me. But then she was a happy person. We had always talked after the weekly journalism lecture from that first fateful time I saw her across a room crowded with newspapers. Perhaps that was because I always made sure I walked past her at the end of each lecture?

Was she like the Duchess Browning wrote about? Did she "like whate'er she looked on, and her looks went everywhere"?

Still, there was no denying what had happened at the final lecture the previous November when a photographer was assigned to get a picture of the Journalism class. There was a spare seat next to Sallyanne in the front row, and she turned right around, patted the seat of the chair next to her, and asked me to come and sit there for the photo!

I lay in the stiff white hospital sheets and looked at that small black-and-white Journalism class photo, which I now carried everywhere in the blue poetry book we had studied for English I: *Seven Centuries of Poetry*. Sallyanne and I were in the centre front of the photo. We both had huge smiles and, as I studied it for hours, I was amazed by her lips, her hair, her elegant jawline, and those big eyes.

She truly was created of every creature's best.

Because of my knowledge of poetry I had passed English the second time around. Not only that, I got a credit for my first go at Journalism.

Olive was really proud of me. In her eyes I was now an unqualified success: a journalist who had passed something at Uni. "I knew you could do it," Olive had said, kissing me through her smile, as if I had done it just to please her.

What Mum didn't know was that I had passed for Sallyanne.

I didn't want Sallyanne to think I was dumb: especially since Sallyanne, like all the girl cadets, was exceptionally bright and bound to do well at Uni. Most of the girl cadets had scored straight A passes for Senior, whereas the boys generally had a mixture of As, Bs and Cs. We got jobs as journalists because all the boys who got straight As were doing Medicine or Law or Engineering.

Thus, because of SAK, I stayed up all night before each exam to catch up on what I hadn't learned during the year. I was so desperate to pass that I didn't even go into the exam room for the ten minutes they gave you to read each exam paper: I stayed outside studying, believing I could plug huge gaps in my knowledge in those ten minutes.

And I did, too.

The English exam was the worst. After staying up all night, I had to do a three-hour paper in the morning, writing about the tone and intention of certain passages, with another three-hour paper in the afternoon on poetry. Then I stayed up all night again to do another three-hour English paper the next morning on plays and novels.

My writing was slowed down by cramp in my hand because I wasn't used to doing a lot of writing with a biro. The edges cut deep furrows in my fingers and I had to continually stop writing and flick my fingers violently to get the blood to flow.

I asked the English Department if I could use a typewriter for the exam in one of the private rooms available to nervous students. But they wouldn't allow it, though they stopped the second paper to listen to the Melbourne Cup, and the supervisor wrote the first four place-getters on a blackboard. If that wasn't disturbing enough, when a thunderstorm struck half an hour later hundreds of students were allowed to clamber out to put car windows up. Anyway the whole exam system was flawed. None of the supervisors knew who any of the students in the gymnasium really were: which was why some blokes I knew paid others to do exams for them.

It wasn't that Sallyanne was the only girl on the horizon, though she was certainly the prettiest.

I had already had a couple of close calls with some other girls.

There were several pretty girl cadet reporters on the *Courier-Mail*, including one I got on really well with, though I wasn't madly in love with her.

Once I got to drive her home from a journos' party in Fred's Zephyr. I thought I knew her well enough to give her a surprise by pressing the lever that lowered the back of the front bench seat to form a bed — something built into the car years before for our camping trips.

As I expected she only laughed and gave me a quick kiss.

A few months later this girl left the paper without saying goodbye and a rumour spread that she had had a fling with an older reporter and had gone and got herself pregnant. Everyone agreed this was a crazy thing to do since it would mean total disgrace forever more. That was why people often used to say when you were going out: "Be good. And if you can't be good, be careful. If you can't be careful — then don't name it after me!"

Apparently the people who ran the paper were really nice about it. It was said that they paid for her to go out west and have the baby — though I am not sure of this because we never saw her again.

There was another rumour that the Editor asked her to name the man responsible, and I must admit I was a bit worried. The Editor had reason to think I was a bit of a Ladies' Man because, when I first arrived at the paper, this very sexy woman reporter with long, straight black hair who wore high stiletto heels and white blouses with frills, sat on my lap in the Reporters' Room for a joke with the other reporters.

Since both our ancestors were from the Gold Coast, she said we were practically cousins.

It was an ultra-thrilling experience for me. For a moment I was breathless. But my mind soon returned to reality when the Editor stuck his head into the Chief-of-Staff's office and looked straight at me through the glass wall as I sat staring back with the most beautiful woman at the paper on my knee.

I knew what the Editor must be thinking, because over the years I had developed the theory: "if they hold hands in public they must be doing it in private".

He shut the door, but he had seen it all.

Just before my ear operation, I took a blonde copy girl down to the coast to the Chevron Hotel Playroom on a Friday night to hear the Maori Hi-five. She asked me to take her after hearing me boast how Fletch and I had driven the Alpine from Queen Street to Surfers in 51 minutes 40 seconds — a journey which took Fred in his Zephyr an hour-and-a-half.

Of course, I didn't tell her I had lost the car the week before on the way back from the coast when I unexpectedly came to an S-bend just as John Weinthal was pointing out that I had reached 96 mph.

Luckily, that morning John had taken me to a Rootes Group gymkana where he demonstrated on wet grass how to steer a car that was skidding. I stopped braking as we entered the bend and accelerated through the first half, just missing a thick white guide post. I straightened up by steering into the direction of the skid, but lost it completely in the second half. It was a peculiar feeling as the car, for the first time, did whatever it wanted to do.

We ended up going backwards through a railway crossing, missing all the white posts, and stopping in thick grass. I was shaking as I undid the safety belt Jack had had installed as a Christmas present.

But John seemed undisturbed.

"Well done," he said, "but you overcompensated on that second curve."

On the way to the coast with the copy girl we pulled into a Golden Fleece service station for some petrol. Just as we

170

were leaving some man and his family pulled in and he leaned over and said, "Don't worry I'll pick up the pieces."

The Chevron was crowded out and, as the girl suggested, I bought a bottle of a dark drink called Sparkling Burgundy. It was either that or beer, or a new white drink called Barossa Pearl — and anything had to taste better than those two.

She was right. Although it was more expensive than beer, Sparkling Burgundy tasted like a rich, bubbly soft drink: like creaming soda and raspberry combined. I was finally out with a girl, so I wasn't worried about the price.

It took me a while to work out that I had been tricked. All night this girl sat right up the front staring longingly at the white trumpeter in the Maori band. She wouldn't even leave her position for a dance.

The last thing I remember that night was telling her I knew what was going on.

I woke up the next morning on someone's front lawn with a chow dog licking my face with its black tongue.

The Alpine was parked nearby and the copy girl was sitting in it waiting.

But I had lost the car keys, and had to be at work for the *Sunday Mail* at ten o'clock.

I paid a milkman to start the car without the keys and set off for Brisbane, stopping to lean out and vomit on the road several times. At Mt Gravatt the copy girl discovered the car keys in a packet of lollies as I dropped her off and headed for Jack's place. I couldn't face Olive.

Jack put me under the shower, and cleaned me up. I was still feeling a little crook, so Jack's wife, Lyn, drove us both to work over the Victoria bridge and down Queen Street in Jack's white Wolseley.

I was getting sicker and sicker and, with just fifty yards to go, we got stopped by the lights at Edward Street. It was one of those new scramble crossings where pedestrians could cross diagonally if they wished and, being Saturday morning, hundreds of women shoppers were eagerly creeping over the gutter next to my open car window ready to cross.

I had to hurl.

I looked at a frail old woman in an ironed pink dress right in front of me, and then at the tanned leather seat of Jack's beautiful Wolseley.

I chose the back seat of the Wolseley.

After washing my face down in the Comps' lavatory I sat in the General Reporters' Room hoping to be left alone until it was time to go to the races. But the Chief-of-Staff came running out and said he wanted me to go — of all places — to Coochie Mudlo Island in Moreton Bay with a photographer. There was a new type of seaplane moored there.

On the way we had to drop another photographer off at the red brick Museum. When we got there I started vomiting again, this time in the gutter. To my amazement, my photographer also started being sick. He said he had a weak stomach and always vomited if someone else did. Instead of helping us, the other photographer stood pointing at us both and laughing.

But all that was in the past now, and girls might never be a problem for me again.

A few days after Sallyanne's get-well card, another card arrived at Ward Five. This time it had a big red heart on the front and said "I'm not sending YOU a funny Valentine! .... I think the fact that I'm sending you a Valentine at all is funny enough". Naturally, it was unsigned.

Had Sallyanne sent me a Valentine?

For days I examined the only two letters I had received in hospital, searching for any similarities.

Luckily Jim dropped in with two long red saveloy sausages saying "these will fix you up, Lunn".

Sallyanne's get-well card was addressed in her scrawl, but the Valentine letter was typed. Jim said this was obviously to disguise the sender.

Journalists, Jim pointed out, used typewriters all the time.

Both cards contained a tuppeny and a threepenny stamp and both were "posted pillar box" in Brisbane late at night,

Jim noted. "Cutting a long story short Lunn," said Jim, "it's Sallyanne for sure."

However, the address on the Valentine card was much more detailed than on Sallyanne's get-well card which was merely addressed: "H. Lunn, Mater Hospital, Brisbane".

I hated to even hope. But, since there was no other girl who would send me a Valentine, the weight of evidence was there.

I couldn't wait to get out of hospital and do something about it. But, on the first day out, I developed a cold sore on the chin which formed a large scab. I was still determined to ring SAK, but just as I was reaching for a phone in the General Reporters' Room Bruce Wilson walked up and said: "What's that you've got? Syphilis of the chin?"

Three weeks after leaving hospital I still hadn't rung Sallyanne. I had sort-of been hoping to run into her, but we no longer went to the same lectures.

I wasn't sure what to do.

Fletch was on his third world tennis tour. Jim was no expert on girls. So, in desperation, I asked Bob Macklin. There was something about Macklin that made me feel I could trust him with the secret of the Valentine card: and the terror of being wrong.

Bob was great.

He told me that he too, believe it or not, got nervous asking girls out. Particularly a girl as ravishing as I obviously thought Sallyanne was. The secret to success, he confided, was to slip down to the Royal and have a couple of brandy-lime-and-sodas and then ring her up.

"It's that simple, Hugh old bean," Macklin said, laughing till he sucked in air between his big teeth, and slapped me on the back.

Three drinks later I was on the phone to a clearly surprised Sallyanne at the *Tele*.

I didn't muck around.

"What are you up to Saturday night?"

"Well I'll be down the coast staying with my parents this weekend," she said.

I knew she had been out with a handsome blond bloke called Barney who had a red sports car, I had seen them driving along Coronation Drive.

Perhaps her story was just a cover-up?

"Great. I'll be down the coast this weekend. I'll be around at about seven to see you," I said confidently, ignoring the possibility she was putting me off.

"OK," she said. "That'll be nice. I'll see you then."

It was so easy I couldn't believe it.

As I walked away from the phone, I leapt up and clicked my heels. I was feeling so good, so much on top of things, that I headed back down to the pub looking for my old mate, Bob.

However, by the time Saturday came around I was packing death. I couldn't get out of going down the coast to take Sallyanne out now. But where to take her?

What would we talk about?

The last time we had met was months before. She had told me how Women's College at Uni when she was there had banned girls from hanging their pants on the clothesline "in case it incited the boys".

I laughed at this suggestion: though I knew it was true.

Because Jim also hadn't yet got a girlfriend he realised how important this outing with SAK was. So he turned up on the Saturday morning with a car-load of equipment to get the Alpine ready for the big date. He even used a special soft rubber hammer to remove the chrome three-pronged spinners undamaged, so we could polish them better.

We spent all day cleaning the car. Then, late in the arvo, I got dressed in a pair of strides and a white shirt and threw on my loose emerald-green corduroy coat with rainbow-coloured thin-striped lining, which Rod's mother had made for me out of material I bought myself. It had three leather buttons. You just couldn't get anything like it in the shops.

I was all ready for Sallyanne, and, just before I left to see her, Jim finished things off with an all-over buff with a vibrating wool pad on the end of an electric drill.

The Alpine was absolutely gleaming. Truly in the pink.

174

But I wasn't.

I felt out of tune.

Sallyanne's house was at Southport on the highway just a couple of doors from the sand beach on the Broadwater. This was right where, when we were kids, Fred always used to organise a contest, to see who saw the sea first on the drive down from Brisbane.

I pulled up opposite in the strawberry twilight which so evenly matched the car, combed my fair hair carefully back, took some deep breaths of the cool air that smelt like the sea, and walked across the road uncomfortably: missing the brandy-lime-and-sodas now that I was here.

It was a little white two-storey house with a foreign name on the front: Rumah Putih. I noticed that they were so close to the beach that there was sand in their front yard.

At the top of the stairs I was welcomed by a child, a little blonde girl who turned out to be one of Sallyanne's sisters. She seemed excited by my arrival and rushed off screaming out for her sister to hurry up.

Then Sallyanne came to the door.

She was dressed in a shirt and white shorts! This was something I wasn't expecting. She looked great, but how did she think we were going out if she was dressed in shorts?

I didn't say anything.

She introduced her father, who had played cricket for Ceylon, and over a cup of tea we discussed Queensland's excellent chances of winning the Sheffield Shield next year. Sallyanne's mother, I could see, had once probably looked even more like Judy Garland than SAK herself.

This augurs well, I thought, remembering Brother Freddie's advice at school: "If you think you are falling for a girl have a look at her mother because that's what she will look like in 20 years."

I had another cup of tea with the whole family and, as we talked, with a couple of young sisters sitting on the floor looking up at me, I noticed the slight tremor of Sallyanne's peerless lips each time she started talking, which emphasised the perfectly-placed natural beauty spot above her lip.

175

Her mother seemed pleased to see me. And everyone seemed to enjoy talking, just like at the Lunn household, and — later on — a cup of coffee sounded a very good idea.

By now, I was feeling like a real suitor.

The way things were going, with a bit of luck, I wouldn't have to take Sallyanne out anywhere. Once Macklin's brandy-lime-and-sodas had worn off after I'd phoned her, I realised I had no idea where to take Sallyanne on a night out. The "Twist" was the in dance at the moment, so I wasn't going anywhere you had to dance. I didn't want the whole dance hall watching me trying to twist.

Soon it was getting late. First the young sisters — and then the parents — started going to bed.

"Well I suppose I had better get going," I said.

Sallyanne came down to the gate with me and didn't even comment on the Alpine gleaming — even in the dark — like a pink jewel across the road.

We waved goodbye from two feet apart at the gate.

It wasn't until I was well up the Pacific Highway that I realised that all that work Jim and I had put in on the Alpine had been for naught. She hadn't even noticed the car.

I drove back to Brisbane cursing myself all the way to the Big Gun.

But I hadn't given up.

Not yet.

Next month I would be twenty-one, old enough to vote and drink. I would ask her to my 21st party. I would pick her up and drop her home at Bardon, where she had moved in with some other girls. Maybe I would get a kiss, I thought as I sped along, and felt like the poet who wrote: "Say I'm old, say I'm weary, say that health and wealth have missed me. But, remember, always say: Sally kissed me".

Sallyanne not only accepted the invitation to my 21st, she also dropped off a special birthday card to the *Courier*.

She had made it herself out of folded-over copypaper: "These RED HOT 21st birthday greetings, on good ole copy paper, come to you Hugh from .... (turn page) three REAL COOL copy-cats!" And it was signed by Sallyanne and two of her female cadet friends from the *Tele*, Suzanne and Janelle.

My plan was to take her to the party myself.

Unfortunately, I dislocated my left shoulder the week before the party playing rugby league for the *Courier-Mail* Tigers.

The pain from the shoulder was so intense that I thought the doctors at the General Hospital casualty department were kidding when they told me to stand up for an X-ray. But one of them said: "If you can't stand up, then you're the first person with a dislocated shoulder who couldn't."

Because I wasn't yet 21 — and Fred and Olive were down the coast at Nerang visiting Duncan relatives — the hospital couldn't give me a general anaesthetic. It required parental permission.

So they had to put the shoulder joint back while I was still conscious.

The pain was only equalled by the relief that flowed through my arm after they had pulled it out, and up, and around — something called Cocker's Movement.

It turned my shoulder inside out.

Then they put my left arm in a sling, and tied a binder around to hold it tightly to my side.

It had to be kept like that for three weeks, the doctors said. Then physiotherapy could begin.

Which meant I couldn't drive the Alpine, and therefore couldn't pick up Sallyanne.

The party was at our Annerley house, with Fred and Olive going away for the night. Because it was held at home it was important to keep things fairly quiet, so I got a bit worried when Lawrie Kavanagh wrestled a huge new cadet called Tony Barker: a fierce contest in which both seemed to be exactly equal in strength — which meant they continually rolled across the lounge room floor from one side to the other.

Journalist John Atherton, who had worked in New York, sat on his heels next to the piano watching Gay's hands as she played. Suddenly and inexplicably, he fell straight over

177

backwards — sending scotch spraying across the room. Some of this scotch hit Jack's wife, Lyn, who was so annoyed she sank her chisel-toe shoe into the prostrate body of the man who was later to be Jack's Editor.

There was an unfortunate confrontation in the middle of Ekibin Road when Rod and John Atherton both claimed title to the same bottle of scotch. I had no way of controlling the party properly with my left arm tied so tightly to my side so Jim, for once in his life, spent most of the night as peacemaker — pulling journalists and others apart as they rubbed each other up the wrong way.

For some reason, Sallyanne and her girlfriends from the *Tele* didn't seem to be having a great time. The three of them just seemed to hover around the kitchen together all evening. And, because I had to look after everyone, I didn't have much time to talk to them.

So just before midnight Jim suggested I should escort SAK home.

"You bloody idiot Jim," I said, "I can't drive like this. I can hardly walk."

Jim's smile showed teeth made whiter by his brown skin. He held up some car keys.

"Cutting a long story short, what I am trying to tell you is this. Lunn, you can take the Plymouth — you dog. The gear buttons are on the right. In any case, it's automatic and you won't need your left arm. I'll take the Sunbeam."

What a great idea. Why hadn't I thought of it?

Sallyanne agreed to be driven home when I explained the car was an automatic.

We walked down the back stairs past a game of football in the backyard where journalists were having a great time using a beer bottle as a ball, and the garden hose as the tryline. Peter McFarline nearly collided with Sallyanne when he went over for a try near the tank stand and slid yards along the wet grass ending up in the monstera deliciosa.

I thought Sallyanne would be impressed by the size of Jim's green American Belvedere, but she didn't say anything about it.

As we cruised along Annerley Road towards the Grey Street Bridge, I gunned the engine a few times without even meaning to. For I had other things on my mind: I was silently making my plans against her.

In five minutes' time it would be now — or never.

This time I would have to make a move. Not a grope. That was uncalled for. More of a lunge.

It was clearly going to be difficult.

SAK was on my left-hand side across the wide chasm of the Belvedere, yet the top half of my left arm was tied to my side, with the forearm bent upwards and held securely in a sling.

Somehow I would have to manoeuvre her on to my right-hand side.

It was very important I keep her away from my left shoulder. I hadn't been able to wash under the arm for two weeks, because even to lift the arm an inch made me want to faint. Olive had used soapy cotton wool on the end of a knitting needle to try to get under the arm to clean the armpit for the night. But — because of the pain the movement caused — it hadn't worked. Even Olive said she couldn't bear to see me suffer any more, and stopped.

Sallyanne's flat was on the crest of a hill at Bardon overlooking the city and, as I pulled up outside, I made the long-thought-about move I'd been rehearsing all along.

I twisted my whole body around to try to come at her from the right side. But, as I did, I tipped sideways heavily against the back of the front bench seat. My left elbow hit first, forcing the arm forward several inches through the sling and binder.

The sheer panorama of the pain made the blood drain from my face.

I had learned from a dozen Christian Brother football coaches to "never let the opposition know you're hurt", and so managed to quell the cry that had made it as far as my front teeth. I squeezed my left wrist with my good right hand as tightly as I could, as if to re-assure the arm that it would never have to move, even a fraction of an inch, ever again.

This took a deep breath plus several seconds of intense concentration.

When the worst of the pain had flowed away, I straightened up again by throwing my torso back around to the right, in front of the steering wheel, without uttering a sound.

My sister Gay often complained about boys who belonged to the "WHS" — the Wandering Hands Society — but there was absolutely no chance of my joining that club here.

The pain had momentarily brought tears to my eyes, which now had made my nose start to run. It was imperative that I blow my nose before making any further romantic advances.

This was just what I didn't want to happen.

I was always having to blow my nose. But I had hoped it wouldn't happen just as I found myself alone in a parked car for the first time ever with SAK.

Unfortunately, Olive had put my clean white handkerchief deep in my *left* pocket, and it was very hard to reach with my right arm across the bound left arm.

I was worried now that Sallyanne might wonder what this silent lurching around was all about. I looked up to explain, but she was already out of the car saying goodnight, and before I could say anything she had disappeared across the road.

All the pent-up pain hit me at once and I collapsed head over heels back across the front seat and lay there until I was strong enough to drive back to the party.

Jim was disappointed — and a little disgusted — that even his mighty Belvedere hadn't worked, but I was relieved that at least the worst of the pain was now over.

# 13
# Trapped in the Indian Death Lock

In 1962 I found myself back in Sport, but this time not just typing up results. The new Lord Mayor of Brisbane, Clem Jones, had surprised everybody by suddenly legalising Sunday sport: which meant a lot of extra sports reporting jobs on Sundays. I was thrilled at the news because these sports journalists were all much older than me and happy to answer questions about girls.

There were several famous football writers with Catholic names: Jack Reardon, vice-captain of the 1937-38 Kangaroos; Lawrie Kavanagh, who had played rugby league for central Queensland; and the rugby union writer, Frank O'Callaghan.

Two old sub-editors sat up the far end of the lounge-room-sized office, which was isolated from prying eyes in racing by a wide cupboard, and from the long corridor outside by thick frosted glass panels.

One of these sub-editors was named Arthur. It turned out that he was the bloke who wrote under the by-line "Northerner" in the pink Sporting Globe. I had enjoyed reading his stories for years and was impressed to meet him, though I didn't let him know. He wore glasses, but was tall and with black hair combed straight back he looked more like a lawman from the American west than a sub-editor. Arthur spoke quietly and sensibly and, after a while, I started calling him "Arthur the Anchor", because he seemed to hold the Sports Department together when everyone else went to the Royal each night to drink.

The other sub was an ugly old coot with a bulbous nose, who scratched and grunted and talked to himself. He even interrupted our conversations all the time, without even looking up or bothering with our replies.

The Sports Editor, Harry Davis, claimed to be the youngest Sports Editor of a metropolitan paper in Australia, though he must have been well into his thirties I guessed.

Most of these men were surprisingly open about sex.

When a judge ruled in a Brisbane court that a rape could not have occurred in a VW "because there isn't enough room inside", they said they knew a few reporters who could prove the judge wrong.

When Frank, who was a bachelor, went down the coast to cover the life-saving carnivals, the others complained how lucky he was spending the weekend meeting beautiful girls in bikinis. After I had been there a few months I got sick of hearing this and said: "Hold on. All of you are married with wives at home. Poor Frank has to chase all over the Gold Coast in the hope of getting on to a girl — and yet all you lot have to do is go home and there is a woman waiting for you to win on."

To my amazement, this caused much mirth.

"Boy have you got a lot to learn," said one. "We all have to sleep out on the verandah."

I didn't believe it for a minute. These blokes were sharp.

When there was no time for staff to go to the Royal, Harry used to pull an old brown teapot out of his drawer, fill it with Bundaberg Rum, and start pouring "cups of tea" for the older men. Alcohol was banned from the building.

After Harry had a few of these he would advise me to be nice to all the journalists on the way up: "because, son, you will meet them all on the way down".

There was only one thing that caused ill-feeling in this happy room: the battle for space on the sports pages.

Frank would get upset if his rugby union story was cut back to allow more space for rugby league. And the league writers couldn't stand the union story to be the most prominent. This was understandable, because the best way to pick a fight at the O'Connor Boathouse or Cloudland was to start saying one rugby code was better than the other.

Lucky for me I had played and followed both.

The rugby union supporters said rugby league was "played on the dung hills of England", and that league players were tough, but unskilled. Whereas the league people said union was played by "public schoolboy sissies" who wouldn't last a minute in the professional code.

"Get a load of these names," Lawrie Kavanagh said, when the Queensland union team to play New South Wales was announced: "Ashley Girle, Trevor Wardrobe ...."

That winter of 1962 Rod Laver won Wimbledon and Lawrie, who was also the tennis writer, wrote a wonderful feature about how his mate, the boy with "one thousand and one freckles" from Rockhampton, had become world champion.

"Laver, the skinny freckle-faced kid with magic in his left arm .... Laver, of the shy grin which hid a spirit as tough as goat's knees .... Laver, who came out of Rockhampton to take on and conquer the world ..." Lawrie wrote.

"Arthur the Anchor" picked up Lawrie's thick wad of copy paper, got his big blue pencil out, and started slowly, but deliberately, crossing paragraphs out — until Lawrie could stand watching it no longer.

He protested loudly, but Arthur merely pointed to the page layout drawn up by Harry Davis.

The layout showed only 20 inches had been allowed in black lower case in the middle of the main page: "And that includes losing space for a dotted border and a head shot of your mate with all the freckles," said Arthur, as always, calmly.

Arthur was enjoying this because he disagreed with Lawrie's assessment that Laver was the best player ever: Arthur reckoned it was another Australian called Jack Crawford. But Lawrie said "Crawford played in long pants".

Lawrie then harangued Harry.

This was a Queensland son who had won Wimbledon. This was the Rockhampton Rocket; the southpaw from sunny Queensland; the unlikely lefty lad who had beaten the best in the world.

Lawrie said he had put his heart, and his soul, into the story. Now they were going to cut it in half. Into less than half.

"Never underestimate a journalist's love for his story," said Arthur, smiling benignly in his corner as he waited, pencil held gently and horizontally in both hands, to show he had stayed proceedings.

Harry, who was famous because he used to appear on television on *Meet the Press*, always seemed to have a quick answer for everything.

"You're right Lawrie," he said. "It *is* a great story and you have done it proud. But we have one main page and lots of other stories must go in. Newspaper people always have to remember, Lawrie, that three into two doesn't go."

At this, Arthur resumed the large swipes of blue .... and Lawrie left for the Royal.

I liked Lawrie because, although he was a star by-line sports writer married to a beauty queen, he didn't act big time. He was the opposite of me: olive-skinned, black-haired, confident, and handsome: yet he always described himself as "a Woolworths shopper", and reckoned the best restaurant in Brisbane was "the pie cart in Edward Street". Although he had done National Service he said it was no big deal: because he could type he had got a job as a secretary to an army General.

Lawrie told funny stories against himself. Like the time he ran into two people from his home town of Maryborough at an inter-state league match and he couldn't remember either of their names: "So I just said 'Orrerah, I'd like you to meet Orrerah', and as they shook hands I couldn't believe it when they both said 'Nice to meet you ... Orrerah'."

When he imitated people making speeches he always started: "I'd like to thank the ladies for the lamingtons, and the RSL for the use of the 'all."

Once Lawrie stopped in at Fred's new cake shop at Chermside and bought some pumpkin scones. Unfortunately, they were the first batch of pumpkin scones Fred had ever made without using a pumpkin.

A traveller had sold Fred a bottle of a brand new product called "Imitation Yellow". Fred didn't like the idea, but the traveller said all the modern pastrycooks were now using the colour because it was better, quicker, easier, and cheaper than cutting up a pumpkin and mincing it into the scone mix.

"Just two drops will do a whole batch," the traveller said.

Fred tried two drops but, being used to cooking by estimate, he didn't think such a tiny amount could possibly do a whole batch of scones.

So he tipped in "a shade" more.

Then "just a dash" to make certain.

Fred shouldn't have been doing this experimentation with colour because when we played snooker at the Irish Club I used to have to tell him which coloured ball was the green, which the blue, and, particularly, the yellow.

He was totally colour blind.

Unfortunately, just as the scones came out of the oven Lawrie turned up for a pie. He didn't want any scones, but Lawrie said he couldn't resist these. He brought them in to work — a dozen scones that looked like a western sunset mixed with tangerine and he held them up for everyone in Sport to see.

"I've got a scoop, a world first: Freddie Lunn has just made the world's first technicolour scones," Lawrie announced.

Though he was funny, Lawrie was also very, very tough. Not pretend tough. Tough tough. On holidays he went hunting wild boar on foot in the bush by himself and came back with horror stories of just escaping long tusks by inches.

The first time I was lucky enough to get to have a beer with him in the Royal I got worried when he looked malevolently up and down the bar — to see if anyone stared back. It was said God help anyone who did.

Lawrie said he didn't like the look of one of the drinkers,

and kept an eye on him along the bar. I was glad the fellow had to leave after he finished his first drink.

Lawrie was also pretty smart.

One day at Lang Park after a rugby league Test I was having a drink with Lawrie, who was surrounded by people telling him what he should write about the match. Lawrie pulled out a full packet of cigarettes, put one in his mouth, and threw the packet on the floor of the crowded club.

I tried to tell him he had just thrown away a full pack. But he motioned for me to shut up.

When we left an hour later, Lawrie bent over and picked up his packet.

"I'm sick of that mob bumming cigarettes," he said.

Once when our journos league team played a match I went down very, very badly injured after a couple of minutes. My bad ankle was once again severely twisted. I was crippled, and I could hardly keep the tears of pain from wetting my eyes or from streaking the dust on my face.

So was I glad to see my captain, Lawrie Kavanagh — who had reputedly scored a 100-yard try against the touring French — running over to help me even though the match was continuing on.

"Thanks Lawrie," I said gratefully.

"Get up," he said.

"What?"

"Get up."

"I can't, my ankle's gone," I said.

"Get up anyway," said Lawrie — who had come to Brisbane to play league professionally, only to be told that like all journalists he had to work Saturday and Sunday.

It wasn't that I didn't want to get up. Arthur the Anchor had come to see me play, and I was desperate to succeed because he always joked about when he went to see me play for the Tigers: "I drove up just as they ran on. I looked down to turn the ignition off, and when I looked up again they were carrying Lunn off," he would say.

"Get up," said Lawrie, "we're two men short as it is."

I tried to stand, but sat down again with the pain.

Just then the ball came bouncing along the broken surface of Hamilton Oval and Lawrie swooped on it as thirteen men charged through to get him. At least this would get rid of him.

To my amazement, Lawrie turned and passed the ball to me as I sat on the ground.

"Get going," he said, and — despite the pain — I started running to avoid several ugly opponents.

The next afternoon at work, Lawrie came over to my desk, lent over, and congratulated me on getting on with the game.

"We couldn't have won without you. Not three men short," he said.

It made my day despite the three-hour wait at the hospital, and the crutches they lent me for the next three weeks. Even the Chief-of-Staff's warning that I should stop playing football or I wouldn't be paid for time off didn't faze me. No one could ever take away the recognition of the toughest reporter I had met.

Jack told me that in his first match with the Tigers in the Commercial rugby league competition he was playing next to Lawrie.

"What's our match plan, Lawrie?" Jack asked.

"The match plan is if you see a head, hit it; if you see a hand, stamp on it," Lawrie answered. Not surprisingly that Tigers team — with Jack and his rabbit killers playing inside Lawrie — lost very few matches.

Lawrie also had an artistic streak.

The Royal held an art exhibition in 1962 where Lawrie met an artist from the bush called Hugh Sawrey who won the competition. Out of all the hundreds of journos who drank at the Royal, it was Lawrie the sports writer who saw the talent in the strokes. Late one night in the Blood Room Lawrie stood and recited "The Man from Snowy River" to inspire Sawrey to paint "that terrible descent", in front of cheering and jeering reporters.

As Lawrie sent the flintstones flying, Sawrey kept his

187

head and painted on a sheet of canvas a man on a horse galloping down a mountainside.

Sawrey said he had painted murals on the walls of bush hotels for bed and beer for many years. I asked him why he did his paintings on walls, and he said the first time he saw a city artist painting he asked someone: "Why's he painting on a board?"

Hugh Sawrey liked to drink with us, and occasionally came up to Sport to wait for Lawrie: or anyone else for that matter. I liked him because he was the only other person I knew whose name was Hugh. But I got a bit annoyed one night when, while he was waiting, he drew all over my brand new white desk blotter with a lead pencil. And he wrote on it: "Aboriginals around a campfire".

New white desk blotters were hard to come by at the *Courier*.

However, I knew the secretary in the Chief-of-Staff's office — Beryl — and was able to get a new one to replace the one Sawrey had ruined.

I wasn't sure what all these men in Sport thought of me. In fact, it wasn't until I tricked Arthur one night that I really felt accepted.

The first edition of the paper for the country areas of Queensland used to be printed before midnight. So most of us waited around after work to have a look at our stories while the two sub-editors went through correcting any errors for the Home Edition.

This was always a time of much discussion as everyone saw things they liked, or disliked, in the paper.

Arthur was particularly critical of a story on page one that a "speed reading" course could teach people to read a novel in just five minutes. He reckoned this was impossible.

It made the paper look ridiculous.

"You wouldn't even have time to turn all the pages," Arthur said angrily.

Knowing these older men all thought cadets going off to Uni two nights a week was a waste of time I had a bright idea. Flicking through the paper, I read a couple of stories until just over five minutes had passed. Then I stood up and slammed the paper down with a flourish.

"Finished!" I shouted.

Everyone looked up, wondering what I was talking about.

"I've done the speed reading course at Uni, and I've just read the paper," I said.

To my surprise, Arthur the Anchor took me seriously.

He said he didn't believe it. It was impossible.

"Pick a story, Arthur, any story," I challenged.

Arthur turned over a couple of pages, read for a few moments, and asked me the name and age of the man who had appeared in court charged with breaking and entering by removing glass louvres on a verandah.

Because Uncle Cyril had enclosed our verandah at home with louvres it was the only story I had read closely.

The room erupted with delight when I answered correctly.

Lawrie Kavanagh, still smarting from the Rod Laver incident, leapt up and shook hands.

Luckily, Arthur didn't ask any further questions because of the uproar, and the debate that followed. Though, after that night, Arthur always called me "The Great Lunn .... spelled G-r-a-t-e".

A few Saturday nights later Tom Linneth, the Sports Editor of the *Sunday Mail*, asked if I could sub.

Before I could stop myself — on the principle I had learned at school to lie first up to avoid trouble — I said I could.

I wasn't too worried about this lie. I thought Tom would give me a story to cut, or a headline to write: surely I could manage that after almost two years on the paper. Instead, he threw me some page layouts with only the advertisements marked on them. Plus a bundle of stories and pictures.

"Do these pages up will you," he said.

They were inside sports pages. One of the photos was of a racehorse in full gallop. I had heard just enough about subbing to order the front half of the photo deep-etched, which meant cutting around the outline of the front of the horse on the metal photgraphic plate, so that the front of the horse would be surrounded by white and appear to be leaving the page.

Then I drew a rough layout, the way I had seen Arthur do, and got a type pad and started writing headlines in the various type faces shown in the book.

Like "72 metro bold lower case".

I knew that it didn't matter if the headline didn't fit: because the compositors would send it back up to be changed marked " 1TL (one too long)" or "2TL" — meaning it missed fitting by one or two letters.

I had seen this happen to subs a lot as they strove to write headings that were catchy and intriguing but also would fit the space cxactly.

To my surprise, nothing came back up from the Composing Room on the floor below the whole evening. Not only had all my headlines fitted perfectly, but the pages came out looking just as if Tom Linneth had subbed them himself.

"Well done son," Tom said, as I handed back the glue pot and razor blade he had lent me for the job.

Just as I had always thought: subbing was easy.

The following Monday night in sport Arthur pulled me aside when the others slipped down to the Royal.

He put his hand into a bottom draw and pulled out bundles of copypaper with my hand-writing on and held them up. Some of the headings were marked in blue pencil in huge letters.

One said: "17TL! — who is this idiot?"

Arthur had been working in the Comp Room that night putting the pages away. He said my pages had made it on time because he re-wrote all my headings in his head. To do this he had to read all the stories backwards and upside down in metal.

Arthur the Anchor had done it again.

He had saved me from a whole lot of trouble, and he wasn't even angry about all the extra work: at least not until he remembered the racehorse.

"Never, never, ever, ever deep-etch a picture when the paper has to come out in a hurry. What would we have done if someone had broken a front leg off your deep-etched horse with the page due to go?"

I decided after that to stick to writing. But writing was much more difficult than I expected.

I had imagined I would be writing about Sheffield Shield cricket and inter-state rugby league but, instead, I ended up covering sports I knew nothing about. One of my first jobs was to cover, of all things, a golf tournament at Indooroopilly Golf Club. Golf was a game only people with money played but, luckily, I had played it once, and so knew that the idea of golf was to sink the ball into a hole with as few shots as possible.

But it wasn't as simple as that.

At the golf course the man in charge told me that they were playing a "four-ball-best-ball stableford" championship. I didn't even know what the words meant. So I pulled out my notebook and, for something to do, wrote down: "four-ball-best-ball stableford".

I guess I sort of hoped that writing it down would expose its meaning. But it still meant nothing.

Under a large tree there was a blackboard with names, and scores, and columns on it and I studied this for some minutes.

The only thing I could figure out was that the competition must be like some sort of raffle.

Then I got a reason to be even more worried. A golf official brought a handsome, fair-headed man in his 30s towards me.

"Hugh, you probably know Max Hawkins, your opposition from the *Telegraph*."

Max Hawkins! I had been reading and enjoying his rugby union stories for years. He was one of Brisbane's most famous sports reporters. I was bound to be scooped.

"How's it going Hugh?" Max asked, as I turned away from the blackboard to shake hands.

"Great. Just great, Mr Hawkins," I lied.

I wasn't going to admit things had gone haywire, and that his presence had practically given me brown shoes.

"Do you understand this four-ball-best-ball stableford game?" he asked, feigning innocence. But I knew he was on to me.

"Yes," I lied, as nonchalantly as I could.

Shortly afterwards I saw Max interviewing some of the golfers near the ninth hole. I hurried over to hear what was going on. I had noticed that one of the golfers had hit someone else's ball.

"Does this mean you're disqualified?" I asked the golfer.

Max swung around, took my elbow and walked me up a slope.

"In this particular version of golf *the whole idea* is to hit each other's balls!" he said. Max practically wrote my story for me after that.

Then he saved me some further embarrassment.

There were two toilets at the Indooroopilly Club. One was marked Members. The other was sign-posted Associates.

Knowing I wasn't a member, I went through the other door. Max burst in and dragged me back out to explain that Associates were women golfers. Because they were women they couldn't be members.

Impressed by my solid performance on the golf story, Harry called me aside and said he was giving me my big chance as a cadet reporter. He was going to get me to cover a World Championship!

I was thrilled by this news, until I found it was the World Championships of water-skiing. Who cared about water-skiing? As far as I was concerned it wasn't even a sport.

I was given an office Holden and drove down to the Gold Coast, returning that evening to Brisbane with a great story — even if I said so myself. I had interviewed the Japanese champion. Although he couldn't speak much English, I managed to find out why he hadn't done very well.

"The water in Australia was much harder than the water

in Japan, according to Japan's leading water-skier," I wrote. But the paper didn't run the story.

Normally, I wasn't game enough to complain, but this time I felt the paper was wrong and complained to Harry Davis.

"Hughie," Harry said, "the first thing you have to learn on a newspaper is that stories don't get into the paper for a multitude of reasons. Every newspaper needs to have too many stories so that a selection can be made. Sometimes even really good stories don't make it. And, just occasionally, the stories are just no good and the reporter can't see it. You should know by now that newspapers are cut-and-paste jobs, Hughie."

I accepted what Harry said. He was the boss, so I had to.

But why did so many stupid stories get in? Like basketball.

A few weeks later Harry sent me to Kangaroo Point to write about some American Mormons who were trying to start up a new competition in Brisbane: Men's Basketball.

What a complete waste of time. I knew no blokes in Brisbane would be caught dead playing a girl's game like basketball. But I was determined to get on well in Sport. I had a new philosophy at the paper: to be like Huttons and "don't argue".

So I went and did the basketball interview, and wrote the story, which, to my surprise, got in the paper.

Then I was sent out to Greenslopes to meet a couple of businessmen who said they were going to set up a new sport on the site of the old theatre: indoor bowling. They reckoned people would come and hire special shoes and large heavy balls with holes in them to knock down skittles.

I didn't even bother writing that one.

Soon I began to notice that some stories I wrote were guaranteed a place in the two sports pages, no matter how bad they were or how limited the interest of the public. Stories on wrestling and the Speedway.

The wrestling at Festival Hall on a Tuesday night was so obviously not ridgy didge that I found it difficult to write a serious story about the masked *Zebra Man* using his right leg to get the *Bulgarian Shepherd*, Nikolai Zigulinoff, in the Indian Death Lock. This was a slow, ever-tightening strangle-hold — unnoticed at first — but applied gradually on an unsuspecting victim.

The thing about this Indian Death Lock was that there was absolutely no escape once it had taken full hold. Except surrender to its inexorable power.

I started to jack-up about covering the wrestling, but, like the Bulgarian Shepherd, surrendered when I was told the family that owned Festival Hall also owned a lot of our paper. So I reached a compromise. I was allowed to go to my Uni lecture in Political Science from six until nine, as long as I dropped in at Festival Hall on the way back to catch the last hour of the wrestling.

Then I wrote six paragraphs which always got in the paper.

At least the Speedway attracted large crowds to the Exhibition Ground every Saturday night to watch the cars and the motorbike races on the round dirt track, although it held absolutely no interest for me.

All the riff-raff went. The place was as rough as guts. Yet I had to walk through the crowds dressed in a suit and tie, and carrying a large black telephone: to phone through results and stories because of the early Sunday paper deadlines. A phone was obviously something no one ever carried around in public, so people whistled as I passed and asked if they could make a call. Some threw pennies from up the back of the grandstand while I was on the plug-in phone.

The man who owned the Speedway came in to Sport every week and took some of the senior staff for a drink at the Royal: but I never got to go, even though I gave him some pretty good write-ups.

I even made the Speedway sound much more exciting than it really was.

Instead of writing about the deafening noise, the acrid smell of burnt fuel, the red dirt from the track that sprayed

194

over the crowd every time the pack churned past, I wrote of the roars of the crowd and the skill of the drivers.

Though once I overdid it, and Harry Davis called me over.

"Where did you get the crowd figure of 20,000 people at the Speedway on Saturday night?"

Suddenly I knew the figure must have been wrong.

I had written 20,000 — even though there was nowhere near that many there — because I thought no one would complain. It would just make the Speedway (and my story) seem more important. More people would go. The paper would write bigger stories. The nice man from the Speedway would be happy.

"I did a block count," I said, knowing that this was not a good answer. The *Courier-Mail* Style Book said to always ask a copper when estimating a crowd. But what would they know?

"What's a block count?" said Harry, bemused.

"I estimated the number of people in various parts of the ground and multiplied by the number of parts."

"Well," said Harry, "you found too many parts. There were less than 8,000. You can't go around saying there were 20,000 people if there weren't. You will get people into trouble."

People who collected the money at the gates, I guessed.

Harry was a good man. He unapologetically pronounced *w* instead of *r*, and his loyalty to Queensland was unmatched. At the start of every summer he bet Golden Casket tickets with anyone who was game that Queensland would win the Sheffield Shield that season. So he lost dozens of tickets every summer, but always paid up.

A Queensland boxer had also just let Harry down badly.

The boxer — a man called Marshall — won the national light-heavyweight title, but wasn't picked in the 1962 Commonwealth Games team. Instead, a southern fancy dan called Madigan — who had fought a split decision at the Rome Olympics with a Cassius Clay in the final — was cho-

195

sen: even though he hadn't bothered coming back from New York for the Australian championships.

Harry was incensed. We had lost the Sheffield Shield yet again and he said this was another example of a Queensland champion being overlooked by national selectors.

So he had an idea.

As *Courier-Mail* Sports Editor, Harry publicly challenged Madigan to be game enough to fight Queensland's Marshall in Brisbane at Festival Hall, saying the paper would pay all expenses for the fight. Surprisingly, the national boxing body and Madigan accepted.

This would show them, said Harry,

Unfortunately, Madigan knocked our Marshall out a few seconds into the first round. Harry lost a bundle of Casket tickets, and announced to a gathering of everyone in Sport that we were never to mention the fight to him again.

I wasn't having too much luck myself.

When I had to write an athletics story for the *Sunday Mail*, which they said was bigger than *Ben Hur*, I couldn't for the life of me think of an intro.

When the deadline got close, a sub stood next to me — as happened often on a Saturday evening — to take each sentence out of my typewriter as it was written so it could be marked and sent for setting in type.

In the end, I was so desperate that I used a Latin phrase "Oh Me Miserum" in the intro. This caused the sports sub to shout across the room: "I know you went to a GPS school son, but you may be surprised to learn that most people in Queensland don't speak Latin!"

It was even worse when I disagreed with one of the comps who was up in Sport giving his opinions on football. When he said I wouldn't know, because I was too young, I asked him how come he wasn't up on the third floor with us instead of downstairs with the comps if he knew so much.

Arthur the Anchor had to hold onto him until he calmed down.

The very next week I was sent to cover the annual general meeting of a large Queensland sporting organisation. There must have been a hundred people there in row after row of chairs.

I took a seat at the back. It was pretty boring as the old president — who was a famous man in Brisbane — read out his annual report from up the front. Then he suddenly said something about "half-asleep reporters whc get their stories all wrong". Before I realised what I was doing I was on my feet.

"I object to that statement on behalf of the Australian Journalists' Association," I said.

"You can object all you like sonny," said the president angrily.

After the meeting was over I returned to the office feeling not unlike a hero. I had publicly stuck up for all my colleagues.

A frowning Harry Davis was waiting for me in the doorway to Sport.

"What the hell did you say at that meeting?" he asked.

After I told him, he left the room saying he had to see "the boss".

Half an hour later an obviously relieved Harry returned and said: "I have just been in to bat for you Hughie. Next time someone criticises journalists don't start making speeches. Just take a full note of it and bring it back and report to me."

As his Casket tickets on Queensland in the Sheffield Shield showed, Harry would always go in to bat for an underdog.

# 14
# Night sport

Now that I had made it to Third-Year cadet, Jack popped around to Sport from the political round to say hello. He didn't want to interfere, he said, but it was time to write my first by-lined feature story.

Otherwise I would never get graded.

Every day, the *Courier-Mail* ran a feature on some important subject on the top of page two, with the name of the writer at the start. I had always wanted to write one of these, and thus get my name in the paper. But I just couldn't think of any subject to write a feature on.

Then, shortly after Jack's visit, a notice appeared in Sport. The Editor suggested someone should do a feature on the growth of night sport under lights in Brisbane. I determined to volunteer. But could I do it?

Harry Davis had taught me how to do what he called a news-feature: sort of half news, half feature. But you didn't get your name on those.

The first news-feature I did was on a champion Ipswich cyclist who trained by riding 40 miles a day to and from work in Brisbane. I interviewed this rider for hours, but couldn't think of a way to start the story. I tried beginning "Meet Bill Smith ....." but Harry handed the attempt back saying: "Never start a story with 'Meet'. It just shows you can't think of anything interesting to say about the person."

Several hours later Harry came over and sat next to my typewriter.

"Try to think of a start that will interest a lot of people," he said. "For example, most people commute to work, so you could begin: 'If you happen to be a commuter, then spare a thought for this bloke who rides to work from Ipswich'."

Once I had that intro I was right. After that I just typed out what he'd said.

My second attempt at one of these was a picture-feature on a tiny nine-year-old tennis player from Sandgate. She hadn't won a tournament or anything, and she was only playing B grade, but tennis people told me she was going to be good. So I had to think of something to write that showed she still had a lot of improving to do.

This time I was very pleased with my idea:

"Not tall enough to see over a tennis net; not much bigger than her racquet, but Wendy Turnbull, 9, has already shown she is a future champion."

But, still and all, there was a big difference between this sort of writing and producing a feature of more than one thousand words.

I rang all of the sports bodies in Brisbane to find out how many extra teams were now playing at night, but that only gave me a list. And I soon found you can't write a feature with a list. What I needed was a theme: plus some quotes from someone in authority to back it up.

Then Harry once again came to my aid: "Presumably night sport must keep young people off the streets. Why not make that the theme — and ring the Police Commissioner for some quotes to give the story substance?"

Good idea.

When I rang police headquarters and said I was from the *Courier-Mail* I was surprised that I was put straight through to the Police Commissioner himself, Mr Frank Bischof. No questions asked.

This caught me off-guard because I thought I would have some time to get my questions ready.

"Hello Mr Bischof," I said nervously. "My name is Hugh Lunn and I'm writing a feature on the growth of night sport in Brisbane. I was wondering if I could get your opinion on whether night sport is a good thing?"

"Night sport," he said. "That night sport is a great thing

199

eh. There's nothing like a bit of night sport. Yes sir, a bit of the old night sport is always a lot of fun."

"I understand," I said, "that it keeps people occupied two or three nights a week. Is that enough?"

"Yes, I'd say two or three nights a week is definitely enough night sport," the Police Commissioner said, with what sounded like a chuckle.

"But I was wondering if you thought it had beneficial side effects?" I asked.

"Does it what! There's nothing like a bit of night sport after work. Does a man the world of good that night sport."

Was I hearing correctly?

Was the Police Commissioner of Queensland cracking dirty jokes?

Maybe I was mistaken.

"I was thinking of the night sport at a lot of the new venues around Brisbane?" I said.

"Yes, all those new drive-in theatres. Great place for night sports those new drive-ins," he replied.

He was ruining my story.

There was no way I could use those comments in the paper. Ours, Kev O'Donohue always said, was a family paper.

I didn't know what to say.

After a long silence Mr Bischof said: "Seriously though, the more youngsters that take part in healthy sport and recreation the less idle time they will have on their hands, and the more that delinquency will be reduced."

That was it! That was what I had wanted. At last he had said it.

I had my story.

Now all I had to do was write it.

It took several days in my spare time, but eventually I came up with an intro I was very proud of:

"A silent revolution against juvenile delinquency is gaining ground in Brisbane — a rebellion that is keeping 20,000 youngsters healthily occupied at night".

Then, before quoting the Police Commissioner and listing the growth in various sports, I wrote: "The aim is to channel youth's excess energy and high spirits into the sporting field so these boys and girls do not have to roam the streets to find adventure and find recognition. They are kept occupied an average of two to three nights a week."

My feature appeared in the paper surrounded by a black star border a week later with "By staff reporter HUGH LUNN" in capital black letters on a grey screen background. I cut it out and glued it onto the first page of my scrap book: a page I had been saving for more than two years for just such a break-through.

As far as I was concerned I had, at last, made it. And I knew I had when Olive cut it out and showed it to customers in the cake shop, like she had done with Jack's articles.

I was feeling pretty good after that, so when Harry said he wanted me to cover the Girls GPS athletics at Lang Park all by myself I didn't worry at all.

Not now that I was a feature writer like Arthur Richards.

I got a haircut especially for my first major sports assignment alone and put on my best Anthony Squires sports jacket — a green and brown small check — and tight light-green strides, sunglasses, sand-coloured brothel-creeper desert boots and slender black tie. As I walked along in front of the main Lang Park grandstand I realised that I was probably the only male — except for a couple of elderley athletic officials — at the ground among thousands of beautiful girls.

The area was so thick with these girls that I couldn't make my way through them to the small wire gate that led out on to the track. This was not a problem, however. In fact it was an advantage.

The chainwire fence around the field was only waist high and would present no barrier to someone as young and fit as me. I sauntered over to the fence in front of the crowded grandstand without bothering to look back at the thousands of girls looking down at the track.

Would they be surprised when, with a flick of the left wrist on the top bar of the steel fence, I bounced over into the field to land nimbly on my toes. Wasn't I fit enough to swing my leg over the parking meters as I walked through town?

It had to look good, so I hit the top of the chainwire fence hard, and took off like a coiled spring.

Unbeknowns to me a sharp piece of wire was sticking out from the fence. And, as I went up, it ripped straight through my left trouser leg from top to bottom halting my leap halfway. I fell heavily on the grass on the other side with my left leg totally exposed and looking much whiter because of my dark clothes.

There was a thick, deep cut clean through the fleshy part of the leg just above the knee: and blood was starting to ooze out. Without looking up at the grandstand I quickly grabbed the trouser leg and held it together hard against my cut knee and walked, bent almost double, rapidly along the fence away from the grandstand. This took me to the most isolated corner of the ground.

When I finally stopped to inspect the damage, my hand was full of blood.

I had to get to a hospital, but all of the ground gates were padlocked. The only way out was back through the thousands of girls at the main entrance.

I wasn't going back there.

In desperation I found a slight dip in the ground below the fence around the Outer, threw my Anthony Squires jacket under first, and squeezed through on my back between steel and dirt.

I drove to the Catholic Mater Hospital, but an official in a white coat wouldn't let me drive in, though I was covered in a mixture of dirt and blood.

The nearby South Brisbane Hospital, on the other hand, let me park right out the front of casualty and within seconds I was on a bed covered in a sterile sheet with a special hole over the knee. A doctor painted the leg with red antiseptic and stitched the wound up and bandaged my leg from shin to thigh.

But I still had to cover the girls athletics. So when I got

home to Annerley I didn't just change trousers. I changed my whole outfit, putting on my grey suit. I dispensed with the sunglasses and returned to Lang Park hoping no one would recognise me. For a while I thought I had got away with it. But, as I was leaving the field with my story, a group of giggling girls in blue gym tunics ran over and held the gate open for me.

I didn't mind because I had a good story: some girls had cried when they were disqualified for breaking.

Following these successes I was elected Editor of the *Courier-Mail*'s internal monthly newspaper *House News* by the other cadets. I was a bit suspicious this was because none of the others wanted the job: since it was unpaid and you had to do it in your spare time. But Peter Thompson said it was a great opportunity to learn about bringing out a newspaper.

Each department was supposed to supply news for the comic-book-sized six-page paper, and — with some other cadets to help — I would organise pictures, write headlines, and make sure it came out.

It was good fun being the boss.

The page proofs had to be passed by the General Manager, Mr Sherman, but I managed to get in a photo of the beautiful Tina Cleary with a koala bear in her arms above the caption: "Tina (left) was overjoyed...."

This was revenge for her telling me at that party that I looked ridiculous when I lit up a Viscount.

I also started a column of snippets called "Headlines Round the House": with a specific plan in mind. Sallyanne had announced she was leaving the *Tele* to live in Sydney, which was headline news to me .... so I determined to get the story of her leaving into our paper.

MY paper.

Arthur the Anchor said I would never get this in *House News*: because Sallyanne didn't work in our "House".

Harry said I would be foolish to try.

But they didn't understand that I just had to get this in, because it would show how much I thought of her.

So under "HUGH LUNN AND ... Headlines Round the House" I wrote:

"The sun over the House dims a little next week when well known young Brisbane journalist Sallyanne Kerr leaves for Sydney. Sallyanne, formerly of the Brisbane *Telegraph*, will now work for the Sydney *Telegraph*."

With this I ran a special picture of Sallyanne I had secured, in which she was all made up for a photo to go with an article she had written for the *Tele* on fashion make-up. In this picture she looked for all the world like Cleopatra: her hair tucked up all around her face, her lips outlined starkly against her face, her eyebrows raised high above dark eye-shadow, her eyes looking demurely to the right.

I was very proud when I saw the page proofs of that September 1962 edition of *House News*. My page one picture showed police roundsman Winston Coates in a cap, smoking a cigar, and holding the trophy as Queensland's champion pistol shooter. "House roundsman top State shot" fitted the four lines of heading perfectly. And, for the front page splash, I had a story about the paper's new building at Bowen Hills reaching its highest point: "NEW HOME GOING UP" was the headline with the "UP" in type twice as high as the rest of the heading.

But then I ran into a problem. The journalists had beaten the Tigers in a Wednesday morning challenge match and the comps wanted me to play a match for them.

No way, I said. The metropolitan league was far too rough.

"No play, no page proofs," one of the Comp Room bosses told me succinctly.

So, to get my paper out, I agreed to play.

There was no way the General Manager would notice the small Sallyanne story at the bottom of page two. Not with all these big stories at the front. Weren't we told in journalism classes that page two was the least read news page in a paper?

However, when the page proofs came back, Mr Sherman had crossed Sallyanne out in words and picture.

It was the only change.

Now I had to either defy the General Manager, or quickly replace Sallyanne with something more mundane. Harry said there wasn't really any choice. So in place of her paragraph I wrote "Thought for the Month. Definition of an optimist: A young man falling from the top of a skyscraper who, on passing the seventh floor, exclaims: 'Well, at least I'm alright so far'."

Sallyanne was leaving for Sydney by train from South Brisbane station the following Saturday afternoon, and I was invited along to see her off at the platform with everyone else. But I couldn't go. I had to go to the races and phone through the gee-gees.

I trudged up the stairs to the racetrack press box at Doomben that Saturday afternoon and wearily dialled the phone and spelt out the names of horses to a copy-taker. It seemed incongruous that I was stuck in this ugly room behind a shadowy grandstand half-full of gambling no-hopers, while Sallyanne, all sweetness and light, was leaving my life.

By train. Probably forever. I might never see her face again. I stopped doing the race results: I no longer cared if the *Sunday Mail* came out before or after the *Sunday Truth*. Instead, I wrote on the coarse, yellowing, dusty copypaper a poem which ended:

I should be at the station
To see off Sallyanne.
I should be at the races —
In fact, I damn well am.

I suppose I'd better do my work
Or else I may be fired.
But bugger it: I'll shirk the work,
I'll get my car,
And drive till I'm tired.
I'll catch that train,
I'll see that girl,
And I'll know I was — *Inspired.*

But I didn't go. Instead, I folded the poem up, put it in my wallet, and phoned through the result of the Maiden Handicap.

# 15
# *Frightening Olive*

A few months after Sallyanne left town I came up with the perfect excuse to go to see her in Sydney. To sort of, you know, meet her on neutral ground. A place where we wouldn't be surrounded by families, and other cadets.

Fletch was back in town from overseas and wasn't looking forward to playing the traditional October-November state tennis championships. He was pretty unhappy, because he had blown a chance of playing Rod Laver in the 1962 Wimbledon singles final the previous July.

"Tell me Hugh," he said, and I knew by this opening that he was going to ask something important.

"Do us a favour and come down to Melbourne for the Victorian title." Ken said that if I took holidays and went to Melbourne we would be able to get on to some birds for sure and certain. When I said the problem was that any girl I liked down there would be bound to go for him instead of me he said: "Listen, you pick yours — whichever one you want — and then I will pick mine."

"We will have a few laughs," he said. "I could do with someone on my side at the moment. The Big Fella is against me."

To Ken, "The Big Fella" was God.

Ken was still religious, and believed in Jesus Christ and the Holy Catholic Church. But three trips around the world had imbued his Christianity with a touch of irreverence: though Ken would have seen it more as friendly familiarity.

God, to Fletch, seemed to be more of an unseen travelling companion than an omnipotent being. An understanding roommate, willing to overlook the occasional error, provided certain rules — like Mass on Sundays — were observed: with Ken occasionally going out of his way to prove his worth. Like a daunting trip to the Confessional, or a visit to Lourdes.

To Ken, God would understand all this because He could not be that most evil of people: what Ken called "a fair weather friend".

Perhaps this strange religious partnership had developed because, more and more, Fletch found being a travelling tennis player for ten months of every year purgatory.

He was lonely.

Being an only child with parents much older than average, Ken craved the company of his friends. But I envied him, not because he was a tennis champion, but because he didn't have an older brother to live up to: and he never had to "set an example" for younger sisters.

However, unlike Ken, I quite liked being alone, because there were always plenty of things to work out in my head. I was usually busiest when I was alone. But Ken always used to say: "When you're on your own, you're by yourself."

He was, of course, friendly with a lot of the younger Aussie tennis players. But real friendship was impossible because they were his constant opponents. Also, Ken was the only big name tennis player from Brisbane and — except for his fiercest rival, Martin Mulligan, of Sydney — he was the only Catholic in his group. Tennis, overall, was not a game of the working caste.

This made it hard for the other top players to get close to Ken who even had his own Brisbane way of talking.

If he was absolutely certain that something would not happen Ken would say that, if it did take place, he would drop his trousers "and walk down Queen Street to Bayards in my jockstrap". If he was going to see you later he would say he was going "to see Ron" — which meant "later-on". If he was angry with an umpire he would get away with shouting "two-to-the-Valley". And if Fletch didn't like someone's looks all his analogies were from his own distinct background: "a head like a half-sucked mango" or "a face like a twisted sandshoe."

Being from a largely unsewered Brisbane, he didn't mind referring to the lavatory as "the dunny".

In conversation Fletch liked to dwell on things Catholic, and I always thought he would have been a priest or a Christian Brother had it not been for his unique ability with a tennis racquet.

He talked to me for hours, night after night, about his visits to Lourdes, and the miracles that had occurred there over the decades. He favoured books by Catholic writers like Morris West. Even if we were on the beach at the Gold Coast Ken would have such a book with him. He would lie in the sun while getting me to read aloud from under a beach umbrella — to protect my pink skin — a page from *The Shoes of the Fisherman*, and he would insist on reading the next page above the sound of the crashing surf: while I had to listen.

I couldn't imagine southern tennis players putting up with that.

And when Ken said — as he often did before an important trip or a tennis match — "Say three Hail Marys for me", few realised that he really meant it.

Ken believed implicitly in the power of prayer to God and — like all Catholics — especially to the Virgin Mary.

But this did not stop him from having fun.

Ken's jokes were not usually those which would appeal to the more urbane world traveller. And many involved religion. Like:

"This girl went to see her doctor and found out she was pregnant. 'But doctor,' she said. 'I've never had sex'. The doctor rushed across the room, threw open the window, and looked up at the sky saying: 'The last time this happened, a star rose in the east, and I'm not going to miss it this time'."

Ken also could go a bit over the top with irony, and southerners would not see it.

Once, when he was accused by a Melbourne reporter of being a bad sport for throwing his racquet, Ken said: "Me?

209

No I'm not a bad sport. You could never say that well. Bad sportsmanship is something I abhor ... I just hate losing!"

He did too.

There was the unfortunate incident overseas when Ken did his block and grabbed the net and shook it in frustration after a bad call by the umpire. He got the fright of his life when the whole net collapsed in his arms. "There I was standing in the middle of the court holding the net up with thousands of people laughing," Ken said. This made headlines, so it sounded much worse than it was.

In the Italian championships, against the European champion, Ken — in the fifth set — played his personal trick shot of catching up to a ball lobbed over his head and hitting it back underarm while running away from the net. I had seen him do this dozens of times. But when this shot went for a winner the umpire said it was impossible: "You must have hit the ball into the ground first."

Naturally, Ken disagreed, but then some Italian in the crowd started yelling at him to get on with the game.

Fletch made headlines again because he walked over to the grandstand and pointed at the spectator who was calling out and said: "One more like that and I will punch you right on the nose."

Scenes like this made Ken hate some umpires. He said if this sort of thing continued then one day he would go "completely ape" and, instead of just pulling the net down, he would walk over to the umpire's stand after a bad call, look the umpire fair in the eyes ..... while slowly pushing his high chair over backwards.

Ken worried me when he talked like that. Everyone else thought it was a joke. I worried he might do it. Because, whatever else he was, Ken was game.

I loved to hear him telling stories about what it was like when he first left Brisbane for overseas. Like when he first arrived in Singapore.

"It took me a long time to sleep but," he said. "I slept on this verandah by myself, and all I could hear was the sound of the wind through the vines. It howled. I couldn't sleep without the trams going past on Ipswich Road.''

Ken had so many stories to tell on his short return trips to Brisbane that he would jump quickly from one amazing escapade to another.

One minute he would be telling me about the prostitutes in Paris: "Fair dinkum they would follow me into a shop and poke me with their umbrellas and try to get me to go out with them for a bit of nooky. And I would have to say 'No way, sport!'''

Next he would be talking about South America.

''Would you believe I was having lunch at this table, and one of the blokes was called Jesus? I was having a great time thinking of things to saying like 'break me off some bread please, Jesus,' and 'what have you been up to lately, Jesus? I haven't seen you around much'.''

I guess we got on so well because we had been through a lot together. Not only had we been as kids "bottletop Lunn and bottletop Fletcher", but we had been friends since before either of us was old enough to remember.

Thus Ken never included me in any of his criticisms of society. Years before, when he arrived back at Brisbane Airport from his first round-the-world tennis trip to be met by dozens of relatives and well-wishers, Ken pulled me aside — alone of them all — and said: "God Hughie, listen to all those terrible bloody awful 'stralian accents!''

Ken would always back you up, not that I always wanted it.

One night we were pulled up by a motorcycle cop while cruising slowly through Caloundra in the Alpine. The leather-jacketed policeman — who had cheated by following with his headlight off — stood aggressively beside my open window and asked to see my licence.

"We saw you following us with your headlight off. What's your game mate?" said Ken, as I made desperate hand signals in the car for him to shut up.

"I believe you've got a heavy foot, sonny," the policeman said to me, pretending to ignore Ken, and unable to accuse me of speeding that night.

"We throw the book at lairs like you."

I was in trouble, and Ken was going to make matters worse.

"You'd better watch out who you're dealing with here sport," said Ken from the passenger seat. "This fellow's one of the *Courier-Mail*'s top reporters. He'll write you up all over the front page of the paper."

Now Ken had really blown it with lies like that.

The policeman asked us to get out of the car and, as we did so, he walked around and stood at the front.

"I'm interested in this car. What's it like?" he said nicely, as he folded up his book and put it away. For a few minutes the three of us chatted about the Alpine and the number of horse-power it delivered. Then he waved a smiling good night and got on his motorbike, turned his headlight on, and drove off.

Ken's aggression had worked that time, but it only seemed to get him into trouble on the tennis court — and it threatened to get him into much bigger trouble in real life.

He turned up on the Tarragindi bus into town one day packing a natty little five-shot silver revolver with pearl handle. He was wearing it in a tan-coloured leather shoulder-holster beneath his sports jacket like Eliot Ness and pulled it out and showed the gun around the back of the bus.

Unbeknowns to his parents, Ken had bought the gun overseas after some jerk had pulled a knife on him over a girl at a dance in Beirut.

Ken said it gave him a good feeling to wear the gun into town, and one night he lent it to me.

He was right. I strode confidently up Queen Street and down George Street packing this silver gun beneath my coat in the shoulder-holster, looking for anyone who might want trouble, and wishing Sallyanne was still around in Brisbane so I could show it to her. As I sauntered along I whistled the theme tune from the TV show *Bat Masterson*, altering the words in my head:

Back when Bris-bane was very young,
There lived a man called Hughie Lunn;
He drove a car and wore a gat:
They called him that, that Hughie Lunn.

But the gun lost all its glamour for me when Ken and I dropped into the Milano in a basement in Queen Street for lunch. We were a long time getting served.

"You can't complain about the service in this place. There isn't any," Ken said angrily.

Bored, he pulled the gun out of its holster and placed it on the table between us. Then he put Frankie Gorman's hat over the top.

Although Ken had won the Philippines national championship, on crushed coral, plus the New Zealand National championship, he was depressed at what had happened at Wimbledon.

That year — 1962 — Ken had made the last eight at Wimbledon. There he played an unseeded player, a man Ken would normally have beaten in straight sets. In fact, Ken said, as we sat waiting in the Milano, he was all ready to serve for the match to win in straight sets.

This would mean Ken would play Martin Mulligan for the right to meet Laver in the Wimbledon final. And, as Mulligan was a claycourt specialist, Ken would have been heavily favoured to win on grass. Though he had never beaten Laver, Ken always fancied himself as a good chance. Not just because he saw Laver as a country boy from Queensland, but because Ken was a very unusual player in that he was extra good against left-handers. He and Rodney had always had close tussles.

But when the Wimbledon umpire awarded Ken the point for the final break of serve in the quarter-final, Fletch was so confident the match was won that he looked up at the chair and admitted to the umpire that he had just brushed the net with his racquet in winning the point. So that point was awarded to his opponent.

Somehow, from there, Ken lost the match.

When the Milano waiter finally arrived, Ken lifted the hat to reveal the silver gun.

"Two spaghetti bolognaise. Pronto."

"He's only joking. It's a toy," I said to the waiter, afraid that he would scream, or run and get the police. But he was too scared to tell on us and we got the meals immediately.

Ken lost the gun after that. His father found it in his room and took it to the Fairfield dump.

Even though Ken always openly discussed sex, I found that at home no one talked about it. When I asked Olive why she hadn't told us anything about sex she said: "Don't bring the bedroom into the lounge room!" Fred said he assumed the Christian Brothers would have told us.

But what would they know?

Olive knew so little about sex that one night at the dinner table she made everyone drop their spoons and practically choke on their soup when she said to Fred "you poofter". As soon as she saw our reactions Mum wanted to know what she had said and what the word meant. The whole family, especially Fred, couldn't stop laughing.

No one ever used four-letter words at out place but one night Olive stood on the cat and it screamed and rolled over. I got a hell of a fright and, before I could think, I said: "You've killed the fucking cat!"

The cat was alright, but I was distraught. What was Olive going to say about my language? To my surprise, she didn't say anything.

When I asked Ken about sex he said: "I am not a sex maniac, but I'm all for it."

He was the sort of youth girls described as having "a bit of a reputation".

His letters from overseas described the girls in each country, or told me to keep an eye out for them at home. "Next week we go to Beirut then to Athens and on to Arabia — so I might buy an oil well. I will bring back a sort from Paris for you, all the best, Ken."

Ken would say he told girls that they had bumped into his torch when he kissed them, or: "That's a Coca-Cola bottle in my pocket.'' He talked openly about wet dreams and knee tremblers, but then he would stop and announce: ''My conscience is bothering me, we have completely deteriorated.''

Still, his supply of jokes on the subject never seemed to dry up. Like the girl who said to the boy who put the hard word on her: ''Mother won't like it''. Then Ken would lower his voice an octave and say: ''Mother's not getting it!'' Then there was the bloke who asked for his girlfriend's hand in marriage, telling her parents there were four things they should know about him: ''I don't gamble; I don't swear; I don't go out with bad women ..... and I'm a hell of a bloody liar.''

At Slazengers Ken and the others would send any new boy up to the brothel at the corner of Albert and Charlotte Street to give a message to ''Miss Box''.

Once Ken almost got into big trouble when he came home from a trip. His mother was in tears lying limp and distraught in a lounge chair. She had found a condom in the pocket of his trousers while ironing.

''I had to quickly explain that these terrible blokes I was playing cards with had put it there for a joke.''

I asked him if that was what had really happened, and Ken leaned across the table and whispered that he had something to tell me, which I should not repeat to anyone. Not to anyone at all.

''My next one will be my second,'' he said, and pulled his face away from the table as far as the chair would allow and stared at me.

I could hardly believe it.

''You know what they say,'' he said. ''Never knock one back, because that's one you'll never get again.''

So Ken had finally done it.

''What's it like?'' I asked.

''I dunno,'' he said.

''But you just said that your next one would be your second?''

''Yes,'' said Fletch. ''I've given up hope for my first!''

215

So — with Sallyanne halfway between me and Melbourne — I agreed to go with Ken for the two weeks of the Victorian tennis championships that November. This would be an important time for Ken because he would have his last chance to make the four-man 1962 Australian Davis Cup team to play Mexico in front of his home crowd in Brisbane, starting on Boxing Day.

It would be tough.

Rod Laver, Roy Emerson, and Neale Fraser were all certainties: so Ken would have to get the fourth spot ahead of people like Mulligan, Hewitt, and Stolle. He even had to watch out for a new younger champion, John Newcombe, from Sydney.

But Ken wasn't worried about Newcombe.

"I won't say Newc couldn't beat time with a stick, but the one thing I can always say after playing all around the world: I've never lost to anyone younger than me," Ken said.

And he hadn't, either.

# 16
# The Oh Shit! Club

Ken was waiting at Melbourne airport with a Slazengers car when I arrived. As was his habit whenever he saw me, he shook hands.

Shaking hands was something I knew how to do really well. Olive had told Jack and me never to shake hands "like a dead fish" and so we had practised shaking hands together as teenagers using a firm grip.

Ken said that, as it was my first time so far from my family, he would drive me into town to the post office every couple of nights to phone home, and he drove me past the Catholic church in Toorak where we would go to Mass.

He advised me not to carry money in a wallet, but to fold it in half and put it in a pocket. That way I wouldn't lose it.

The house we were staying in was rented by Dunlop and Slazengers for their top tournament players. It was at 56 St Georges Road, Toorak, within walking distance of the championships at Kooyong.

I was surprised what a mansion it was. A double-storey white house with large windows, it had carpet or tiles in every room — no bare wooden floors at all, and the lavatories were inside the house. A woman came in to to cook the meals, and Ken startled me by giving orders to a grown up man who had met us at the door.

"Toby, unpack Hugh's bags and get us a pot of tea."

Toby was the butler, Ken said.

"He likes to be told what he has to do."

There were half a dozen tennis champions staying in the house, including Rod Laver — who had that year won the Grand Slam of tennis titles: the Australian, the French,

Wimbledon and the U.S. — and John Newcombe, along with Newcombe's former junior doubles partner, Geoff Knox.

Most of these players had travelled round the world together in Australia's tennis team with Ken but, although they were champions, they didn't seem to mind having me with them. Rod Laver was particularly friendly, perhaps because I had spent an hour with him alone on one of the most important nights of his life the previous month in Brisbane.

Lawrie Kavanagh was such a good mate of Rod's that he got the first word that Laver was considering turning professional for 110,000 pounds after the Davis Cup final against Mexico in Brisbane that Christmas of 1962. After a few drinks in the Royal, Rod and Lawrie came up into Sport and were having one of Harry Davis's special cups of tea. Rod seemed fifty-fifty about giving up his crown as king of amateur tennis to play Hoad and Gonzales every night of the week.

I told Rod he should go for it, thinking that with him out of the way Ken would have a much better chance of winning Wimbledon.

Then over the telex came news that President Kennedy had blockaded Russian ships to stop them taking missiles to Cuba. The Reds would have to back off, or the United States would go to war.

World War III, everyone said.

Reading the latest telex rushed around by an old copy boy, who always carried them hanging out of his trouser pocket, Lawrie said: "If I were you Rod, I'd take the money now. You never know what the future doesn't hold."

Laver nodded his head.

"It looks like the time has come to take on the pros," he said.

Harry Davis and Lawrie leapt out of their chairs so quickly at this statement that I thought the Rocket might change his mind.

Because Lawrie had to write the story, and Harry had to do the page, they shut me in a small features office alone with Rodney behind white-frosted glass with the instruction: "Keep him here. Don't let him go on any account. We don't want anyone else to speak to him until they've read the *Courier-Mail* tomorrow."

Luckily, I knew Rod — who was three years older than me — from being at the tennis with Ken, and he was easy to talk to because he was so forthcoming.

Yet he looked very sad that he was, by turning pro, giving up the chance of further Wimbledon championships — which were restricted to amateurs only.

He was the type of person who always looked into your eyes as he spoke, and, as he did, I noticed that his eyelids seemed to dip at the bottom like a cocker spaniel's: which made his blue eyes look even unhappier.

Even though Rod knew I was a close friend of Ken's he was happy to talk about Ken's game, using his tennis nickname "Norm".

I was very pleased when he said Ken definitely had more ability than himself. "I reckon Norm's so good that he could beat me tomorrow if he only thought he could," Rod said. "But you've got to question a player like Norm who has that much ability — who has been around the world several times — and still hasn't won a major singles title."

"How can you be a champion if you go around talking to everyone during a match?" he said of Ken.

"I can remember playing Norm recently in the Queensland Hardcourt at Milton. I fell over near the net and — instead of ignoring me — he came in and stood at the net and started cracking jokes about me falling over. That's not the way to concentrate."

I got him talking about Wimbledon, and the French clay title, and his tours and victories around Europe. About the adoring crowds and the excitement of touring. The trouble was, the more I talked to him the more he seemed to be inclined to remain as an amateur and revoke his previous decision.

So much so, that by the time Harry and Lawrie returned just before midnight, I was able to report that Rod and I had been discussing things and he wasn't so sure now about the decision to turn professional.

Rodney agreed that there were arguments for both sides.

Harry gave me an ugly look and spoke to Laver. "You hear that rumble Rod, that vibration from downstairs? Well that's the presses rolling. You've turned professional: it's in the paper. So congratulations." And everyone in the room — including Rod — laughed and shook hands.

The next day I raced around to see Ken and told him what Laver had said. Ken's reaction surprised me.

"What he doesn't know is that I DO believe I can beat him, and I will today well," Fletch said.

I sat in the front row of a grandstand next to Lawrie Kavanagh to watch their match in the semi-final of the Queensland state title. I told Lawrie Fletch would beat Laver, even though Laver had just become only the second person in tennis history to complete the Grand Slam.

Lawrie just laughed.

After Ken easily won the first set, Lawrie said: "Rod's a slow starter, he'll eat him now."

But Ken walked over near us and, without looking up, said confidently: "I'll fix his wagon today."

During the next set he announced that he was "doing alright".

When Ken won the second set with several booming forehands, I turned to talk to Lawrie but he had gone to sit somewhere else.

I gave Ken our special arm-up sign which we exchanged whenever victory was certain, but Ken — when he came to fox a ball — said: "Don't count your chickens just yet."

Ken broke Rod's serve early in the third set. He seemed to be too quick to the net on the dark green grass for Laver. As opponents, they always had exciting cross-court rallies — from Fletcher's famous forehand to Laver's infamous backhand. Today each player seemed to believe he could destroy the other's topspin strength by belting it off the court.

Then, Ken got a very bad baseline call from an elderly woman on the line.

Right in front of me.

He did his nana, belting balls into the net while muttering "cheats never prosper".

Then a linesman footfaulted Ken, causing him to double-fault. It was a big point, and anything could have happened as he walked deliberately across with fists on his hips and stared at the linesman.

Fletch had told me how on such occasions he usually said: "Do you realise who you've just footfaulted?" But this time he spat on the ground in the general direction of the linesman and said "Deary me, Deary me."

I knew Ken was gone when — after they had sat down next to the court on the grass while everyone listened to the Melbourne Cup — he stood with his racquet on his left hip and looked at me and pointed with his right forefinger at the sky: he was blaming the Big Fella.

Afterwards, when we got home, Ken said of the five-set loss: "The bloody Big Red Rooster. He's as cunning as a shithouse rat. He'd get out of Boggo Road."

In Melbourne, Laver seemed to like having me around the house. These tennis players were all used to sitting around waiting for matches to start, or rain to stop, and so they played cards — usually a game called Hearts. Ken never joined in, because he only played cards for money — and Rod and the others didn't. Rod, who always seemed bored by the cards, didn't seem to care if he won or lost. So he talked to me while everyone else earnestly figured out what cards they were going to use to win.

Whereas Ken talked about the girls in the crowd at Wimbledon and the dinners afterwards, Rod described what it was like to play there. He said it was the enthusiasm of the crowd which made Wimbledon the greatest championship. Thousands of people who couldn't get in to the Centre Court would stand outside and cheer and clap the outside scoreboard whenever it changed.

"It's amazing," he said with what sounded like a slightly American accent. "There I was playing the final and I would win a point and hear loud applause from the crowd inside and, just as that would stop, there would be more applause from outside. It was like an echo. Wimbledon's the only place in the world where you get clapped twice for the same shot.''

He said Lew Hoad had told him years before that tennis was all in the knee. "If you get your knee in the right position pointing at the ball you can't go far wrong," he said.

We also talked about ways to get more people to go to the tennis in Australia. He seemed quite interested in my idea that he and Ken should both arrive at courtside with a rifle or revolver each, and hang the guns over the net posts to show they meant business.

When he was preparing for a match, Rod didn't walk around and around the house like Ken did. Instead, he would sit in a lounge chair in his white shorts and tennis shirt, with a pile of his Dunlop Maxply wooden racquets at his feet, a roll of pink sticking plaster in his hands, and his white Dunlop Volley tennis shoes off. Then, for an hour or so, he would fiddle with the racquet grips.

"Hugh, come and sit here and let's talk," he would say quietly. But then he wouldn't say much. He would reply with lots of "mmmmms" and "yahs". It was a bit like talking to Fred when he was icing cakes: his eyes never looked up; his concentration never waivered from what he was doing.

I wasn't even sure what he was up to myself.

Rod would remove the leather grips from half a dozen racquets, exposing the thin, tapered wooden handle of the Maxply "bats". Then he would get the pink plaster and wrap it around and around the exposed handle of one of the racquets. After replacing the grip over the plaster, he would swing the racquet around in a slow arc right out in front of him with his muscular left arm — without leaving the lounge chair — to see how it felt.

Once the racquet was in his arm it looked much smaller, like a toy racquet, as his arm muscles stood up.

His eyes would carefully and hypnotically follow the path of the racquet back and forth, back and forth. Invariably,

Rod wouldn't like it, and would take the grip and plaster off and wrap it again: this time putting more plaster in one place than the other.

He would methodically do this three or four times to each of several racquets until they all felt just right.

The Rocket was the antithesis of Ken, whose pre-match preparation was to grab a couple of Slazenger Challenge racquets, whack the strings against his left hand, and listen to the ping to see if he liked the sound.

Rod seemed a much gentler person, so I was surprised that he hung on in tennis matches longer and harder.

Perhaps, I thought, this pre-match ceremony had something to do with it. Certainly, on the court Laver never talked or looked up: unlike Ken who would talk to the sky, the umpire, the spectators, and to me — if I was there.

Lucky for me, Ken didn't have to practise and train all the time like the others. He said he played enough tennis in the competitions because he always got close to the finals in the singles and the doubles. So we had plenty of time to go to town to the movies.

On my second day in Melbourne — after Ken had beaten another also-ran: the national junior champion — we went to see *How the West was Won* with James Stewart and Debbie Reynolds. On other days we drank lots of cups of tea in the clubhouse at the tennis courts in Glenferrie Road, Kooyong.

Ken then easily beat his doubles partner, Newcombe.

I got worried when Ken lost the first set, because the early rounds were only three-set matches and John — though he was younger — was much bigger and taller than Ken. But Ken reassured me through the fence.

"I have just formed a company called Stickdealt & Company, now watch me deal out some stick."

After that, the result was never in doubt.

Although Ken surprised me when he gave away a point. In the first set, when the umpire called a Newcombe serve out, Ken corrected him saying the serve was in. Ken had said he would never give away another point after what had happened to him at Wimbledon, but later he explained his action.

"John was up forty-love when he aced me. He is a big boy with a big serve and I had no hope of breaking him from there. So I gave away the point so the umpire would think I was a good bloke. Then he might believe me if I got a bad call on a vital point later in the match."

Glad and all as I was to see Ken win, it was a pity he had to beat poor John, because — even though John was a couple of years younger than me — we got on well.

We even managed — once he was out of the tournament — to get onto a couple of birds at the tennis.

I saw this pretty pink-cheeked blonde in the grandstand with ribbons in her hair. She stood out not only because she contrasted strongly with her dark-haired girlfriend, who was at least as tall as me, but also because she was wearing an unusual white-pink colour which Olive would have called "elephant's breath".

From a safe distance I bravely waved and, to my surprise, she waved back.

I told John about them, and later we asked them out to a dance and headed across town in John's VW sedan, as I marvelled not only at the number of beautiful trees in Melbourne, but the exquisite turf-pitched cricket ovals that were everywhere. No wonder we were having trouble winning the Sheffied Shield, with our charcoal covered grounds in Brisbane.

I tried kissing the blonde in the back seat, but the VW bounced around so much that we kept clashing teeth. But she let me hug and kiss her in the lounge room back at St Georges Road.

Now I knew why Ken lost a tennis match to the Italian champion at Wimbledon after hugging and kissing a Norwegian girl the night before. He said it sapped his energy.

At the dance we got a table and bought four Cokes.

I burst out laughing when my partner told me she was the daughter of a Protestant Minister. She didn't seem to like me after that, because I could see she kept angling to dance with John Newcombe. But Newc was no fair-weather friend, and he stuck to our agreement and danced all night with the other girl.

As he said later, he didn't want me to end up dancing with a girl who was taller than I was.

Ken was now through to the quarter-finals. His next hurdle was Bob Hewitt who was renowned for three things: his imposing appearance, big and tanned with black hair; his brilliance as a stroke-maker; and his quiet, friendly nature which changed dramatically once he walked on to a tennis court.

He and Ken were the two fieriest players on the circuit, even including all the non-Australians. So everyone wanted to see this match. Especially as Ken had to beat Hewitt here if he was to make the Davis Cup team.

Fletch had beaten Emerson in the New South Wales title — coming from two sets to one behind — but Hewitt had beaten Laver in Queensland the day after Ken let Rod off the hook.

It would be close.

To try to shake Hewitt's confidence I had a bet on Ken's behalf with a friend of his — offering four-to-one — not because I thought they were good odds, but because I hoped this would worry Hewitt.

It was not unusual for Ken to back himself in a tennis match. In the first letter he ever wrote to me from the Melbourne courts in 1959, when he was still a junior, Ken said: "At the start of the tournament a bloke gave me 10 to 1 that I would not win it and I won me a fiver."

Ken lost the first set to Hewitt, but I knew he would win because early on he gave me the signal: holding up his clenched right fist and saying aloud: "The game is up. The game is definitely up."

He easily beat Hewitt to secure yet another match with the Big Red Rooster. This was such an important match that it seemed strange to me that several of us went into town to the pictures that night together — and Rod and Ken sat next

225

to each other, as if nothing was going to happen the next day.

We saw a film called *The Dark at the top of the Stairs* about a nice boy who tried to commit suicide after being kicked out of a club dance with his girlfriend, just because he was Jewish. It brought tears to my eyes. I turned and looked along the row of tennis players and noticed tears welling in Rod's eyes as well.

I liked Laver even more after that.

That evening Fletch was performing his usual ritual of dabbing metho on his feet — which he said hardened his calluses — and cutting off the white dead skin with a razor blade. I asked him how it was that he got on well socially with Laver, even though they were such on-court rivals.

He said it was because they were both members of the same exclusive club. This made all the tennis players in the lounge room erupt with laugher.

"What club?" I asked, knowing that Ken never joined anything: not even tennis clubs.

Fletch said they were both in something called "The Oh Shit! Club".

This was a club the tennis players had formed to protect themselves from the numerous bores who cornered them at functions to tell them how they should play their matches. How to hit their backhands, and where to stand at the net.

"They are always telling me not to keep walking to the corners of the court to get the balls myself: to let the ball boys do it for me. What they don't know but is that's the only way I can get a rest," Ken said.

It was difficult to get into "The Oh Shit Club" because there was only one way you could become a member, and this was what made it so very exclusive.

"You have to look one of these squares fair in the eye while he is boring you to tears and say 'Oh Shit!'" he said.

The next day it rained, the thousands of spectators went home disappointed at not seeing the clash of Laver and Fletcher, and the two rivals played a game of squash at Kooyong for a bit of exercise. The match started slowly, but

226

soon it was turning into a Wimbledon final as both strained harder and harder. Some tennis players came over to watch and were surprised to see Ken matching it point for point. They thought Laver's strong wrist and superior fitness would tell quickly on the squash court. But Ken had been St Laurence's handball champion when he was only eleven: and handball is won or lost by effectively using the walls.

So Ken moved Laver around the court off the walls.

At two sets all, and with a crowd of international tennis players elbowing for positions above the court, Rod and Ken had to agree to stop and save some energy for the next day.

That night we all took it easy.

Rod, as he did every day, noted down in a little book all the money he had spent and other details I couldn't see because they were in such tiny handwriting.

These tennis players did not smoke or drink, so we sat around the lounge room telling stories — with Ken occasionally breaking into verses from one of his favourite Irish songs: "Galway Bay" or "Rose of Tralee".

Ken explained to the Protestant players about his trip to the Confessional. "You have to form the desire of amendment, or your sins are not forgiven." Then, realising he was being a bit serious, Ken added: "Then there is the propagation of the faith .... that's going out with a Protestant."

It was as if, as he sometimes said, he was always "wrestling with his conscience".

I was worried I wasn't contributing to these nightly conversations. I tried to get them interested in poetry, and for a moment I thought I'd succeeded when Ken said he knew a poem. But it wasn't really a poem:

She offered her honour,
He honoured her offer,
And, all night long,
He was on her and off her.

To try to show how a poet could say things in a superior way, I got each in turn to describe a girl getting undressed

227

.... and then contrasted their prosaic attempts with Coleridge's lines from *Christabel*:

> Her gentle limbs did she undress
> And lay down in her loveliness.

I also told them how our Political Science lecturer that year had spoken glowingly of Karl Marx and Communism.

Fletch reckoned he was going to go and see this lecturer when he got back to Brisbane and put him straight.

"I've been there with the Australian team and they've got nothing," he said. "The Russians are such no-hopers they bought my tennis gut and my old racquets and even the soaking wet tennis shirts off my back after I played."

He said ordinary people were so badly off that there were no free hospitals like in Queensland. Instead there were magnificent hospitals for sportsmen only: he had been treated at one when he wrenched his knee in a final.

Fletch said the Communists were so desperate to hang on to power that the Aussie team had been warned that even their hotel rooms were bugged.

"But I didn't worry about that," he said. "I was really annoyed I'd lost the Moscow final to some Russian because I'd sold all my best racquets and gut. So when I got back to my room I shut the door and let them have it with what I thought of their Commo regime and where they could put it. I hope they got it all down on tape."

The morning of his match with Laver I was surprised to find that Ken did not seem his usual confident self. He walked around and around the room in the white boxer-short underpants he preferred to Y-fronts, unable to stand still.

Had Stickdealt and Co. been wound-up?

As we sat in the dining room eating, he seemed to me to be talking about the match too much: alternating between being positive and being downright negative.

"Uneasy lies the head that wears the Crown," he whispered as we both looked out to where the Grand Slam

Champ sat relaxed — red knees splayed outwards — playing cards.

I told Ken that I liked Rod. Ken agreed he was a good bloke, but said they could never become close friends because of tennis.

"He makes me feel like I've got an eagle on my shoulder. I always know that if ever I am going to be the best in the world I've got to somehow put the block on him," Fletch said. "Look at him. He thinks he's God Almighty .... and maybe he's right."

As Ken said this, he wrapped his right hand around his left forearm: a gesture the other tennis players always made when they talked of the man known as "the Rocket". Even though Olive always said Laver looked like "a chewed up piece of string", his left forearm, unlike his right, was the size of Popeye the Sailor Man's. It was something other players looked on in awe: a thigh-thick, tight bundle of freckled steel-rope tendons and iron muscles covered with red hair. That forearm could twist a racquet to any angle at any moment — and keep doing it all day.

"Look at him, the bastard's got an arm like a mud crab, thick and red," said Fletch, whose playing arm looked just like mine

"I think when I get out on Centre Court tomorrow, I'll turn around and serve into the bloody grandstand."

"Why would you do that?" I said.

"Because they say, when trying to do the impossible, always do the unexpected."

Ken said Laver was harder to beat than anyone else because he hit the ball at an indiscernibly different speed every time.

At one set all, Ken had a chance to go two-sets-to-one up at the break. But the ball hit the tape on top of the net.

"You choker," Ken called out and and picked up a ball and belted it low and hard across the net to the other end, where I was sitting ten rows back in the grandstand.

I suddenly realised the ball was coming like a rocket. I had never seen anything come towards me that fast — not even a car — and it lifted in flight like a bottle-top thrown into the wind.

An old man hardly had time to panic as the ball cannoned into the sloping back of the seat next to him and ricocheted straight up into the air.

"Wouldn't it root you," Ken called out.

Eventually, he lost the third set after a long tussle and the players returned to the dressing rooms for the ten-minute break.

I followed and saw Ken sitting by himself looking at his feet, half-smiling, with a far-away look in his blue eyes. I thought it best to wait until Ken chose to speak. But he didn't.

He smiled up at me, but just sat there resting, recovering and thinking.

"I'll have to guts this in," he muttered after a while. "I mustn't do my lolly."

From the other side of the line of high grey steel lockers there was an earnest voice which was slowly becoming more audible.

It was talking tactics.

Tennis tactics.

Something about Ken's backhand.

Fletch leapt into the air and raced around the lockers to where we were surprised to see Australia's Davis Cup coach, Harry Hopman, standing over a seated and silent Laver and lecturing him sternly on the way to win the match.

Ken did his block and called Hopman a few names.

"That's a dingo act, Hop," he said. And Ken did value loyalty above all else.

Hopman tried to calm him, saying Australia needed Laver at the peak of his powers for the Davis Cup final next month.

The scene only lasted a minute because the players were called back onto the court. But Hopman's advice must have been good, because Fletch faded right out of the match after that.

Ken was really depressed that evening.

He said he was whistling down the ghosts if he thought he would ever win Wimbledon, even though Laver was turning pro. He had dropped his bundle against the Big Red Rooster after the break; he probably now wouldn't be picked in Hopman's Davis Cup team because of the argument; and he had received a nasty note from relatives of the man in the grandstand he narrowly missed with the ball. But within a couple of hours he was his old self again.

"It's all down to having fun," Fletch said.

We went out to a tennis function and Ken came home with an admiring girl, who couldn't believe it when he pulled his jock strap on over the top of his dark strides and stood on the lounge wielding his Challenge racquet — showing everyone the shots he *should* have played that day.

When he showed the ones he *did* play in the fourth set, he played them with a limp wrist.

The next night Newc and Ken played Hewitt and Stolle under lights at Kooyong in a doubles semi-final. Hewitt and Stolle were considered the best doubles combination in the world. But John and Ken had beaten them at their last meeting in Holland. Ken said Stolle and Hewitt had great understanding because they were the only top players who signalled behind their backs to each other.

These two doubles combinations were so equal that the match was still going at one o'clock the next morning. Every set went to advantage, and nearly every game to deuce.

Fletch was really enjoying himself hitting trick shots and, when John fell over, Ken sauntered across and said loudly so everyone could hear: "Ever see that movie Newc, *Elephant Walk*?"

Hewitt and Stolle eventually won the match, but I was proud of Ken because he won something too: the prize from the ballboys for the nicest player. Ken was particularly friendly to them because they were from an orphanage.

So that the players could pocket their tournament air fares, several of us headed for Sydney in two VWs — Newc's and Geoff Knox's.

There I would see Sallyanne.

A young English tennis player, Chris Bovett, came with us. When we got to Gundagai we stopped at the dog on the tucker box. Chris couldn't understand what the dog was there for. I carefully explained it until I could see in his face he understood.

"Aye, yap yap on yum yum," he said.

For that we stripped him in the back of one VW and passed all his clothes to the other car as we sped side-by-side heading for Sallyanne's Sydney.

When we hit Sydney, Ken continued north in one car with fellow Brisbane player Jimmy Shepherd and I stayed on at Newc's house. John's father was a dentist, so they had a nice house. But I was surprised to find a cricket bat in John's room.

John, who was just eighteen, was flying north to Brisbane the next day, and he suggested I forget the fantasy of this girl in Sydney who I hadn't even taken out.

On the road north from Melbourne, I had discussed the problem: relating what had happened at my 21st birthday party when my arm was in a sling.

Ken said my chances didn't sound very hopeful to him.

"She sounds like the sort of girl who wouldn't say shit for a shilling," he said.

I now faced a choice: fly to Brisbane with John and be there to meet Ken and Jimmy when they arrived. Or, stay in Sydney by myself and go into the *Daily Telegraph* and see Sallyanne.

I pulled out the crumpled letter I had brought down with me and read it again, for the 60th time. Sallyanne had written that my letter saying I was passing through Sydney was a "nice surprise and very upcheering".

That sounded good.

She said she had been converted to my love of cricket by meeting Australian captain Richie Benaud and "chatting to him for hours".

That was bad: what hope did I have up against Richie Benaud?

She was going to buy a pink portable typewriter "just like those goldfish we used to laugh about".

That was bad. What goldfish?

She wrote a couple of words in French, which I didn't understand.

Also bad.

She said she had only done two stories that day — about a new look for railway waitresses, and the presentation of a medal to a 71-year-old entomologist.

Bad — I was lucky to do more than two stories in a week.

Sallyanne had written the letter on the *Telegraph*'s copy paper to show me how it was joined up in threes, and signed the letter "Yours, Sallyanne".

Was this good? Was she mine? Or was it, as seemed more likely, a shortened form of Yours Faithfully or Yours Sincerely?

Then the news came through on the wireless in John's room.

Kenneth Norman Joseph Fletcher, of Annerley Junction, Brisbane, had been selected in the Australian Davis Cup team for the 1962 final in Brisbane: Rod Laver, Neale Fraser, Roy Emerson ... and Uncle Ken.

It seemed a good enough excuse to head straight home: and so I caught the plane north with John.

# 17
# *The Queensland Quartet*

After the Melbourne trip I realised that, if I was ever going to get a girl to fall in love with me, I was going to have to become a success. To make good, no matter how hard that was going to be.

By now I had been at the paper for almost two-and-a-half years. Jack had been graded within such a time. Yet here I was, still the bottom person in the lowliest department except Social: as most journalists saw Sport.

Peter Thompson was already a graded journalist, working as a sub-editor. And Bob Macklin — though he was still a Third-Year cadet like me — already possessed the confident swagger of the fully-fledged journalist, that special ability to walk into a room filled with people and say: "What's happening here?"

But there were some positive signs.

Not only had I ghost written Frank Sedgman's newspaper column on the Davis Cup in Brisbane that Christmas of 1962, but I had once again passed both University subjects.

I amazed even Olive by finishing second in the whole state in Journalism B.

Normally I would have considered such a result a mistake. But this time I knew I had done well. Jack did the subject with me, and insisted I take a week's holiday and move into the spare room at his house so we could study together. He said Journalism B was the hardest exam at Queensland University. There was one paper on the history of journalism in Australia, the U.S.A., *and* England; and another on law in journalism.

Jack's approach was exhausting. Each morning he woke

me early so we could study for an hour before breakfast. While we ate our corn flakes he insisted we discuss what we had learned. Then more study until lunch, and after lunch we would each write an answer to a question from a past paper. Over dinner we would coach each other with a question-and-answer sesssion — and then study until midnight.

Some aspects of the law, Jack insisted, could only be learned by heart until we could say them like a Catholic prayer:

*"Any imputation concerning any person by which the reputation of that person is likely to be injured, or by which others are likely to shun, avoid, injure, or despise him is said to be defamatory and the imputation of the matter is said to be defamatory matter."*

But it paid off.

What a feeling when, for the first time in my life, I walked into the examination room and picked up the paper and knew the answers.

When Jack got the results at the newspaper he rang me at home: "Guess who came second in the whole state in Journalism?"

"You," I said. "Congratulations, Jack."

"No I didn't," he said, "you did."

I couldn't believe it.

It seemed an impossibility that I could, at long last, do better than Jack.

"But how come I beat you?" I asked.

"Guess who came first?" Jack replied.

By passing Journalism B and History III, Jack, aged 24, had become one of the few journalists at the *Courier* to complete the University's Diploma in Journalism: which required three-quarters of an Arts degree, plus two Journalism subjects.

Now Jack was going to continue on to get a degree in Economics.

This made him the centre of much attention. He was written up in House News. Mr Bray congratulated him personally, plus he gave Jack an extra ten shillings a week in his

pay — saying the paper wanted University-educated journalists.

Even Fred took notice. As he made pies in the new shop
on the north side of town, Fred said that he could never have
imagined, as he rode his bike around Western Australia
after leaving the Salvation Army orphanage, that any son of
his would ever get a University qualification.

"Jack's brains are worth bottling," he said.

Olive confidently predicted to every customer that many
more University degrees lay in store: "for both of them!"

I thought she was taking things too far, and advised her
not to include me. But she came back with one of her favourite sayings:

I can't is a mean little coward,
A boy that is half a man;
Set on him a wee little doggie,
For the world knows, and honours, 'I can'.

It seemed to me now that the path to success lay through
these Uni exams: I could see that girls soon worked out who
was succeeding in life, and who wasn't. I was feeling extra
confident because I had also passed my other subject, Political Science I — despite going to see *Lawrence of Arabia* at
the Metro the night before the exam.

So I determined to study hard throughout 1963, and see if
I couldn't finally "make something of myself" — as Olive
used to say.

When the first term History assignment — 4,000 words
on "Protestantism therefore Capitalism" — was handed
out, instead of complaining about getting a three-word
question I got stuck straight in. I read about a dozen books
on the idea that there was somehow a relationship between
moral philosophy and economic behaviour.

I was aided in this effort by the Alpine. Because my car
was so narrow, it fitted between the sandstone columns of
the colonnade at Uni. Thus I saved time by being the only
driver who could park just inside the Great Court next to the
Library.

236

The subject interested me because it involved finding differences between the philosophies of Catholics and Protestants. Were poets more inclined to be Catholic, and businessmen Protestant? I had often wondered this myself. Did Protestants therefore study and work harder? This question had intrigued me when I was at school. Once I spent a whole day adding up all the A, B, and C passes in Senior gained by my Catholic school, Terrace, and its Anglican equivalent, Churchie. Then I divided each total by the number of students. I didn't tell anyone about this because I found Churchie scored a higher proportion of As, though Terrace students passed more subjects.

In my essay I concluded that — rather than Protestantism being responsible for the creation of Capitalism — Capitalism had changed Protestantism "from its original strict form, to its modern lackadaisical attitude".

To my surprise, I got a Distinction for the essay. The third-year History lecturer, who had an American accent, wrote up next to my name, as a separate comment: "It is a great comfort to find someone at this University who can write intelligible English".

Bob Macklin and Peter Thompson were unimpressed. They cautioned that success at Uni meant only that I was repeating everything the lecturers wanted to hear. Uni assignments were just a collection of quotes from various books, not original thoughts.

Macklin had deliberately failed his assignment — despite the *Courier*'s policy of paying fees, providing books, and almost demanding that cadets pass. Instead of answering the History question, Bob wrote a long dissertation on his year as a jackaroo.

Thus I swung my attention back to what Peter Thompson called "serious journalism", and decided to get out of Sport. I spent too much time, anyway, in Sport just looking up copies of Wisden to answer cricket questions from drunks in hotels all over Queensland. Harry Davis said we had to answer these as a service to the public.

237

I applied for a job with the ABC as a sports broadcaster, but missed out after I failed the voice test in a studio.

Then I got a break.

When Queensland's wicket-keeper, Wally Grout, was finally selected for Australia — many years after he should have been — he was out travelling and no one could get hold of him.

I tracked him down by phoning all five hotels in Toogoolawah and wrote the conversation verbatim beginning with what the switch girl said:

"Hello Wally Grout, connecting ...."

They ran it on page one in black and in a box.

The man who was even at least as important as the Chief Sub and who subbed page one — Fred Haselwood — came all the way around to Sport to thank me for the story. Shortly afterwards I was transferred to the subs desk.

A feather in my cap, Jack said.

After being issued with a glue-pot, paint brush, steel ruler, 42-page typeface book, and a razor blade, I could hardly hold everything in my hands as the Chief Sub, Jack O'Callaghan, pulled me aside: "Hugh, you will get a lot of reporters coming in to complain about what you do to their stories. Always remember one thing: *we* are always right."

He said to look for the key word in the story, and make sure it was in the headline.

"Try to cut out unnecessary words in every story — if every sub could save one line in each story we would have an extra column to play with."

The system was that the Chief Sub "tasted" all arriving stories to decide where they would go in the paper. After consulting his layout, he would write on the top front of the story the number of inches it was allocated; the page it was for; the space the headline would have to fit; and the typeface to be used: "P3 12 in. 4 X 48 metro bold l/c".

To find out how many letters would fit in this heading — fourteen — you looked up your typebook, which had examples in each typeface. You had to know to count an "m" as one-and-a-half, and an "i" as a half.

When you needed another story to sub, you leaned across and took one of these marked stories from the central basket.

That first night, I noticed two stories stayed in the basket. So I picked one up.

"Don't touch that, son," said the old sub on my left. "Those two can't write."

"Well, let's throw their stories back out the door," I said.

But the sub said these reporters were more powerful than the subs because one had great contacts, and the other perfect shorthand. Subs, he said, hated reporters with great contacts, or perfect shorthand: "They write absolutely every word they are told."

The subs talked a different language. They measured things in lots of different ways: ems, points, words, picas, columns, and inches. They said the *Courier-Mail*'s columns were nine-and-a-half picas wide, but 22 inches long. One of these columns would hold 1,100 words of the paper's normal seven-point type.

They knew things you would never guess at. Such as that a column-inch of eight-point Metro bold would take 37 words; but nine-point Ionic would take only 25.

They used lots of familiar family words to talk of type: widows, orphans, and bastards.

At first I only subbed fillers. But slowly I learned what was meant by dinkus, sidebar, reverse and dropped cap.

While most of the subs worked diligently all evening, with the only sound the sucking of the cannisters swishing up and down through the pipes, two of them seemed to get drunker and drunker without appearing to drink anything. Yet they left the table only to go to the water cooler where the strongest thing consumed was Bex headache powders. One sub took so many Bex that he could undo the complicated white paper wrapping one-handed, before tossing his head back and tipping the white powder onto his outstretched wet tonque.

There were lots of stories told about these subs.

One was said to have bumped into the water fountain one

night and told it: "Sorry, madam." Another, it was said, had recently come up the stairs from the Comps Room on his hands and knees. But this was told in a positive way: here was a sub so good that he could put the paper away even though he was too drunk to walk.

The Comp Room below was where all subs ended up going at some stage of the evening to check their pages. I didn't like the place. The whole floor clanged and clanked, as banks of ten-foot-high black steel linotype machines cranked out line after line of lead in all shapes and sizes.

It looked not unlike a torture chamber.

Men in shorts and grey ink-stained coats never looked up from large typewriter keyboards as they sat feeding letters to these machines of a past century. As each line of type was made, a long lead bar — a pig — hanging from a hook high above each machine melted imperceptibly into its own small steel pot of silver and black creating a hot, heavy, acrid atmosphere.

The melted lead was so hot that subs lit their cigarettes by touching the lead with the end and sucking. But these pots were not witch's cauldrons. They did not bubble or steam. Instead they resembled cool silver pools: which made them all the more dangerous.

The comps in their grey coats and bare legs called this melting of the lead "dunking the pig".

The liquid lead was syphoned off to form each new line of letters, instantly turning earth's ancient metal into man's latest ideas: as wheels, springs, levers, cogs, and pulleys operated as one.

Perversely, the wheels on these machines were not even round. It was as if they had been designed by someone from up the line. The biggest wheel looked, at best, like the letter "a" gone wrong. Yet each machine could set three lines of type per minute.

Each story was taken away from the linotype in a long metal tray called a galley. Long strips of paper — galley proofs — were printed from these metal trays so the story could be checked for mistakes made by the typesetter. Then the galley went to a high steel table on wheels: the stone. This was the flat newspaper-page-sized bed on which the inch-deep lead lines of type were set out as a page before being locked up.

At the stone, the sub read the lead type, even though from his position it was upside-down and back-the-front. He did this with a comp partner who fitted the columns of type into the page. Often the sub and the comp played golf together once a month which helped things run smoothly.

On my first night in this whirling metal underworld, I wanted my fillers on a page and so, when I saw a perfect-sized hole in the bed of type, picked up the filler story to stick it in.

"Drop it," said the sub, and he looked across to the comp. "He's just a cadet."

They both told me never, ever, touch the lead lines. That was the comp's job, and it was a strict union rule.

Normally, mistakes were picked up by people employed as readers. These worked in pairs in little alcoves where they read the galley proofs aloud to each other. But, even so, sometimes mistakes got through from galleys to the stone and were only picked up in the page proofs late in the evening. By that time the only way the mistake could be corrected was to use a special blue piece of paper with "Rush Stone Correction" printed in red across the top.

After a while I got to like working with these old subs. They cracked jokes in barely audible tones: mostly without looking up. Most of these revolved around slightly altered words.

To the subs the Australian slogan "Populate or Perish" quickly became "Copulate or Perish". Instead of "all the news that's fit to print" they said "all the news that's print to fit". One told me newspapers weren't liars: "we just print what a lot of liars say".

Writing headlines that fitted was extremely difficult. Because of the constraints of time, it was sometimes better to send the story down with "Head to Come" written on it.

241

That way the body type could be set at three lines a minute while you wrestled with the headline.

One night a mouse raced around the Subs Room creating a rare diversion. A frustrated sub lashed out with his steel ruler, as if a reporter with perfect shorthand had come scurrying through the room. He scored a direct hit: the ruler chopped the mouse's head clean off. While everyone wanted the mess cleaned up immediately, one of the subs picked up the body of the mouse, attached it to a piece of copy paper, wrote "head to come" on the top, and slipped it neatly into a cannister and sent it downstairs.

Luckily, the comps also enjoyed the joke.

I couldn't believe how many things I had to learn to be a sub-editor.

Not only did they know the little marks on the front of the paper which identified which edition was which, but somehow they knew automatically what the big stories were.

When someone overseas claimed he had transplanted a kidney from a dead man to a dying man it was big news, apparently. As was the opening of a compulsory mass X-ray campaign in Brisbane to combat TB, and Menzies being awarded "the Most Noble Order of the Thistle" by the Queen. But the story that really set the desk buzzing was when the Russians and Americans agreed to set up a "hot wire" between the two countries for instant communication.

Although "Japs" was an everyday word, the rule was it was only to be used in headlines "at a pinch". "Telephone" was not to be shortened to "phone". Names of poisons were not to be published. Racehorses were to be treated like people, by using "who" instead of "which".

We had to make sure "finance" was not used in a story where "money" was meant. Married women were not to be identified by their first names. Honours like C.B.E., degrees like M.A., and decorations like M.C., were not to be used after names at all. But the Style Book added: "The exception is V.C. It is always used."

Legal problems were numerous.

The word "adultery" was not to be used in headlines on divorce stories. "Infidelity", "desertion", "an affair", and "a romance" were all dangerous. "Misconduct" was safer, but — because this word was used as a euphemism for adultery — it was not to be used in other stories.

It was dangerous to identify someone in a photo at the races "with his wife" — in case it wasn't, and the real wife sued because all her friends were now pointing at her and saying she had never married her husband.

The manner of witnesses and counsel in court cases was not to be described.

The word "incest" was not to be used in stories.

"Rape" was "usually to be avoided" in stories, and banned from headlines.

Subs had to ensure that the plea of an accused was always in the story: guilty or not guilty.

Even words like thermos and cellophane were banned — because they were trade names of certain products. Thus subs changed thermos to vacuum flask and cellophane to transparent wrapping paper.

I was sorry I ever volunteered to leave Sport. Life was much simpler there.

Why, for example, was the word "Aussie" banned except in a direct quote?

But there were advantages.

Subs didn't start work until six at night, so I had the whole day off. It was important to have this extra time because I had become good mates with the big cadet who wrestled Lawrie Kavanagh at my 21st, Tony Barker. Unlike Fletch and Jim, Tony was as interested as I was in football, and we also shared a love of folk music which was becoming more and more popular.

We had so much in common that we started talking near the lift one night, and a few hours later we were still talking.

Then a few nights later he helped me out. At a journos party that had been going 24 hours a large reporter, who didn't like me because I was Jack's brother, came over and looked down his nose at me from so close that I couldn't focus.

He told me to stop singing.

This left me with no alternative but to keep singing.

The large reporter said that if I didn't stop, he would make me. Just then a heavy hand landed on the reporter's left shoulder and turned him around.

It was Tony's hand.

Tony might have been one of the youngest on the third floor, but he was certainly the biggest. The reporter smiled, and started singing along joyously with me.

Tony — who was the oldest of about a dozen brothers and a sister — liked to go out on Moreton Bay in motor boats and I started going with him.

Now that I was a sub there was no problem. I could spend a day driving around eating with Jim listening to his elongated stories about cars, and engines, and electric motors, and inventions, or wetting the masonite to help him do up his West End flat; have lunch talking about life overseas, tennis, and girls with Ken; then spend a couple of days exploring the Bay with Tony — and yet still get along to all the journo parties after subbing.

It was important I made these parties. I was now part of an exclusive club of male cadet mates which had evolved from singing *The Third Man* theme until dawn.

It started with Peter Thompson, Bob Macklin and myself one night, but Bill Richards and Bob Cronin were immediately admitted: so that The Third Man theme applied to any of the five of us. Sort of one more than the Three Musketeers. Any one of us would only have to arrive at a party for the others to start up a loud repetitive chant of: "Down da down da down da down, down da down da down da down, down da down da down da down ...."

When Peter married one of the girl cadets, Stephanie Bright — who he got to know after a tackle at a boys versus girls football match in Yeronga Park — all five of us stood in a circle in dinner suits at Lennons and held hands and sang for the last time: "Down da down da down da down

244

....'' Peter was off to sub on the *Sun* in Melbourne, and we were all going to miss him. We had been through a lot of nights together.

Peter, Bill, and myself were attacked at the Windmill hamburger joint on Petrie Terrace after work early one morning by the biggest man I had ever seen. As we sat at a table he came over and, for no reason, punched Peter who'd objected to his chair being pulled. Then this guy pushed Bill backwards against a wall.

I could see that Jack's rabbit killer wouldn't work here. So I looked around for something heavy.

Lawrie Kavanagh had lots of rules about fights, and all I could think of at that vital moment was Kavanagh's fourth rule. ''A smaller man fighting a much bigger man is allowed to use an object which weighs no more than the difference in weight between the two of them''.

However, all I could pick up in a hurry was a small salt and pepper set.

As the giant turned on me he scoffed at the tiny objects in my hands and lunged forward — just as an Aboriginal soldier, no bigger than any of us, came over and spun him around. The white giant shaped up to the Aborigine, but saw a calm and a confidence that should not have been there. He wrapped his arm around the soldier and walked off with him.

Olive was right to like Aborigines.

The only fighting I did was with a younger cadet, Bob Howarth. Bob was a strong, blond-haired bloke who was unusual in that he had been to a state high school — Indooroopilly — and had played Australian Rules football.

Bob and I developed a great party trick which used to get everybody going. When a party went quiet, Bob would call me a ''Catholic shit'' across the room and I would scream back ''You Protestant bastard.'' We would get into a slanging match about religion until everyone at the party was watching. Then we would agree to fight it out in the backyard.

We would lairise around and have a good old wrestle,

245

crashing through bushes and over pot plants, without doing each other much harm. After people had pulled us apart we would shake hands, and say how ridiculous it was to argue over religion.

This was great fun, until one night someone hosed us like a couple of dogs in a fight. I wouldn't have minded, except my new desert boots got soaking wet.

Just about everyone had a trick for those parties.

I thought I was on to a good one when I bought a book of great speeches and learned by heart some of Winston Churchill's. I stood up on a chair at a party: "*I say to the House, as I said to Ministers who have joined this government, I have nothing to offer but blood, toil, tears, and sweat ....*" But no one listened, except Bob Macklin, who congratulated me on learning the speech.

Jack had a couple of good tricks. He could stand up from a crouched position using just one leg, and he was the beer skolling champ.

No journalist could compete.

Jack would stand at the table with an opponent: each with one hand held behind the back, and two seven-ounce beers in front of them.

On the signal of the umpire, Jack's hand would flash out, tip the beer down his open throat, and hit the table again as if nothing had ever happened. People couldn't believe it.

I could. I had seen him practise with a glass of water at home.

Older University students — repeating second or third-year medicine for a number of years — would somehow find their way to these parties. They were not unwelcome, but there was some tension because the students had published a couple of disrespectful papers called the *Courier-Wail* and *The Yellowgraph*.

One night they brought along a bloke who they said could beat Jack. They were anxious to win back the money they'd lost at previous parties, and so substantial bets were made — before the Uni students gleefully revealed that their bloke was in the Guinness Book of Records for skolling beer.

Even that didn't shake our faith in Jack. How could any-one drink a beer faster than in one gulp?

The two champs lined up at the pink formica kitchen table next to the wooden 10-gallon keg, both bent forward towards their beer glasses, hands raised claw-like in front.

"Go!" — and they moved as one.

Both grabbed their beers ; both tipped; both banged on table.

Jack's glass made it first: but only by a whisker.

The Uni students were shocked. But then some creep pointed to a drop of beer trickling down Jack's cheek.

"Spillage!" "Spillage!" they cried — and demanded a re-match.

But the journalists wouldn't budge.

The scene was getting ugly. Jack didn't like the accusa-tion, and I sensed trouble as soon as I saw his left hand start to fiddle with his collar. As a boy Jack, a left-hander, had worked out that people don't watch left hands. He had de-veloped a very effective blow he called his "rabbit-killer" where he struck with the outside edge of a straightened left hand. He could strike like a snake, before an opponent could twitch a muscle.

If Jack was fiddling with his collar, he meant to strike at the adam's apple.

Perhaps it was the look in his eye, but Jack was thereafter unanimously declared the winner.

Then I happened to mention that, rather than skol beer, I could skol vodka.

Some of the newer cadet reporters were surprised to hear this. I was on to a new party trick.

They called others over to watch, and I did it again. Then everyone wanted to see it — especially as this time I said I would skol a whole glass.

To their amazement I did.

I was complaining that there was no more vodka left, when I saw a bookshelf coming straight for me. I couldn't understand why a bookshelf would be moving. Then some-

thing hurt my left arm terribly, and the bookcase flew past
my head.

I was on the floor.

Lawrie Kavanagh had caught me by the arm on the way
down. He volunteered to carry me out to a car to be driven
home. He grabbed me by the ankles and threw my body upside down over his back like a sack of flour with "use no
hooks" on the side.

Out the front, the lawn sloped rapidly up from the house.
My weight must have been too great for Lawrie, because we
collapsed and both rolled down the grass and hit the front of
the house.

I was sick for two days after that, and almost missed out
on a Sydney holiday with Jim.

Jim had had the brilliant idea of taking half a dozen of his
mates on a quick drive to Sydney for the Easter Show, something all of us had heard about, but none had seen.

Actually, I wasn't that keen to go. Not since Jim had lost
the Belvedere in the rain at night in Petrie. As the car spun
around and around up the middle of the road he took his
hands off the wheel and shoved me onto the floor saying:
"Get down Lunn". We hit a lamp post side-on, and ended
up on the other side of the road facing back the way we had
come. I told Jim I had been packing death, but he blamed
me for telling him to speed up.

How was I to know the tyres were bald?

Then he wanted to go back through all the details of a recent incident in which I just missed a garbage truck loaded
with bottles which turned right as I was overtaking it on the
way to Uni.

"You made a bad mistake that day. That isn't an insult
Lunn, it's a fact," he said as we sat in the battered Belvedere. Jim was more like an elephant than his favoured hippopotamus — he never forgot anything.

But still a trip to Sydney would be fun. Who knows I
might bump into SAK.

At 6 p.m. on Easter Thursday 1963 several of Jim's mates
turned up at his place, as arranged, for the trip. To our sur-

prise, there was the green Belvedere *up on blocks*. Our old classmate Barry Culhane, and Jim's mate Cliff Matfin, couldn't believe it.

"Cutting a long story short," Jim said, "all jokes aside, we are up shit creek without a paddle."

The brakes were buggered.

Everyone was in despair.

The holiday they had talked about for months was off.

Faced with so many long faces, Jim put the wheels on and drove to the Valley that Easter Thursday night looking for spare parts for an American car. Somehow he knew someone who opened up a wreckers yard and by midnight we were on our way: but only after Barry's mother had doused the car in holy water to keep us safe from Jim.

Jim piled on the pace through Aratula reading off the speedo to "see what it will do": 120, 130, 140 .... miles per hour.

Barry read off the thermometer.

The water was boiling.

"I have got to relax the pressure in the radiator," said Jim in the torchlight.

"Don't touch that radiator," said Bernie Burke.

He could see it was too hot to handle.

But Jim replied with his favourite non-swear word: "Up your arrr....mpit".

Using a piece of wood, Jim got the lid off. Suddenly we were standing next to a volcano of red hot lava as the accumulated gunk of years gushed out the top of the Plymouth in a cloud of boiling, evaporating water.

Everyone took off.

Back in Aratula, Jim knocked up a garage at 5 a.m., bent the pressure cap to decrease the pressure: and we were off again.

Over Cunningham's Gap we landed in Warwick, touched down in Tenterfield, but at Glen Innis the exhaust system fell off when the Belvedere bottomed out. Jim found a garage and, because the mechanic didn't have an exhaust system for such a car, he had to make one out of old tractor pipes.

It took hours.

When he finished we couldn't find Jim anywhere. We looked in the toilets, out the back, up the road, in the shop — but he had miraculously disappeared, and we couldn't go without him.

It was only when the hoist came down that we found Jim — who claimed to only need three hours sleep a night — having a snooze in the car.

We were so happy to be on the way again that everyone — except Jim — started singing. Barry had a deep, trained voice and had sung opera, so he led the rest of us in his favourite *Danny Boy* as we sped through Armidale.

Barry was also the navigator and, as we finally put down in Sydney, he announced that we had been on the road just ten hours — "and in the air for four".

The next day, on the way to the Easter Show from our motel, Jim took a wrong turn into a one-way street and reversed at 35 miles per hour in the centre of Sydney, to show how American speedos registered in reverse.

The Sydney Easter Show was a disappointment because it wasn't as big as the Ekka. But they did have something we didn't: the 2GB Talent Show. Hundreds were queued up outside a broadcast van listening to the amateurs perform on a program that was being broadcast clear across Sydney.

Jim slipped around the back, and a few minutes later reappeared with some startling news: "I've been talking to the DJ. In any case you're in the show. They're really excited because, cutting a long story short, I told them you were The Queensland Quartet from the Wentworth Hotel and, Lord and behold, without word of a lie they believed me."

"There's no way, Jim, that I'm singing on Sydney radio with this lot," Barry said, pointing at us.

"Bugger-me-dead you'd be a perverted little agent Culhane. Do you want to go down in a screaming heap? It's all arranged," said Jim. "I told them you were staying at the

Wentworth to improve your image. I even told them you had made a record."

Barry was a big bloke, a rugby league footballer who had put the shot at Terrace. He wasn't the type to take any nonsense, even from Jim.

"Jim, you didn't perhaps tell them that this imaginary record was in the Top 40?" said Barry suspiciously.

"Er er not the first Top 40," said Jim, who never had time to do such a mundane thing as listen to the radio. "But, er, I said it made .... the third or fourth Top 40."

"You're being ridiculous. We can't go on," said Barry. "What would we sing?"

"I told them you will sing *The Danny Boy*," said Jim. "They said they liked *The Danny Boy* very much."

Before we knew it The Queensland Quartet of five was singing *The Danny Boy* in a sound-proof studio at the Sydney Show in front of hundreds while all of Sydney listened.

The DJ cut us a bit short, taking the mike from Bernie and saying: "Let's thank The Queensland Quartet, the boys from the Wentworth. Those guys will probably make a record one day — if they ever relax."

As we flew back into the Gold Coast on Easter Monday night the Belvedere's radio announced: "Queensland roads have been fatality free over Easter".

All of us — except Jim — burst into laughter.

251

# 18
# Fishing for girls

The glamour of the subs desk soon wore off, because there was no way you would ever meet a girl while working there. So was I glad to once again end up back in the General Reporters' Room.

At least as a reporter I went out to cover things and meet people. I even got invited to the occasional cocktail party at Brisbane's main hotel, Lennons.

Sometimes, the invitation said "and partner". But I didn't have one.

Before he went overseas in the Australian team for the fourth time, Ken had introduced me to a pretty, black-haired Italian girl, Maria Ventura, who worked for the Catholic Church in the Cathedral grounds on the other side of the GPO. So, one day — now that I had turned 22 and was on the shelf — I rang to ask her to a cocktail party at Lennons.

We arranged to meet under the GPO clock after she finished work, and I went out and bought some Old Spice aftershave to make sure I smelt OK.

Everyone stood around at the cocktail party not knowing what to say to each other. So the best part of the evening was when I finally got Maria home and met her family. They were a happy lot who laughed out loud at every story. For the first time I understood what Jim meant when he told me of his success at a recent dinner party: "I told a few jokes Lunn, and without word of a lie they were rolling themselves."

One of Maria's sisters, I was shocked to learn, was a nun: so I was glad I hadn't tried anything on.

Maria's mother was a big woman who reminded me of Olive: the way she ran the family and the finances. She held court from a crumpled lounge chair in the vast old wooden New Farm mansion which she had turned into a boarding house for men.

I asked the mother — who complained she always had spare rooms — why she didn't take women in as well, to fill up the boarding house.

"Where there woman, there trouble," she said.

"Oh, I can agree with you on that one," I said, and to my surprise the mother and her daughters split their sides laughing.

After that I dropped in occasionally for a cup of tea, and Maria and I sometimes went out when I got free tickets that nobody else at the paper wanted, like to Shirley Bassey at Festival Hall.

I guess I wasn't meeting many girls because Ken was away most of the time, and Jim didn't seem to know any. He had only ever lined me up with one date, and even that was to help him out.

Jim had met a "pretty little girl" at Uni who wouldn't go out with him, unless she could take her sister along. So Jim got me to go too.

They were, as Jim said, little. I was surprised, because Jim described all girls as little.

After the pictures at the Boomerang we ended up going back to the nearby Lunn residence at Annerley for a cup of tea. We were all getting on very well: Jim with one sister, and me with the other.

Jim and I could have a lot of fun in this sort of situation. We could communicate with each other without the girls knowing what was going on. This had evolved over the nine years we sat next to one another at school. Thus, if we had no chance, Jim would say "Comes the Butt." If one of us got in the other's road with a girl, the other would say "hinder" or "hinder on the court".

One of the things Jim often did was to quote our Junior

teacher "Basher" when he wanted me to know that he knew I was up to something.

So, while the younger sister and I were out in the kitchen making the tea, Jim thought I was taking so long that we just might be playing up. To signal he thought this, Jim — imitating Basher — called out in a threatening voice from the lounge room where he was sitting with the other sister:

"I'm coming Lunn, I'm coming!"

Olive thundered out of her bedroom in her nightdress, dropping on the wooden floor the thick murder mystery she had been reading, and shaking the boards of the house as she swept down the hall. She looked bemused as she saw the four of us, with tea cups and tea towels in hand. We asked what was wrong? In a low voice Olive did something she had never done before, she kicked us out.

"Come on, it's late. I think you had better take these girls home to their parents," she said. And that was the end of our evening.

Some of the mini-skirted copy girls at work were very attractive: though I had never managed to flash on to any. There was one in particular I had played against in our boys-versus-girls football matches. Few girl cadets played in these matches, since they were a bit too uppity. But lots of copy girls and switch girls used to join in.

I had marked this copy girl in a game, and we had been involved in a number of off-the-ball incidents. Jim, who watched that game, said she was keen on me. But he didn't think I should go out with a girl who played football: "So young, and so untender," he said, quoting King Lear. It was something Jim often said about girls.

Once, just mucking around, I asked her to meet me in the photographic dark room, and was surprised when she accepted. But I was suddenly sent out on a job, and so asked another cadet to go to the dark room and tell this girl the problem.

He said he would fix things up.

A few months later they were married. Olive was right

once again. She had often warned me: "Never introduce your donah to your pal."

I got on very well with a copy girl called Gwen, but fate intervened to end our most promising chat. While we were talking, Gwen sat up on the desk, which I took as a good sign. We were laughing about all sorts of things when our conversation was interrupted by a lot of activity.

The Sports Editor raced past.

The Chief-of-Staff, and his deputy, both vacated their office on the other side of the glass.

The Finance Editor and Social Editor headed quickly for the Editor's office.

"Must be something big going on," I said to Gwen. "You watch, whatever this is about will be tomorrow's splash. This story I tell you is headline news, 84-point caps at least."

Gwen, I could tell, was impressed by my knowledge of news.

Seconds later the Editor's red-haired secretary, Sheila Carver, appeared from nowhere next to us.

She asked Gwen to stand up.

On the desk was a machine called a Dictograph — a heavy black phone handle on top of a varnished box with five-inch-long black toggle switches sticking out from one side, and a red toggle. Each of these switches could be used to call various department heads by flicking them up or down.

Gwen had sat on all six switches while we were mucking around — summoning half the department heads non-stop to the Editor's office, while at the same time completely blocking the entire newspaper's intercom system.

Sheila said she would explain the electrical fault to the Editor, but suggested we leave the Dictograph — and each other — alone.

Girls were becoming a more and more distant possibility. Rather than chasing them, I was spending more and more time in boats out on Moreton Bay exploring the uninhabited islands with Tony Barker. And at night Tony introduced me to other folk singers besides Joan Baez — like Pete Seeger, Odetta, Josh White, and songs of the American Civil War.

After work we would sit and listen to these records until near dawn, and my favourite song became Josh White singing "Nobody Knows You when You're Down and Out".

*As soon as you get back up on your feet again,*
*Everybody wants to be your long lost friend; mmmmmm,*
*Mighty strange, without a doubt: mmmmmm,*
*No girl can use you when you're down and out.*

We could hardly wait for Joan's third and fourth LPs to come out on Vanguard records, to hear her sing in her whistle-pure Irish-Spanish voice "The Battle Hymn of the Republic", "Kumbaya"; "Danger Waters"; "Don't think twice, it's alright"; and, of course, my all-time favourite: "*Plasir D'Amour*".

*Joys of love, are but a moment long;*
*The pain of love endures the whole life long.*

But Pete Seeger — who was little known in Brisbane — was our hero. Like Joan Baez he sang the battle hymn of the integration movement in the southern states of America: "We Shall Overcome". He even wrote some of the verses.

All of Pete Seeger's songs contained messages about things I had never thought about before and that you just didn't hear anywhere else.

*What did you learn in school today?:*
*I learned that Washington never told a lie;*
*I learned that soldiers seldom die;*
*I learned that everybody's free ...*

Like Bob Macklin, Pete Seeger was not too impressed with Universities: even though he had been in President Kennedy's class at Harvard. In "Little Boxes" he sang how everyone lived in little boxes "made of ticky tacky, and they all went to University where they all were put in boxes, little boxes just the same".

These folk singers were really catching on. They were different from Buddy Holly and Elvis and other rock-and-rollers. They didn't dress up, they just let their hair hang down, and they were for true love and against things all the older people were for: like study and uniforms and war — and even atomic bombs.

One folk song writer who seemed to capture in a particularly poetic way the dangers that faced the world, even though he was a year younger than me, was a singer-writer called Bob Dylan. He saw a devastating future for us all now that both sides had the H bomb: particularly in "Hard Rain's A-gonna Fall" which overflowed with frightening images from a young "blue-eyed son," like me, who had seen into the future:

*Saw 10,000 talkers whose tongues were all broken ...*
*Heard the roar of a wave that could drown the whole world ...*

Although he saw bodies burning, the line I found the most frightening of all, but couldn't understand said: "Where black is the colour, where none is the number". Nor could I understand what Dylan meant by: "Where the pellets of poison are flooding the water..."

Tony and I were living right on the edge of Moreton Bay and swam in it every morning. The only danger in that water was the sharks. It was also shallow and difficult to negotiate so that occasionally when boating we got stuck on uncharted mudbanks, or beached in fierce storms. But we found our own lagoon with a waterfall and swam at isolated sand beaches or explored deserted islands.

We loved the bay so much that we set up a pad in the boatshed about five yards from the water's edge next door to Tony's family home. And we began to live the idyllic existence of reporter-beachcombers: running along the sand, eating his mum's cooked breakfasts, playing cricket with his many younger brothers, and then dashing to work — after a swim and lunch — as fast as the Alpine would go.

It was great fun. But I couldn't help feeling this life made meeting the girl of my dreams more and more unlikely.

When we finished work too late to head down the Bay, Tony and I would stay at Annerley and — no matter what time we got home — Olive would get up and cook a hot meal. Her speciality was a delicious serving of heated-up leftovers.

Olive knew what it was like to be hungry, "so hungry you could eat a horse, and chase the rider". She agreed with Jim that food kept you healthy.

Or we would eat with Dracula, if Fred hadn't yet gone to bed. Whenever I asked Fred how the shop was going, he would say "fair to middling" and, if Tony or I complained we had to write a 3,000-word Uni assignment, he would say without sympathy: "That'll hurt ya."

Fred would insist on letting our brindle boxer dog — "Arolia Todman" who we called Droopy — sit up on a chair at the table with us "for company". Fred loved Droopy so much he wanted to start a "boxer dog farm" on our ten acres at Southport when he retired. Fred said he liked the way Droopy tried to talk to him.

Afterwards, Tony and I would play folk songs in the lounge on Gay's radiogram, or five sets of table tennis under the house. When the bats broke, we played with bread-and-butter plates — using the top for the forehand.

It was an advantage starting and finishing work late because there was no traffic at midnight. One night we stopped a milkman in the middle of the Story Bridge and bought a bottle of milk. Sometimes I would sit the Alpine's tyres in the tram lines, after the trams had stopped for the night, and drive a few miles along Ipswich Road without having to touch the steering wheel.

Fred said I was living the life of Reilly, but he had his own business and didn't know how hard it was being a reporter working for a newspaper. While I could write a news story, I often didn't know what to say or do when meeting different important people on my nightly assignments. I went to lots of Rotary dinners, for example, and while one hundred men sang their song "Firm as a wheel fitting cog to cog"

258

what was I — the only non-member — supposed to do? Stand up and sing? Or sit down all alone and watch?

Sometimes a reporter from the *Tele* would beg me not to do a story, so that he didn't have to bother. But I always wrote one even if they didn't say anything worthwhile.

Just in case.

The task of introducing myself each night on arrival at these functions was made much more difficult by my unusual name. No one seemed to be able to get "Hugh Lunn" right first up. When I said "Hugh" they would think I was saying "you". One elderly athletic official said after I introduced myself: "No, I no longer run. Gave it up years ago, in fact. Though I was pretty quick over the 220 I can tell you."

I even had a few people say, after I introduced myself as "Hugh Lunn": "No, I'm not Lunn ... that could be him in the leather jacket over there."

Organisations were always pleased to find the Press covering their function, and so I was often introduced publicly by the chairman: wrongly. At a function at Victoria Park Golf Club the chairman announced that they were very proud to have "Mr Hulun" covering the dinner for the *Courier-Mail*.

This "Mr Hulun" mistake had happened a couple of times, so I decided I would have to leave a bigger gap between the "Hugh" and the "Lunn" when introducing myself. I practised it in front of a mirror at home.

The very next night I was sent to cover a meeting of the Asian Society. When I arrived the meeting had already started. The woman in charge stopped talking and rushed over to me. I took a deep breath and, remembering Mrs Leggatt's elocution lessons from school, said:

"My name is Hugh ..." (long pause) ...

She interrupted.

"Where are you from?" she said quickly.

"*The Courier*," I said.

She seemed delighted. A broad smile cracked her face. She turned to the 80 seated delegates and announced with obvious delight:

"Ladies and gentlemen, attention please. Quiet everyone. We have, as a very special guest tonight, for the very first time ever" …. and she pointed both open-palmed hands at me … "Mr Hu, from Korea."

Everyone stood and applauded loudly.

However, there were compensating factors being a general reporter. Sometimes I got to drive the Police Rounds car — a green Holden Special with an aerial on the roof and a large black radio-phone on top of the dash-board so everyone could see it. It was the sort of car that looked both mean and important at the same time. I was first given this car to drive after someone rang the Chief-of-Staff to say they had seen a Chinese Junk, of all things, sailing up the Brisbane river. I herbed along Hamilton Road next to the river not really expecting to see anything. But there it was coming up the river: a dead-set Chinese Junk. Excited by the find, I lifted the black phone, pressed the button on the mouthpiece, and said: "VHK 47 calling *Courier-Mail*; VHK 47 calling *Courier-Mail*, Over."

When the Chief-of-Staff answered I shouted so he could hear me: "Have sighted Chinese Junk. Repeat. Have just sighted Chinese Junk."

I was disappointed when the voice at the other end said: "OK. OK. Keep your shirt on."

That was the one day I really missed having a girlfriend. Not only could I have driven round to see her in the Police Rounds car, but the next day there was a page-lead story in black type with a black square-dotted border "By a Staff Reporter" with my great intro:

*Up the Brisbane River yesterday sailed a real-life, genuine Chinese Junk.*

Anyway, at least Tony Barker liked it. And, on top of that, I had just come up with a plan to combine our life on Moreton Bay with a couple of good looking sorts.

Ken on his trip home had got Gay to introduce him to a girl he liked the look of on the Tarragindi bus, a Margaret McKeirnan. It turned out that she was one of no less than six sisters, and their father was an old sub on the *Tele*. He had made newspapers his life, so I got on well with him when Ken took me around there.

I introduced Tony to the family and he fell for one of the McKeirnan daughters, while I liked two others. This was the advantage of families with lots of daughters. Both of the ones I went for were very pretty, small brunettes with brown eyes. But one had just been named Dux of her school and was going to study medicine. And the other was too young: she would be 14 that year.

I asked one of the older women reporters for some advice: "What happens if you get on to a 13-year-old girl?"

"You fall off," she said, and walked away.

Ken didn't see it as a problem. "Thirteen shouldn't worry you, Hughie, as long as you're not superstitious!"

We all went to the pictures, but only as a group, and after a while I began to realise the disadvantage of a large number of sisters: you could never get one of them alone.

So I worked out a plan. I got Tony to hire a motorboat, and to leave the rest to me.

The day before a public holiday I worked out that four of the sisters all had things to do: except for the Dux and the one Tony liked. They were a good Catholic family — with an older brother a priest — so it was going to be extremely difficult to get permission for two sophisticated adult cadets like us to take two Catholic teenage daughters out on a boat in Moreton Bay alone for the day.

The night before the trip I dropped in with Tony for a cup of tea in their kitchen. Tony was under instructions to say nothing. I told Mr McKeirnan — who seemed to trust me — that Tony and I had a problem. We had booked this large motorboat which was licensed for four — and the other two cadets had pulled out at the last moment because of urgent journalistic asignments.

Then I confidently sat back and waited for it to dawn on Mr Mac, as I called him, that we could take along the two daughters who had nothing to do on the public holiday. To sort of look after them for the day.

But, instead, he merely said: "That's too bad."

261

"It's a great pity," I said. "The weather will be perfect tomorrow."

"What are you planning to do all day?" he asked.

At last some interest!

A definite break-through.

"Well ... " I said, "... we are going to fish."

Fishing sounded nice and innocent. It was the sort of past-time that kept both hands constantly busy.

"What time will you be leaving, and when will you be back?" the protective Catholic father said.

This was it! I looked across at Tony and raised my eyebrows ever so slightly.

"We were planning to leave about ten o'clock tomorrow morning ... back by five .... well before dark," I said.

To my surprise, Mr Mac leapt up out of the chair that he was usually slumped in all day and, with an energy I had never suspected, said: "That's far too late!"

He hitched up his trousers with his thumbs and licked his lips. "The fish are gone by then. You're right Hughie," he exclaimed. "It is too good an opportunity to miss. *I'll come.* But we have to leave by five so we don't miss the run." And he rushed under the house — re-appearing within seconds with a long rod and a fisherman's basket covered in cobwebs.

The next morning, as Tony and I drove, half asleep, to pick up the father in the Alpine at 4.30 a.m. Tony annoyed me all the way by imitating me:

"Oh leave it to me Tony. I'll fix it up Tony. You'll see. There won't be any problems Tony. You just wait. Just the four of us all alone at sea. Just those two beautiful girls, the boat, some deserted islands, and us ..."

We drove down to Moreton Bay at dawn in silence, Mr Mac squeezing his bulk sideways into the back of the Alpine with his fishing rod held firmly along the side.

We were forced to fish all day, but it wasn't too bad. Tony caught a three-foot shark, and I hooked a whiting as big as a beer bottle.

But we would have preferred a couple of girls.

# 19
# Stomping with a spider

Just as the winter of 1963 was at its bleakest, the July edition of *House News* arrived, and I couldn't believe the story that jumped out at me from page two. The beautiful photo of Sallyanne looking like Cleopatra that the General Manager had wanted removed when I was in charge a year before, was back in.

"There will be a sparkling new face on our floor from now on," *House News* said. "Sallyanne Kerr has come from the *Sydney Telegraph* to work as a journalist on the *Courier*."

Holy mackerel!

SAK was back!

And she had landed smack bang in the same boat with me.

It sounded like good news, at first, until I realised something that I had never thought of before. People always got rises when they changed papers, everyone said. That was the way to get promoted quickly. So, no doubt SAK was at least a D grade by now — possibly even a C grade. Yet here was me — a year older than her — and still a cub reporter. And that wasn't all. I had just become a Fourth-Year cadet — the only Fourth-Year cadet anyone could remember. Gradings were considered so important in journalism that SAK wouldn't be able to help noticing this gulf between us.

Nice and all as she was, to her I would just have to be a failure.

And what if I never got graded at all at the end of the next 12 months — as was entirely possible? She would be there to witness the disgrace, to watch me pack my notebooks and pencils and leave after four years of fruitless apprenticeship.

I wouldn't just be losing my job, I'd be losing my whole reason for living. So many people would be disappointed, and not just Fred and Olive. Bob Macklin would say I followed instructions too closely; Peter Thomson would know I hadn't read the foreign news page; Tony Barker would realise I wasn't as far ahead of him as I pretended. And Sallyanne — I wouldn't be around to run into her.

I didn't know exactly when SAK was due back. But a few days later, as I stepped out of the lift on to the brown third floor lino, I knew she was there even before I saw her.

The General Reporters' Room seemed to be less smoky — less untidy — less degraded. Some of the reporters even looked as if their suits had been dry-cleaned.

The Chief-of-Staff waved as I walked past his glass.

I peeked behind the thick green pillar in the middle of the room, and there was Sallyanne cooing into a large black phone that seemed too heavy for her slender hand. In that smoke-stained room she stood out like Wordsworth's violet by a mossy stone: "half hidden from the eye! Fair as a star, when only one is shining in the sky".

She was all dolled up in a tailored red linen two-piece suit with three-quarter sleeves which revealed her only ornamentation: a watch and a bangle on her slender left wrist. There were four buttons down the front of the jacket, covered in the same red material as the dress. Two pleats at the front of the skirt emphasised her slenderness.

As I walked around the room I noticed that she was wearing those new seamless stockings. Her dark shimmering hair was pulled back tightly from that pale face with a white band which caused the hair to flick up at the neck, exposing the narrow nape. Bright red lipstick emphasised the Madonna smile on her lips, and at last I understood what the girl-chasing Lord Byron meant by his phrase: "she walks in beauty".

Lucky for me I had finally got hold of a suit which looked good on me, a zoot suit with a drape shape. It was a single-button job in a thick-weave wool in a greenish-grey. To go with it I had a tan crocodile-skin belt and some green suede shoes which were so pointed I could have stabbed someone with them.

The outfit hung lightly o'er me and gave me confidence, and I adjusted the jacket with both fists — lifting it up and out to fall back into shape — as I sauntered casually over after SAK hung up the phone. "Welcome back," I said, as nonchalantly as I could.

She seemed pleased to see me. She had moved into a flat in Sandgate Road, Clayfield, with some girlfriends: a two-storey red brick block of flats called Hampton Court. She had continued her University subjects by correspondence while in Sydney, and coming back meant she could now go to the lectures. By lucky coincidence, we were both doing Pol Science II. There didn't seem to be much to say after that.

To break the resounding silence of the General Reporters' Room I said: "I'll bet I can guess how much you weigh."

I instantly regretted the remark. Guessing girls' weights was something I was pretty good at. But I also knew that — while I had got a lot of girls' weights right — I hadn't got any girls.

"Oh come now Hugh," SAK said, laughing nicely so she showed her upper teeth as if they were a set of ivory jewels, "that's what they do with the bull at the Brisbane Exhibition. I hope you're not saying I remind you of him."

She was right. Every year in August at the Ekka a bull was put on display and there was a prize for guessing his weight. Everyone in Queensland used to enter, except me. I had no idea what bulls weighed. Sallyanne was about six stone 12 pounds, I reckoned, but I was too shrewd to say anything.

That night, after SAK had left the office for the day, I sat down and wrote a poem about her which ended:

Her blush makes blushing dead;
It makes pink roses, red.

With different days off, and assignments out of the office, we didn't run into each other again for a couple of weeks.

Then, of all the luck, in mid-August, we were both assigned to cover the Ekka on the last Saturday. This meant we would be together all day in the Press Box high above the Main Ring at the top of the double-decker Ernest Baynes Stand.

Not that I was really looking forward to it. I had been covering the Ekka all week, and yet I had failed to get any good stories in the paper.

It wasn't for the lack of trying.

Jack said this was a big opportunity for me.

"If there are 10 million stories in the city of New York then there are 650,000 stories at the Ekka," he said, "because that's how many people go there."

On my first day I was told to find and interview a man who had competed with some success in the dog trials. Before heading off to find the dog man, I joined the throng to Sideshow Alley with a girl I had brought along with a spare press ticket. We had met at Cloudland, but — just my luck — it turned out she was in my younger sister Sheryl's class at school.

This time I was going to make sure that if there were any strippers lurking in tents out the back, then I wouldn't miss them.

It was hard to move in Sideshow Alley, so I had a brilliant idea. I shouted the girl from Sheryl's class to a ride on the ferris wheel for a bird's-eye view. That was when I found out why there was no queue for the ferris wheel: with a freezing westerly blowing it was ten times as cold at the top.

At the end of each ride the two blokes in dirty white overalls running the wheel would only let as many people off as were queueing to get on. And very few were opting for a ride. It seemed to me these men knew that full ferris wheels look much more attractive to the public than empty ferris wheels.

Several rides and more than half-an-hour later we were

still doing cold circles. I had by then discovered the awful truth about ferris wheels — there's no way off unless you're in the bottom seat. And with the monster still turning, I was getting no closer to the dog story. Eventually — just like a number on a Chocolate Wheel — we were lucky enough to be the bottom seat when the wheel, and the music, stopped. But the two men in overalls allowed only three off, because there were just three waiting to get on.

The rest of us protested loudly, but the men ordered us to sit down and started up the engine and the music. In desperation, the girl and I leapt out onto the grass. This made the men in overalls very angry. While the girl from Sheryl's class fled, they stood close to me and said: "Get back on the wheel, smart guy."

I thought of running, but one was slowly wiping grease from his hands with a towel as if in readiness to grab me by my checked Anthony Squires sports jacket.

"OK fellas," I said, holding up the palms of my hands to them. "I'm sorry. If you want me to get back on, I'll get back on. I like your wheel, but I thought we were at the end of the ride."

I turned around and lifted my left leg up towards the seat — but then kicked off sideways and ran for the depths of the nearby crowd. One of them just hit my back with his hairy paw as I went.

I had escaped, but I still had to find the story, and the girl from Sheryl's class.

At the pig pavilion I stopped for a look because a tubby old sub-editor at the paper always reckoned he had slept there during the war — in a bed, he said, which was now occupied every year by a sow called Harriet. I couldn't find Harriet, but the pigs were much more interesting than I had thought. There were piebald pigs called Saddlebacks which the pig men said were the best mothers; black Berkshire pigs which they said gave the most bacon; and white Landrace pigs which made the best breeding sows.

Nearby, I found the dog man when I heard shouting and peeked into a large shed. Through a narrow crack in the door I could see him angrily belting into one of his cowering dogs. It was too embarrassing to interrupt, so I waited until after he had finished, and then knocked on the shed. During the interview, I asked for the secret of his success. "Always treat dogs with gentleness and kindness," he said.

I didn't like the man, so when I got back I broke a cardinal rule of journalism and wrote my own story, instead of the one I was assigned to do. This was the type of story older journalists cynically called a "not my idea story", which they said was always destined for the spike because it was not the idea of your boss.

Despite this knowledge, I sat down and wrote my first Ekka story, beginning:

*Anyone who thinks pigs is pigs, is wrong.*

This was, of course, a reference to a famous anti-bureaucracy book I had read for Uni about a man trying to send two guinea pigs by rail freight. The porter looked up the price for pigs — instead of domestic pets — and charged the man fifty times what he was expecting to pay. The man pointed out that there was a big difference between fat farmyard pigs and little guinea pigs.

But the rail porter was unmoved.

"Pigs is pigs," he said.

The subs mustn't have heard of that story, because mine never made the paper. But a story on pigs didn't seem that important when Buddhist monks in Saigon were setting fire to themselves with petrol, and President Kennedy's new baby had died.

Still and all, Bob Macklin got a big run with his Ekka story, even though it was one he thought of himself.

Bob spent the night in the cattle stalls. He came into the press room the next day smelling and covered with straw, but still wrote a page-lead story. He also did well with another idea. Bob stood in front of an abstract painting in the Arts Section of the Ekka and asked people what they thought it was:

"They told me it was a tree, a woman getting into a bath, a stove, an aeroplane, and a country scene," he wrote.

I wished I'd thought of that.

No wonder Bob had already been graded, even though he started six months after me.

SAK laughed when I told her of my failure on the dog story, and recounted some of her own. But I knew she had done really well in Sydney. I had heard she posed as a model with a portfolio of pictures — of course easily fooling everybody — when writing about rip-off modelling agencies.

We wandered around the vast Exhibition that last Saturday as it was being torn down around us for yet another year, like a day-dream come to an end. She bought a Kit Kat and shared it with me, which seemed an intimate thing to do.

I was surprised how easy she was to talk to.

When I asked her about the model agency story she said she never expected to get through the front door. SAK surprised me by describing herself as being built "like a spider".

"What do you mean?" I said.

"All long arms and legs," she replied.

It was an awful analogy, especially for me. I had always been scared of spiders, ever since they used to run up my arms when I was sorting the soft drink bottles in the dark under Fred's shop. I didn't think she was all arms and legs.

She was perfect.

But I didn't say anything.

We discussed all sorts of things, even her fascination for hair.

Holding some of her hair between her fingers and casting her big brown eyes sidelong at it, she wondered aloud what hair was, and what it was for.

"Don't ask me," I said.

I couldn't think of anything to say to her while standing so near — pushed closer and closer by hordes of people — and looking at her play with her glistening hair. I realised then and there that I loved listening to her voice because, unlike mine, it was clear and tinkling and sharp — like Olive's crystal bowl.

We went down to the agricultural displays to see the

young farmers from various districts of Queensland take their huge fruit and vegetable maps apart: lifting the pumpkins out of Cape York and the potatoes out of Heartbreak Corner.

Together we devised a story on the pulling down of the Ekka.

On the way back to the press room I told her how I was fascinated by the make-up that chemists sold women — things like "Moon Drops" which were so obviously not moon drops, and how I would like to write a story about that one day.

When we stopped on the several flights of stairs up to the press room, she asked how I shaved in the dimple in my chin, saying: "Cleft on the chin, the devil within". I told her that other girls had asked me that same question, and I always told them a lie: that it wasn't a dimple. "I was shot in the chin by an air rifle when I was young," I used to tell them.

She laughed at that one.

Even though it had been such a wonderful day, I wasn't fooled for a minute. I wasn't going to mistake fellowship and friendship for anything else. What a terrible mistake it would be if I did. How embarrassing to force SAK to say: "No monkey business. I never meant to lead you on." We wouldn't be able to face each other again.

What SAK didn't know was that I had heard she was going out with a doctor, no less. One of the other male cadets told me.

I secretly knew a lot about girls and what went on. I knew, for example, that if they wanted you, they would let you know. So it was no use making any false moves.

I knew they smelt nice because of lipstick, rouge and perfume, but I also knew that there were girls who wore corsets, waist-whittlers, padded bras, and lots of other equipment a boy could only guess at; and girls who got all A passes at private schools, kept a good table, and ate bananas with a knife and fork. The first lot with all the props had to get married before they fell pregnant, while the second mob had mothers

270

who would ensure they got husbands with an assured future. And I knew for certain that no one would describe a Fourth-Year cadet as having much future at all.

Future, of course, meant money.

Older journalists used to point out that while they worked hard and saved their money to marry, their girlfriends would take overseas trips, spending what they had before marrying: because girls were not expected to bring money into a marriage. That was why if I wanted to get a girl, they said, I should go on a cruise ship where girls outnumbered boys twenty to one.

Cars, I was wrong about. Cars were no good for getting a girl at all. But if George Orwell was right that a man's personality was his income, it was even more true that a young man's personality was his prospective income. And my prospective income could be as low as zero.

There wasn't much time to dwell on these thoughts, because within a few weeks I was transferred to Press Service. This was probably the most difficult job a cadet did. I had to send to other Australian newspapers any of our stories which I thought might be of interest to them — and to answer any of their requests. Plus I had to somehow remember every night to monitor the BBC News from London on the radio at 11 o'clock to make sure the paper didn't miss any major world stories. The BBC News always started with the gongs of Big Ben, and an announcer would say: "This is the BBC world service, Greenwich Mean Time is one o'clock."

This job meant starting work at five each afternoon, and finishing after one in the morning. It was tougher because, for the first time, I was competing directly with a reporter from another paper. Sydney's *Daily Telegraph* had their own man — a highly graded journalist — in Brisbane solely looking after them. Like me, he had access to the blacks of all *Courier* stories. It was said that he was very smart, so smart that he owned a couple of taxis around town which he managed in his spare time.

That October of 1963 was a very sad month for everyone on the paper.

A new office complex had been built a few miles out of the city centre, and we all had to pack up and leave the old *Courier* building which had for so long been at the centre of everything in Brisbane. I thought the paper was mad to move. I couldn't see how you could run a newspaper from a railway shunting yard wasteland at Bowen Hills, so far removed from the people. No use putting the Test cricket scores in the window out there, I told everyone who would listen.

There were lots of wakes held in the Royal, and the reporters and subs wondered how they would survive without a hotel next door. "No Blood Room anymore," reporters kept muttering. They said it was like moving out to a pineapple factory.

The boys in Sport were particularly upset, and Lawrie Kavanagh was acting very strange. Lawrie knew that I was keen on SAK and, since he called her Lois Lane, he started referring to me as Jimmy Olsen: significantly the friend who always lost out in the love stakes to Superman. On the night we were all leaving Queen Street, Lawrie stood on a desk among the scores of large cardboard boxes stacked with everyone's glue pots and type books and steel rulers, and started playing the role of Superman.

"Faster than a speeding bullet," he said to everyone below him. "Able to leap tall buildings at a single bound" — and Lawrie jumped over a cardboard carton, much to the delight of all in Sport.

Sallyanne suggested that, while everyone else was drinking in the Royal, she and I should go out to a Sound Lounge for a Stomp. She suggested the Sound Lounge in Elizabeth Street behind the *Tele*, an idea I didn't like because most people who went there were teenagers.

But I readily agreed.

The Stomp was a dance craze which had hundreds of people elbowing for space on dance floors so they could stamp their feet as hard as they could in time with loud music. I didn't like going dancing because everyone would see I was no good at it. But the Stomp was great. Perhaps my years

272

learning tap dancing as a child helped, but I found it the easiest of dances and, for a few hours, SAK and I stomped and stamped around in front of each other on the crowded floor to the music while I wrote a poem in my head as I watched her roll and Stomp:

Is it possible I ask
That God could perform such a task?
To paint such a face
To mould such grace
Into one small space?

Thank God the Creep had gone out. It would have become embarrassing had I been asked to creep slowly around the darkened floor body-to-body with Sallyanne, occasionally catching a glimpse of those eyes.

We went for a coffee and a Kit Kat in the Shingle Inn on the way back to the paper and she told me her mother had told her that, when dealing with men: "Lunch, dear, but never dinner."

It was such a wonderful evening that the next day the *Sydney Morning Herald* was screaming blue murder ... because of me. I hadn't sent the Queensland Sheffield Shield cricket team south, and the highly-graded journalist from the *Daily Telegraph* had.

Harry Davis looked grim when he called me into his office on the first day in the new building which — instead of having lots of cosy private little rooms — was one huge room of hard two-tone tiles, with steel and glass dividers only waist or head-high so everyone could see everyone else *all* the time.

This huge building must have covered the floor area of a hundred houses.

Harry now had deep scars in his forehead from a car accident when he hit the Grey Street bridge late one night after work. But this day they seemed deeper. As he motioned for me to sit down in front of him, he said he would accept no excuses. None. Not even the fact that we had moved buildings the previous day.

"You only had one story that had to go south, and — Hughie — you couldn't even manage that in eight hours," he said.

I told Harry — who had once worked for an international newsagency in Sydney — the truth.

How I got sidetracked by going Stomping with Sallyanne. How the Queensland cricket team — despite the excellent chance of winning the Sheffield Shield that season — had slipped my mind completely as we Stomped around the darkened dance floor. How time just got right away when we stopped for a coffee and Kit Kat together.

To my surprise, Harry's attitude changed immediately. He said not to worry, that he would fix it so that the complaint from Sydney would go no higher.

I couldn't work out what was going on.

As I stood up and walked away, Harry called out: "Hughie, that's the best excuse I've ever heard for missing a story," and a wide smile ironed out his scars completely.

It was Uni end-of-year exam time again, and I was determined to pass — for an amazing third year in a row — because SAK and I were doing the same subjects. I didn't want her to think I was a dud.

Sallyanne suggested we should do some swatting up together after work one night to help each other pass. I thought all my Christmases had come at once. Not only did she have confidence in my knowledge of the subjects, but we wouldn't get back to Hampton Court until after midnight. So, even if we only studied for a few hours, I would be with her practically all night.

But I knew that was all a fantasy.

She was going out with this doctor — whose father was educated at Cambridge. And one of the more worldly reporters — who claimed to have had his first with a girl when he was eight — said that, if ever a reporter did happen to flash on to Sallyanne, she would probably just say: "OOOOops".

I wasn't sure what he meant, but I did get a bit risque with

274

her one day when, before I knew it, I brought my silent thoughts into the conversation.

"I bet you sleep diagonally in bed?" I said.

She looked up slowly, clearly unfazed.

"Why would you say that?"

I had to think fast.

"It's one of my theories that everyone sleeps diagonally in bed — and the wider the bed the more the angle," I said.

She looked back down at her story.

We talked more than we studied that night at Hampton Court. Sallyanne said she liked people who looked her in the eye. Did I look her in the eye? I wondered, looking away.

She was obviously awake up to men. She told me how she had once gone out with an engineering student who had got the job of lighting her up on stage for a Uni student opera.

"He put a light in my hair," she said. "Then he said I really needed a light on my shoulder, so he attached one there .... The next thing I knew he wanted to put a light down my front," she said.

"Ohhh nnno, we don't need that," she told him.

This girl who had been to a private Anglican girls school agreed — to my surprise — that many of the top religious poets had turned Catholic, or had considered doing so. But she thought that was only natural.

"One would have expected poets to be attracted to Catholicism because your church is very much more mystical," she said. "It has exotic language, beliefs, symbols, traditions, stories, costumes, colours, and unusual words. There is a warmth, a ritual, an emotion." She was the first Protestant I had met who had something good to say about my church.

No wonder she was such a good journalist.

SAK had recently written the best story I had seen in the *Courier-Mail*. To anyone else it was just the wedding of a couple of pensioners. But Sallyanne wrote how the elderly couple had met just a few months before on a bench seat overlooking Moreton Bay. They had got talking, and found out they had both lived in the area more than fifty years be-

fore. Slowly they realised they had been in love as teenagers
— when they had not been allowed to marry. They had gone
off separately and unhappily into the world, married, had
children, lost their spouses — and met again on a park
bench, and were still in love.

What a story.

And only Sallyanne had the touch to write it.

After three hours studying at her dining-room table, SAK
suggested we go for a walk to clear our minds.

I was willing to do whatever she liked: walk, study, talk,
go, stay.

I was glad too that I had finally finished the bottle of Old
Spice aftershave, because I couldn't stand putting a smell on
myself anymore.

We wandered around through Clayfield at 3 a.m. and
talked about how the University tutors tipped you off to
exam questions: presumably as a reward for bothering to
turn up for tutorials.

I told her how Cecil Hadgraft had once called me a
poached egg.

We sat on a seat at a bus stop and she told me how different it was working on the *Courier* from the *Sydney Telegraph*. She said she first noticed the difference when sent on
assignment to a country town by the *Courier*. "Ooohh
DDeear. The photographer pulled out a large pistol as we
drove along and proceeded to shoot up the highway signs
out of our car window," she said as I watched her beauty
spot quiver delicately on her upper lip.

Then there was a long silence, accentuated by the quiet of
the night, which I didn't know how to break.

Eventually, I pointed this out.

"That proves we are friends," she twittered. "Friends
can sit in silence together, and it doesn't matter."

So that was something new I had learned about girls.

We went back and studied Political Science II until dawn
when one of her flatmates appeared in pyjamas, with cream
all over her face.

She looked unwell, and didn't try to hide her surprise at

seeing me. But she was buoyantly happy. She had become engaged the night before.

"I think it is only fair that your fiance sees you early in the morning before making a final decision," I said.

For a moment I thought I had said the wrong thing. But both girls just laughed and laughed.

# 20
# *A real knockout*

It was a despondent Fletch who returned from his fourth overseas tennis tour in October 1963, again without having won the elusive singles crown at Wimbledon.

Although Ken had been seeded number three, he had surprisingly lost — for the first time ever — to Fred Stolle. And the unseeded Stolle went on to reach the Wimbledon final, instead of Ken. Yet Fletch had beaten Stolle in straight sets on his way to the final of the Australian championship just six months earlier. In fact, Ken had become one of the few players ever to reach the final of the Australian without losing a set.

I had never seen Ken depressed like this before. There were no flashes of humour, even though he and Margaret Smith had won the Grand Slam of Mixed Doubles — the first pair ever to do it.

He wasn't just upset about his singles performance at Wimbledon.

"Imagine, not only did I lose to Stolle at Wimbledon, but I lost to the worst clay court tennis player in the world on clay in the French," Fletch lamented.

It was supposed to be practically impossible to ace someone on the slow French clay surface, but Ken's opponent — Britain's Mike Sangster — had aced Ken 33 times in just three sets, averaging better than two aces per service game. Sangster's serve was the biggest anyone had ever seen — officially timed that year at Wimbledon at 154 mph across the net.

Ken made no excuses publicly for his losses. But he complained to me that he had tried to have his match against

Stolle at Wimbledon postponed for a day because he was getting over a bout of the flu which saw him pull out of his semi-final at Queens the previous week.

"Workers around the world can take a day off, but they wouldn't even give me a sick day," lamented Ken. "Anyway, imagine being the number three seed at Wimbledon and drawing a finalist in the second round."

After that loss Ken sent an aerogram letter saying he had copped a caning and signed off: "Kenneth Norman, the worst tennis player in the world".

The only headlines Ken made during Wimbledon that year were for a ball he belted in the air after losing set point in a doubles semi-final. The ball bounced around on the Wimbledon roof above the Royal Box, while thousands gasped as they watched to see where the ball would eventually fall. It finally dropped into the lap of some Princess.

"It wasn't anything much really," Ken told me. "There were only a couple of minor royals there."

But it still made the front page lead of the Brisbane *Telegraph*.

Fletch was also unhappy that he had been unable to make his usual visit to Lourdes that year because the Australian team didn't go to Barcelona. A Russian had beaten him in Moscow, and I suggested half-jokingly in a letter that maybe all Ken's prayers were for nought because God had let a Communist win.

Ken replied immediately: "I did not like you saying about my God letting me down against the Russian, because in the end my God will win. Remember old chap my God will not let me down."

The following week in the Queensland championships I saw just how dejected Ken was.

Playing against Newcombe, Fletch found himself unexpectedly down two sets to one at the 10-minute break on the centre court. But instead of going off to shower, rest, and change his shirt — as all the top players did in the break — Ken amazed the Milton crowd by climbing wearily up into the vacant umpire's chair. There, with his sweat-soaked white Fred Perry tennis shirt sticking to his slender chest, Fletch sucked sulkily from a Coke bottle until Newcombe returned.

It reminded me of the scene from *The Hustler* where Minnesota Fats (Jackie Gleeson) returned from the shower, newly-shaven and still powdering his hands, to defeat the more gifted Hustler (Paul Newman) who had spent the break drinking and sitting staring at the table.

Ken lost to Newc in five sets and said when he came off the court: "What do you know Hughie. For the first time in my life I have been beaten by someone younger than me! I guess it had to happen but."

That night Ken said not to tell anyone, but he had a plan. He was going to give up tennis and go back — aged 23 — and do Senior at night to get into University. There he would study, of all things, medicine.

"Q," he said, using a nick-name for me he generally saved for letters, "I want to do something worthwhile, instead of just playing tennis. I want to help people, and deal with people. I don't like just playing tennis all the time. It is playing on my mind, like a Vocation."

Ken said he would be a doctor before he was 30 if he did this.

This was headline news to me. What had happened to the rich eccentric? What would his father say? How could one of the best tennis players ever, in the world, just give up tennis?

I resolved to try to talk him out of it.

I tried to get Ken interested in folk music, so that he could see that the world was now full of such problems, as modern society changed too rapidly. In particular I wanted him to hear Bob Dylan's song "The Times They Are a'Changin'".

I played the record for him, and even copied down the words and read them out to him: "Your sons and your daughters are beyond your command, The order is rapidly changing ..." But even as I read, Ken said: "Tell me son, how are things with Sallyanne?"

Trying to ignore the question, I told him that if he could

just win Wimbledon once he would be rich enough to do whatever he liked. He could travel the world and help anyone he wished. But Ken said he had toured the world four times under Australian managers. They had made him train and go to bed and try in every match. He was sick of having people in charge of his life.

Tennis, I said in a moment of inspiration, was just "a means to an end". A way to achieve bigger ambitions.

To my surprise, Ken went for the idea. But he said that if he was going to do it, he would have to travel alone, outside of the official Australian team. To do this he would need some back-up. What he needed was a friend to be there with him, to make it all seem worthwhile. "If you come overseas with me I think I can win Wimbledon," he said. "We can talk and discuss things. There's a lot of pressure."

Ken talked of his visits to Saint Peter's in Rome, the pyramids, the Taj Mahal, and the lakes in Europe. But he thought the Far East would be the place for us to base ourselves.

"Hong Kong or Japan would be great," he said.

Well that was out of the question. I was still a cadet reporter. A Fourth-Year cadet reporter.

Fletch and I had promised each other that if one of us ever ended up down-and-out the other would look after him. But promising to travel the world was something else. I said that if I ever did manage to get graded I would be in a position to work overseas, and we fantasised how I would write, and Ken would play tennis.

The idea made Ken very happy.

That November I again took holidays and travelled with him to Melbourne for the Victorian championships. If he was going to take the place of Laver (now ineligible as a professional) in the 1963 Davis Cup final, Ken was going to have to beat American champion Denis Ralston. But, after three long sets, Fletch found himself down two sets to one at the break against Ralston and turned to the crowd and said:

"Stop the world, I want to get off."

As he lay back in a long chair in the dressing room with

sweat running down his nose and pouring endlessly on to the green wreath on his shirt, Ken said: "Hughie old son, I'm stuffed, rooted, knackered, knocked-up. In other words, I've had the Royal Order."

Just then Davis Cup coach Harry Hopman came into the dressing room. Ken told him the same thing.

"Well Fletch," Hopman said, "you know all that road training you have done over the years like I told you, and all that gymnasium work? Well in the next hour against Ralston it's going to stand you in good stead." Then Hopman walked out.

Hopman was obviously no longer a Fletcher fan.

Ken reckoned it had nothing to do with training. Hopman had asked him to get the oranges at Davis Cup training and didn't like it when Ken refused, saying: "Hop, there is one thing you are going to have to realise: I'm no orange boy."

What Hopman didn't know was that Ken had been helping to secretly organise most of the top Australian tennis players to rebel against the LTAA. The idea was that all the top Australian players would break the LTAA's March 1 deadline and leave for overseas in January instead of playing exhibitions in small country towns.

Ken lost to Ralston. But he was still selected in the Davis Cup Squad for Adelaide, while I returned to the fishing hut on Moreton Bay. A few mornings later, Mrs Barker came rushing over to the shed.

"President Kennedy's been assassinated. President Kennedy's been killed," she was yelling out.

The whole family — including all the young boys — sat on the steps looking out over Moreton Bay without saying anything. We were all thinking the same thing: the first Catholic President of the United States, the first one to be admired around the world, the first one to frighten the Russians: and they go and shoot him. It made the world a much less hopeful place to live in. Especially for me.

I could have been late-stop sub that night. What would I have done when the news came through on the wire after 3 a.m.? Would I have had the nerve to ring Mr Bray at home and get him out of bed, like the late-stop sub did? Probably not. As it happened, Mr Bray collected journalists on his way in, and ran a special edition of the *Courier* which sold out.

It showed me once again what a difficult job journalism was.

President Kennedy's funeral was on TV and Fred, of course, said he had told us they'll all shoot you. Quick.

A little girl wrote a poem about the President's son watching the funeral which ended: "That's my daddy in that box; the black one, with the six gold locks."

Because of Ken's losses, Newcombe replaced Laver and made his debut in Adelaide for the 1963 Christmas Davis Cup. Hopman didn't even pick Ken to play in the doubles with Emerson, as everyone expected.

That January of 1964 the Australian tennis championships were held in Brisbane — the perfect opportunity to take Sallyanne somewhere. Particularly as I wanted Fletch to see just how beautiful she was. Also, I wanted his opinion on whether I had any chance, because he always said: "I'm the first to judge any sort of cold shoulder."

He said he hoped she wasn't "the type who could go to an Arnotts biscuits-and-cordial party, and enjoy herself."

I had seen SAK recently when I pretended I needed something in the office one Sunday when she was working. I went in dressed in all-white cricket gear from a journos match, sporting blood-splattered gravel-rashed elbows and with a white hankie tied jauntily around my neck.

She agreed to go to the tennis. It was a beautiful Brissie summer's day and, as we had plenty of time before Ken played, we went for a long drive with the hood down out to Cooper's Crossing. I wore a hat, but her dark hair flew around in the air as we raced along the dirt road with the morning shadows of the trees flickering across the car. For the first time, she seemed to realise what a groovy car I had: though she didn't mention it.

Sallyanne was wearing a pale pink strap-topped dress with a thick belt made of the same material tied loosely at the side. She looked a real knockout, which was what I wanted.

At Milton, Ken was, as usual, wandering around in his tennis gear and illustrating stories with arcs of his Slazenger Challenge racquet.

I could tell Fletch was impressed with Sallyanne the way he swung easily into his better accent, while hitting his calf muscle with the side of the racquet and flicking his blue eyes, very obviously, up and down her pink dress.

But I was a bit worried what Ken might say. You could never tell with Ken. Once, when I told him I had taken a Melbourne girl up to Mt Coot-tha, he asked what she thought of the view clear across Brisbane.

"She said it was like fairyland," I told him.

"Did you wave your magic wand?" Ken asked.

I mentioned that she didn't dance because she was Presbyterian.

"Yes that's why Presbyterians are against sex — they think it could lead to dancing," he said.

What would he say to SAK?

"So you're Sallyanne," Ken said at last. "Hughie's told me all about you." And then, turning to include me: "She's a good sort, Hughie. You were right, you were so right."

"Ohhh Ken," said Sallyanne, smiling demurely.

This was just what I was hoping Fletch wouldn't say — but it turned out to be the right thing after all. Sallyanne chatted away easily to Ken, as if he was just anybody, while he took us up to the covered Harry Hopman stand overlooking the Centre Court and told the usherette to give us two good seats at the front.

Ken could see I was a bit bamboozled by it all and so he pulled me aside: "She's a good sort Hughie. She's not Miss World but."

"I've got to get cracking well," Fletch said to SAK. "I'm going to deal out stick to Sangster for beating me in the French. Say a prayer for me will you?" and he disappeared beneath the rows of wooden stands into the steaming arena where a dozen umpires and ball-boys in hats were waiting.

Ken said he would have trouble breaking Sangster's serve, and he was right. It was so fast I couldn't see it till it hit Ken's racquet.

In Melbourne I'd seen Sangster ace Ralston four times in a row, whereupon the American turned to the thousands in the crowd, pleading: "Can any of you people see them? Because I can't."

But Ken had a plan. This time he wasn't going to try to hit perfect returns.

"The secret against Sangster is to concentrate like hell and just struggle the ball back any old how, and, heck, he'll probably miss it."

At 13 games all in the first set Ken had his white washing hat on, it was lunchtime, and the temperature had climbed into the 90s. Sallyanne suggested lunch, but I didn't want to leave Ken in the lurch.

Luckily he won the set 17-15, and I felt safe to go.

When we stood up I saw my Test cricket hero, Ken "Slasher" Mackay, sitting a few seats behind us. I pointed him out to Sallyanne.

I loved Mackay, though I had never met him. He had played so many courageous innings for Queensland and Australia despite having had infantile paralysis as a child. He was a man who never gave in, causing Len Hutton to say: "Bowling at that chap Mackay is like bowling at Westminster Abbey." I read everything I could get about Slasher, listened to all his innings on the wireless when I couldn't get to the Gabba to see him bat, and Fletch even got me a "Ken Mackay" cricket bat from Slazengers for my birthday.

I could not believe what happened next.

"Hello Slash," said Sallyanne, "what about coming to lunch?"

What was she doing?

To my surprise, Slasher stood up and walked out of the stand with us to have lunch in the Milton Club. He insisted on paying and, as I sat and looked at him, I noticed that he had mournful eyes not unlike Rod Laver's, yet wrists that were as slender as my own.

I didn't know what to say, sitting between the two people I admired most in the world, and mainly let SAK do all the talking.

I loved the story Slasher told when I expressed surprise that he ordered a beer.

"I always said I would never have a beer until Queensland beat New South Wales at the Sydney Cricket Ground. I had to wait many years, but when we finally did it — I was batting — they handed me my first glass of beer as I walked through the gate off the field. I liked it straight away."

"Newcombe did really well in the Davis Cup in Adelaide," I ventured to say.

Even though I thought Ken should have been picked in the team, like everyone else I was surprised that Newcombe, aged only 19, took both his American opponents to five sets before going down.

"No he didn't do well," said Slasher, "he lost."

I was shocked at Mackay's straight-forwardness. No wonder he was such a hard batsman to remove. Even Ken had not taken such a hard view of Newc's performance. Ken was more crooked at the performance of Neale Fraser — who was brought out of retirement by Hopman to play the doubles, instead of Ken, with Emerson.

"They should have played the match at Eventide," Fletch said of the vital doubles loss that cost Australia the Davis Cup. Eventide being a large old people's home in Brisbane.

By the time we got back to the tennis, Ken had won easily — revenging the loss to Sangster in Paris — and SAK and I headed off to work. Now I'd be sitting in the General Reporters' Room with her all evening, and we'd probably go and have a cup of tea and a Kit Kat.

In the staff toilets I ran into a younger cadet whose grimace as he looked in the mirror contrasted markedly with my broad smile after my day with Sallyanne.

"What's up?" I asked my colleague.

"I'm going bald," he said, and bent forward pointing to his scalp, which was easy to see because he was short.

"No you're not," I said generously. "Your hair line is just taking its adult shape."

"No. I'm going bald," he said. "It's gruesome."

"Look," I replied, feeling I could be of help to a fellow human being much less fortunate than myself. "We are all going bald. It's part of being masculine. I'm losing hair myself. I see the hairs in my comb too. It's only a problem if you worry about it. Cheer up."

An hour or two later this cadet came walking past, stopped at my desk across an aisle from Sallyanne, and looked down.

"Yes. You're going bald, Hugh. I can see the hair thinning. Hugh's definitely going bald," he announced to the room. Then he walked down the back to his desk, as SAK looked across at me and shrugged her shoulders. This was hardly the perfect end to the day I'd planned.

A few weeks later I arrived in the General Reporters' Room after some holidays and knew something was up. Somehow I knew it wasn't good news. A group of girl cadets were gathered around Sallyanne near my desk.

They were oohing and aahing like girls used to do at the convent when a nun produced a holy picture.

"What's going on?" I enquired of a girl at the back.

"Sallyanne's become engaged. Look at the ring the doctor's given her. Isn't it beautiful. So big, so red. It's the best ring I've ever seen. It's wonderful, truly wonderful."

I was in a real pickle now.

So that was it. No more Sallyanne.

It was like hearing of her death.

Now she would be removed from my society forever more to have children and run a house.

I would never see her again.

No more Kit Kats.

The worst thing was I knew all along that this was going to happen. That I was kidding myself. That I had no chance. But at least I knew it wasn't going to affect me anywhere

287

near as much as when I lost the redhead. This time I'd played it nice and safe, and kept my distance. There was even a certain relief that, now that it was all over, I could forget about her. Her and her brown eyes and her little nose and her beauty spot.

"Remember, we *are* gentlemen": I could hear Ken whispering in my ear from wherever he was in the world that day, now that he had flown out of the country alone to be branded as a rebel by the LTAA.

Then, suddenly, the excited group of girls parted, and there was Sallyanne. She was sporting a large red ruby on the third finger of her left hand. The scene reminded me of the song Olive used to sing us to sleep with in the Hillman when we drove home from Nerang: "Isle of Capri" — "as I bent my head I could see, she wore a plain golden ring on her finger, it was goodbye on the Isle of Capri."

I knew enough to know that girls were not to be congratulated upon engagement — so that it would not be implied that they had, at last, landed a man.

Even though I couldn't bring myself to admire the ruby ring, I did manage to wish her all the best.

Later that night, after SAK had gone home, I told the girl cadet who sat at the desk next to me that she was a hypocrite to have carried on so much about how lovely the ring was, when clearly she hadn't really meant it.

To my surprise she started crying, and ran around to Social.

# 21
# *Generalissimo Lunn*

Early in 1964 I found myself still a cadet reporter after nearly three-and-a-half years on the paper.

Kev O'Donohue had obviously noted this. He congratulated me on again passing both University subjects, and said I was being put back on General. There he would ensure I was given some top stories so I could impress the Editor.

Kev liked me because I had become the cadet representative on the journalist's AJA union committee. Even though he often filled in as Chief-of-Staff, Kev was a strong union man.

He had recently stepped in to save me from trouble.

I was incensed when I arrived for work on Christmas Day only to be told that — for the first time ever — we had to sign a book to get in to the new building. I refused to sign, on the basis that it was bad enough having to work on Christmas Day — without having to sign to get into work: even though the company always gave everyone a Christmas Bonus in the pay packet. A couple of other reporters backed me up, and we stood outside until we were allowed in to work without signing.

"You were right Hughie," said K. O'D. "But you will find it is best to finish your cadetship before taking on management."

On the first day back on General, Kev — who often complained that giving certain reporters good stories was "throwing stories down the drain" — called me in to his office and said he had "a beauty".

A 30-year-old Canadian had been writing to a Kingaroy

woman for two years, and he had now arrived to marry her. Sight unseen.

"Go to it, Hughie, and show them what you can do," he said.

I was really interested in this story, because I didn't realise a girl could fall in love by letter. So I interviewed the couple for an hour-and-a-half at Corinda, and was back in the office by noon. I knew it was a great story, but — once again — couldn't find the right intro.

Over and over again I tried, but always my intro was too long and too complicated.

Five hours later I hadn't even been able to find time to do a Summary for Conference. People were starting to look at me inserting and tearing copy paper out of the typewriter over and over again.

I needed some privacy. There were too many distractions in the General Reporters' room. All of the journalists were laughing at a Scottish reporter who was on the phone to a Barrier Reef island resort asking about an invasion of turtles. Because the Scot kept saying "tuttles" he couldn't make anyone on the island understand him.

Another reporter was trying to write a story about a new type of clock which had been unveiled that day on Ipswich Road. He couldn't work out how to describe this new-fangled clock so readers would know what it was like. Apparently it was a very strange clock indeed, without an hour or a minute hand. Instead, it gave the time in lit-up numbers, like 9.47 or 11.31.

"Call it a clock without a face," someone shouted across the room.

"A clock without hands?" said someone else.

"A numbers clock," suggested the First-Year cadet Markets Reporter.

The reporter finally decided on "a direct-reading clock".

One woman was writing the usual weekly story about the burning down of a Queensland country hotel. You always had to go to the library to look up how many had been burnt down that year, but, because it happened so often, she was hoping someone would remember the current figure.

At the entrance to the Chief-of-Staff's office a group of older journalists were discussing the new paper called the *Australian* which had just started.

"It won't last six months," said one.

I was glad to hear this, since when they went looking for a cadet to hire and grade they took Bob Howarth, my blond wrestling partner: who had started a year behind me.

To get away from these diversions I went around to Radio News, but three hours later it was getting embarrassing there too.

I moved to the Press Service office, knowing that soon the Chief Sub would start to wonder where the story was.

Finally, in desperation, at 9 p.m. I got an intro I didn't really like:

"*The 'postage-stamp romance' of Canadian Bill Lancaster and Queenslander Miss Norma Brunjes ended yesty — and a new romance started.*"

To my relief the paper used it, unchanged.

I covered an Italian wedding at New Farm and wrote how the guests ate: "200 chickens, 800 potatoes, two cwt. of vegetables, 1000 fish fillets, 1000 big prawns, and 400 ice cream pieces." But Kev said I would have done better describing the bride's dress.

On weekends I got the beaches round where I always tracked down a lifesaver who had seen a shark. But then I was told we didn't want a shark story from the Gold Coast every weekend. "The Gold Coast *is* a holiday resort," a Chief-of-Staff said. "We don't want to go *looking* for sharks."

There were lots of traps.

Some things really seemed to upset the subs.

When Australia's aircraft carrier *Melbourne* collided with the destroyer *Voyager* — killing 82 sailors — an A-grade reporter wrote: "The old Australian adage 'never leave your mates behind' came to the fore..." I thought this was very good. But it was spiked on the subs desk with the comment: "The old Australian adage of 'bugger you jack, I'm alright' came to the fore…"

I learned not to write that car accidents were "spectacular".

I even got to review books. When I was asked to do my first book review I refused, thinking I didn't know enough. Anyway, I said, I couldn't possibly read and write about an entire book for just ten shillings and sixpence.

"You don't have to *read* the book," said the journalist offering it to me. "You just read the stuff on the back, and flick through and write a few sentences. That way you not only earn some extra dough but you get to have your say on the issue."

Within two months I was covering the Premier, Mr Nicklin, and Parliament, where I got a good story on how it was revealed that Queensland's policewomen didn't have the power of arrest.

These stories gave me the courage to at last confront the Editor about my grading. I pointed out that Bob Macklin had been graded, although he started after me. Mr Bray was unimpressed, and said I still had a way to go.

Yes, I had passed six University subjects, but had I passed the shorthand test?

I couldn't tell him that I couldn't pass the shorthand test: not at 120 words a minute. Or that I was desperate to get graded now because there was no way I would pass Economics I at Uni. Not since the argument with the lecturer.

This lecturer said Economics was based on a theory called "Marginal Utility" — that the more of a product consumers have the less they want.

"What about Hot Cross Buns?" I asked from up the back of the lecture theatre. "I never eat buns, but every Easter I have one Hot Cross Bun in my father's cake shop and, suddenly, I want another. Then I desperately crave a third Hot Cross Bun, and I would kill for a fourth."

The lecturer said I was being ridiculous. "Economics is not based on Hot Cross Buns, thank God," he said.

Arthur the Anchor advised me to give the shorthand test

a go if I wanted to get graded. "If I were you I'd practise that morning's editorial. They always give you the editorial," Arthur said.

They did, and I passed.

But still no word of a grading, while everyone else was racing forward with their lives.

The Chief-of-Staff booked me into a hotel for three days to cover the 100th Toowoomba Show, my first out-of-town assignment. Kev gave me a special pass which said: "The Bearer, Mr H. Lunn, is authorised to send telegrams collect, and reverse charges. Any assistance which can be given to the bearer will be appreciated."

I was so keen that in three days I got 20 stories into the paper: including one on a man who — I worked out — had judged more than 45,000 pigs in his lifetime. The subs even put "From a Staff Reporter" on my preview of the election: "Toowoomba is a colourful city, with colourful streets and a colourful Mayor ... and it is about to have a colourful Council election."

No one knew that Jack had suggested that intro before I left Brisbane.

When I got back to the office, graded journalist Bruce Wilson came over and said: "Hey Dad, didn't you know that three stories a day is the limit on a trip."

I was thrilled he had noticed.

Some Sundays I did churches, ringing priests and ministers to ask what they had told their congregations. One Methodist minister condemned an exhibition of nudes at the Sydney Art Gallery: "When an exhibition like that can draw from a hardened journalist the exclamation 'WOW!' then we should start to think where the whole thing is going," he said. And an Anglican Archbishop said the world was starting to misuse music "as a vehicle of sensualism".

This was a good story because the Archbishop was obviously referring to a new pop group of four young blokes with long hair who seemed to have adults everywhere worried about where the world was going. The group had an unusual name: The Beatles. Their songs were on the wireless

293

all the time, but adults hated the group because they had hair which hung down over their ears and almost to their eyebrows.

The Beatles were so popular that Brisbane shops sold Beatle suits: thin, tight suits with four buttons up the front of the jacket, with no lapels.

I bought a light grey Beatles suit myself. All the old subs hated my outfit. Like Uncle Cyril, they reckoned Beatle music was terrible, but everyone I knew in Brisbane was walking around humming "I Wanna Hold Your Hand".

We cadets got the old subs back that Easter.

Because there was no newspaper on Good Friday morning, the paper always held an annual dinner dance at Milton tennis stadium on Easter Thursday night. Cadets Tony Barker, Peter McFarline, Gary Stubbs and myself borrowed some guitars and four long black Beatle wigs from Mc-Whirters in the Valley. We recorded three Beatles songs on the briefcase-sized portable tape machine Ken brought me back from overseas, and hid it behind a pot plant on stage.

Then, after Kev O'Donohue had been presented with the AJA's gold honour badge for all his good work on behalf of journalists, we appeared from behind a curtain — all with long black hair — and apparently singing: "*She Loves you, Yeah, Yeah, Yeah; She loves you, Yeah Yeah Yeah; She Loves You, Yeah, Yeah, Yeah, Yeah ...... She said she loves you, and you know that can't be bad; she said she loves you, and with a love like that, you know you should be glad.*"

Arthur the Anchor said he loved the words to the song: "Every word in that song would fit in a Poster."

It was fun being a star on stage at the dinner dance, but it only reminded me of SAK. She didn't love me, yeah, and I knew I should be sad.

It wasn't so much that I missed her. I had never spent that much time with Sallyanne anyhow. But while she was still a single girl there had always been the hope that fate would throw us together in some unexpected way. The idea that she was there. The delicious chance that something wonderful and miraculous might happen between us at any time in the future. A look. A touch. An event. Even an accident. But not anymore. Not now that she was engaged to be married.

I wrote to Ken telling him — in words he would understand — that the game was up. He replied from the Caribe Hilton, San Juan, Puerto Rico, saying: "Sallyanne is finished, so it is too late for you to do anything there. You must get yourself a girl you like. Overseas there are so many girls you will go ape. I have failed to hear from any girls in Australia, so I am well and truly divorced. I am still thinking of returning to study as I have to do something besides tennis, but I hope Our Lady of Lourdes works something out for me. I rely on Our Lady of Lourdes to give me something to do when I finish tennis. Say a prayer for me, and be good."

With Sallyanne taken, I became desperate to escape Brisbane.

I even thought of going to France to study French. But Tony had a better idea. He suggested we resign, buy a Land-Rover, and tour Australia for six months writing stories. I went for the idea and wrote to magazines like *Outback* asking what sort of stories they wanted.

We even went so far as to buy a couple of hunting knives.

To show myself how I was getting on, I kept a graph in pencil on a toilet wall at the paper — above the line for happiness, below for sadness. I wanted to see if Shakespeare's comment that "the sum of tears is always constant" made a straight line on the graph: a constant.

I was surprised to find that it did.

Sallyanne was still around and, without letting her know my graph involved her in any way, on some empty Kit Kat silver paper I showed her the basic idea of the graph. Funnily enough, she said she had a version of this herself.

If things had gone well, and she was suddenly happy, she saw herself as going "up a ladder"; whereas at the other extreme she went "down a snake": just like the dice game we used to play a lot as kids when I always loved the idea of the ladders, but hated sliding down the long, ugly, twisted snakes.

I wrote a poem down by the Bay when I found myself there for a whole night alone. It was called "Dear Anybody," and ended:

I sleep all day,
I dream all night,
All is not well —
I am losing this fight.

She is a fair maid,
A beauty divine;
All is not well,
She can never be mine.

A few weeks later, however, I was up a ladder.

The Chief-of-Staff called me in and said I was being flown 500 miles out west to cover the Charleville Show.

Fred and Olive drove me out to the airport in the Zephyr to see me off on a DC3, my new blue portable Olivetti typewriter in hand. Fred wore his pith helmet to stop the sun giving him a headache, because he had recently lost most of his hair, and Olive wrapped a scarf over her head — worried the wind from the propellers would mess up her hair which was now very grey. They didn't know much about aeroplanes. Olive had never even been off the ground, but Fred had paid a pound to go on a joyflight in the 1920s.

I was lucky because I immediately got on to a big story in Charleville. The Show ribbons had been lost, sent by mistake to Longreach, 300 miles away.

The next day I went down to the newsagent to buy a paper and was thrilled to see more than 50 people queued up waiting for the *Courier-Mail* to arrive from Brisbane. They were all there to read my stories about their Show.

Getting into the spirit of the west, I bought a broad-brimmed Akubra hat and a long-sleeved blue shirt with two large breast pockets with buttoned-down flaps — like all the men out there wore.

I made sure I had these on when I got back to the paper: just in case I ran into SAK.

She wasn't there and, instead, when I walked through the

Subs Room they started having a go at me. But I didn't mind. I felt a bit sorry for them, because they never got to go on out-of-town assignments like me.

They never went anywhere.

"We send him out west for three days and he comes back looking like a cow cocky," said one.

I showed them a colour picture I had taken of myself with a bull.

"So that was where you were getting all your stories," said one.

But I must have done well, because it wasn't long before I got sent away on another story. However this time it was down a snake.

The day I left for the job SAK finished up at the paper for good because she had to go and prepare for her wedding.

We had a last Kit Kat together — staying longer than usual in the canteen — and I had to wrench myself away to head off in an office car for Tin Can Bay to cover an Australian army exercise by 3000 troops: 400 of whom were "enemy".

Six hundred square miles of bush was declared a war zone: no fires, no showers, ration packs, 52-ton tanks, artillery, and helicopters. The setting was supposed to be for "a limited war in south-east Asia" and people kept saying: "we all know what that means," and winking.

But I didn't know, and was afraid to say I needed, like Fred, to be told.

Because it was so hot, I discarded my jacket and just wore a white shirt and tie.

Next day I was taken to the secret Battle Group HQ, a heavily camouflaged group of tents. Within seconds, four screaming Sabre jets came in at tree-top level and a Colonel raced out of a tent screaming: "Get that white shirt under cover. You've given away our position. We are being bombed out of existence."

I picked up a branch and stuck it over my head, but it was too late.

The Colonel contacted the umpires on a radio phone.

297

"We really shouldn't have been wiped out," he said. "This reporter from the *Courier-Mail* was wearing a *white* shirt. Listen. If we're wiped out, the whole bloody exercise is over and we can all go home."

It was a bit like a giant game of Cowboys and Indians.

The enemy were called "Phantoms" and their leader the "Red Pheasant". The Colonel told me our attack on the Phantoms had had to be postponed "because you wrote a bloody article about it in the paper this morning, didn't you?"

I hadn't realised the Red Pheasant would get the *Courier-Mail* home-delivered to the battlefield.

I got a lift to the front lines in a jeep, but we were stopped by soldiers wearing white armbands at a bridge. They said they were battle umpires.

"This bridge has been blown up by guerrillas," one of the umpires said.

"No it hasn't," I said.

"For the purposes of this exercise, it has," the umpire replied.

We were diverted over an engineers' corduroy bridge.

The umpires said I should be wearing a white armband to show that I was neutral. He didn't have any left so, in true Digger style, I improvised. Since Olive had supplied me with plenty of handkerchiefs, I tied a spare white one around my left biceps.

Then I advanced with the front line in attack, taking notes as we went.

"Gunfire echoed around the hill."

The hill got steeper.

"The enemy retreated back up the mountain."

An umpire yelled from above: "You are now under artillery fire," so we dropped back.

"It has stopped," he said — so we advanced.

"Grenades."

We retreated.

"Coils of barbwire."

Someone called for the engineers.

"Use a bazooka," I said, remembering the war movies.

"A what?" an officer asked.

"They're bringing up Centurian tanks," said an umpire, "the biggest thing in their field."

"So were the dinosaurs," said a soldier.

By late afternoon we had taken the ridge, and I had to get back to the jeep to be driven miles to the nearest phone. The very last thing the Chief-of-Staff had said before I left was that I must phone him *before* the Conference every afternoon.

I walked casually back down through our troop lines, waving to the soldiers with whom I shared victory.

Suddenly, I felt a gun barrel in my back.

Four soldiers had their rifles levelled.

"You're a POW," said a Sergeant.

"Look," I said, "I'm neutral. I'm a reporter. Look at my white armband."

"That's not an armband. That's a handkerchief."

"Yes, I improvised," I said.

"It's the Provost Camp for you for 24 hours," said the Sergeant.

I tried a new tack.

"Why do you think I am wearing a white shirt and tie and carrying a reporter's notebook?"

"The last bloke we let through was a religious minister, collar on back the front, and he blew up our supply depot with three grenades," the Sergeant said.

"Look, I've really got to get back to my jeep," I said.

"Jeep? Since when did reporters get around in jeeps?" he said — and they marched me a mile to a Provost Camp in a heavily wooded valley.

A moustached Major sat incongruously at a large six-drawed varnished timber desk, its legs sinking in the dirt of his lounge-room-sized tent. There were about 20 prisoners in a wire compound outside.

By now it was well after dark, and I knew the Chief-of-Staff would be wondering where I was. I explained my situation to the Major.

299

"You're a bloody prisoner-of-war sport," he said. "That's who you are, Right?"

I could see I would have to talk fast. So I explained the grading system for cadet journalists and how I had only a few months left to make it. I really couldn't afford any more muck-ups like the one the previous Saturday, I said.

"Two armed men held up the Moorooka TAB and the Chief-of-Staff came running out of his office and threw me the keys to the blue office VW," I said. "He told me to grab Police Roundsman Peter Hansen and get out there. When we got back two hours later police were also at the newspaper. Someone, they said, had stolen a sub-editor's car from out the front of the office: a blue VW. It was me! It was just rotten luck that the keys to the office car also fitted the sub's car."

This story brought a hint of pity to the Major's face.

But the Sergeant said he didn't believe it. It was too much of a coincidence.

The Major lifted his cap with one hand and rubbed his jaw with the other, wondering what to do. I told him I had to get my story in soon, or it would miss the paper, and the army would get no publicity for its exercise.

"What's the use of the army putting on a display of its might if no one hears about it?" I asked.

The radio-telephone on the six-drawer varnished desk rang.

The Major picked it up, spoke briefly, removed his officer's hat, wiped his brow, and looked up.

"It's for you," he said.

I couldn't believe it. I didn't even know where I was, so how could anybody ring me up?

"Dr Bloody Livingstone, I presume?" said the Chief-of-Staff. "I've been trying to get you for two hours."

"I didn't receive any signal," I said.

"Don't come that army talk with me Lieutenant. What's happening up there?"

"Well," I said, "we attacked a simulated battalion, under pretend artillery fire against an imaginary tank squad-ron. Headquarters was wiped out by a make-believe air attack, but it was the *Courier-Mail*'s fault because the planes spotted my shirt — so it didn't count.''

"Have you been drinking Colonel?'' the Chief-of-Staff asked.

"No. I'm under armed guard. I would have phoned you by now but I've been captured. I'm a POW, a prisoner-of-war!''

"Well Generalissimo Lunn,'' the Chief-of-Staff said slowly and malignantly, "if you don't somehow escape from Stalag Tin Can Bay tonight and cover the Caboolture-bloody-Show tomorrow, you had better stay a POW.''

"The Caboolture Show?'' I said. "But it's only a one-sideshow affair.''

"So's that,'' he said, and hung up.

When I got back from the Caboolture Show — where the winning bunch of 300 bananas was entered by Mr R. Dobson, of Wamuran — a silver-on-white invitation set in old fashioned type was waiting.

"Mr and Mrs Kerr request the pleasure of your company at the marriage of their daughter, Sallyanne, at St Thomas's Church, Camp Hill, with Nuptial Mass at 6 p.m. and afterwards at Wanganui Gardens.''

Tony had also been invited, but we found ourselves still out in the boat on Moreton Bay at dusk. When we finally came ashore we decided to attend the reception. We hadn't got around to buying a present, but I said we would take along the fish we had caught that day.

At Wanganui Gardens all my bravado drained away when I saw dozens of people dressed in tails and white bow ties — and me in my grey Beatles suit.

So I left the fish in the Alpine.

In the vestibule I ran straight into Sallyanne, when I was hoping to just mingle among the guests. She looked like a princess from a storybook. Though she was not quite 22, here she was already a graded journalist, a married woman, and a newly converted Catholic.

Whereas I had just turned 23, and was still a cub reporter.

301

The long sheer white gown showed off her lovely shoulders. It trailed regally behind along the floor. Around her head was a band of flowers holding a white mosquito-net veil which emphasised the darkness of her eyes and hair.

When Sallyanne saw us she rushed over and spun around in a complete circle in her dress to see what we thought.

"You can see your pants through your dress," I confided.

Several men in white bow ties — including the groom — made brilliant speeches, which made me realise just how out of my depth I had been all along. There was no way I could stand up and make a speech to 200 people.

Then the bride and groom left early for a trip somewhere in the Pacific, while I went back down to Victoria Point with Tony.

That night I wrote a long poem which concluded:

Music the deaf doth forsake,
In colour the blind do not partake,
And love, the loveless, doth escape.

Just a few days later, a ladder appeared as if from nowhere: destroying forever my old theory about one door shutting in your face as another door shuts in your face.

On the noticeboard was a *Courier-Mail Memo* envelope addressed to me.

Inside was a note from Mr Bray.

"Dear Mr Lunn," it said, "I am pleased to tell you that as of today's date I have decided to make you a D grade reporter."

I had made it. And with two months and eight days to spare. Wait until Olive hears of this!

As I looked up from the small white note that had changed my life, a young Markets Reporter called Scott McKinlay came over.

"Mr Lunn," he said. "Can you help me with my intro?"

No one had ever called me Mister before.

# *Postscript*

I flew out of Brisbane Airport six months later with Ken Fletcher bound for Hong Kong and destinations unknown.

When I sold the Alpine and resigned from the *Courier-Mail*, Olive cried. It was the first time I had seen her with tears running down her cheeks. She had always seemed so strong, now she was crying at good news. She said I had thrown in a good job, and hadn't finished University. I said I was only going for six months, but Fred, as usual, made things worse.

"You'll never come back." he said. "I left W.A. for six months, and I've never been back."

At the airport Jack made sure I had my scrapbook; Jim threw a friendly farewell punch to the solar plexus and urged me to join him in a hamburger to keep my strength up for the long flight; Gay gave me an ugly Troll doll for good luck; and Sheryl and Gay put a boomerang clothes brush in my port "to make sure you come back".

Fred reminded me that he had his ticket to New York when he met Olive, and I said he was lucky he had found a girl to stay home for. Olive told me to stay out of the night air, always to wear a singlet, never to miss Mass on Sunday, never to eat pork and to be careful of the Chinese Communists. She gave me a book of Banjo Paterson poems in which she wrote: "My Dear Hugh, I hope you will enjoy this book. It is a piece of Australia to cherish."

As I hugged Olive goodbye, Fred kissed the end of his fingers and patted them on the top of my head, like a priest giving his blessing.

Ken left his parents Ethel and Norm and grabbed me by

the arm: "We'd better get going well. It's all down to getting on the plane. That's the hardest part but."

From the top of the plane's stairs they seemed such a tiny and insignificant group: Olive, Fred, Jack, Gay, Sheryl, and Jim. Yet they were all I had: and I was leaving them.

KEN didn't win Wimbledon when I was there with him — but both years it took the winner to beat him in close matches. I saw him win the Men's Doubles with John Newcombe and the Mixed Doubles with Margaret Court.

ROD Laver won the Grand Slam again seven years later — the first time the professionals were allowed to play the amateur tournaments. No one else has ever done this twice.

PETER and Stephanie Thompson arrived in Fleet Street two years later and stayed a few days in my room. Peter rose rapidly to become Editor of one of the world's biggest newspapers, London's *Sunday Mirror*, was appointed to the board of the Mirror Group and later co-authored a controversial biography of notorious media proprietor Robert Maxwell, his former boss. Steph became a Fleet Street columnist. They never returned to live in Australia.

BOB Macklin left Brisbane and wrote several books including a novel, *The Queenslander*, about being a cadet reporter on the *Courier-Mail*.

HARRY Davis died three decades later, without ever having won a Casket ticket on Queensland in the Sheffield Shield.

LAWRIE Kavanagh left Sport in the 1980s and became a fulltime columnist on the *Courier*, still unrepentently kicking heads and stamping on hands.

JACK became Editor-in-Chief of the *Courier-Mail* and *Sunday Mail* in 1991, and Deputy Chairman of the Queensland Newspapers Board.

THE solid stone CIB headquarters and Supreme Court buildings were knocked down, as was Cloudland, the National Hotel, the Royal Hotel, the Roma St Markets, Christie's, and Her Majesty's Theatre. The O'Connor Boathouse was destroyed by fire and a freeway flyover now occupies the space. The *Tele* was closed down, as was the railway line to the old Gold Coast, and the trams. It is no longer possible to park between the columns of the colonnade at Queensland University. The BBC News on Brisbane radio at 11 p.m. is now sponsored by an advertiser. The white picket fence around the Gabba cricket ground was pulled down and replaced by tin advertising hoardings.

FRED and OLIVE: During the seven years I was away, Fred and Olive moved to Chermside to be near the new shop — leaving our family home at Annerley forever. So I never got to see inside it again. Fred did, eventually, get back to W.A. In 1974 he bought a new pith helmet and, in an old second-hand black Rambler sedan he called his limousine, he and Olive — in their late 60s — travelled south once again. They were headed for the mining town of Tom Price in north-west W.A. to see Gay and her family. On the way, they visited Fred's mother's grave near Kalgoorlie at a place Dad always called "Boulder City". His mother died there when he was a small boy — sentencing Fred to the childhood he never forgot in an orphanage. On the way back home the Rambler's engine blew up in the middle of nowhere, and they had to wait more than two weeks for parts. The owners of the local roadhouse — not realising Mum and Dad were both happy camping by the side of the road — put them up. They spent the rest of their lives in Brisbane, living just long enough to see me married, aged 40. So Fred had been right after all.

AND SALLYANNE: Sallyanne went on to become a star of the Sydney TV series *Beauty and the Beast*, but later had her lovely beauty spot removed. She lived with her husband in Scotland while he studied to become a neuro-surgeon,

305

had five children — four girls and a boy — became a Brisbane newspaper columnist and TV current affairs reporter, and in the 1980s was twice elected Lord Mayor in a vote by the entire city of Brisbane.

In 1991 she was quoted in the *Courier-Mail* as saying of her adolescence: "I was always the left-over, the one nobody wanted."